ADROS VERSE EDUCATION S.R.L.

Learn & Retain
French
with Spaced Repetition

700+ Anki Notes for Level I

with Vocabulary, Grammar, & Audio Pronunciation

Bucharest - 2023

Table of Contents

I. Introduction to Spaced Repetition

Remember all the times that you learned something just to forget it when you get rusty after not practicing for a while? Now imagine that there is some way to remind yourself of only the things that you are about to forget before you forget them, without boring yourself with the ones that you have already memorized. You may think that this would be convenient but also impossible, when in fact, it is possible using *spaced repetition*. Spaced repetition is a method of learning new material and then reviewing and memorizing that material over *spaced* intervals. Spaced repetition is often carried out using *flashcards*. The cards that you memorize successfully (i.e., *easy* material) will be reviewed less often, whereas the cards that you stumble over and struggle to memorize (i.e., *hard* material) will be shown more often.

In essence, spaced repetition is an enhancement of the old technique of learning by flashcards. Flashcards rely on cramming the material into the learner's memory regardless of how many times the learner successfully memorizes the material. This makes the learning process inefficient and exhausting. Spaced repetition addresses this flaw by presenting the material to the learner with a frequency that is inversely proportional to his or her ability to memorize it. This way, the learner will ideally be presented with the learned material right before he or she is about to forget it. As you can guess, this technique comes in handy when used to learn new vocabulary.

There has been a lot of research on the usefulness of the spaced repetition of learned material since its first proposal by C. A. Mace in 1932. Since then, it has remained a subject of interest for many researchers and people who seek to improve their memory. In any case, we believe that the improvement that spaced repetition adds to old flashcard techniques, especially in the context of learning a new language, is substantial.

ANKI: THE MOST POPULAR SPACED REPETITION SOFTWARE

To apply spaced repetition to flashcards, we need to decide on many parameters, such as the interval between reviews and whether the interval is fixed or graduated. Many software programs use algorithms to implement spaced-repetition learning. We will not delve into the details of each software and the algorithms they use. Instead, we will pick the most popular software among students and language learners, and that is *Anki*. The word "Anki" in Japanese means "memorization." It is an application developed by Damien Elmes in 2006 that uses an algorithm called SM-2, developed by SuperMemo. The software seems to offer many features while maintaining a reasonable level of simplicity.

In the next chapter, we will walk you briefly through the basics of Anki, how to install it, and how to use the basic features. The Anki software can be used on a desktop device (AnkiWeb) or a smartphone using Android (AnkiDroid) or iOS (AnkiMobile). The use of AnkiWeb and AnkiDroid is free. AnkiMobile, unfortunately, is paid and can be purchased from the Apple Store. Alternatively, if you use an iPhone or iPad, you could install AnkiWeb on your computer and test it for a few days. If you like it, you can continue to use AnkiWeb or purchase AnkiMobile—if you deem it worthwhile. If you create an account using your Anki software, you can synchronize your account on different devices, including multiple desktops and mobile phones.

USING ANKI FOR LANGUAGE LEARNING

There are many studies out there that try to answer the question: "How many words do I need to know to understand X% of a language?" Stuart Webb, professor of linguistics at the University of Western Ontario, asserts that a typical native speaker knows 15,000 to 20,000 word families. A word family is the base form, or root, of a word (e.g., break, breaker, broken, broke, etc., all count as one word family). A language learner who learns only 800 of the most common words in English can understand 75% of the daily-spoken language.

Research done by Francis and Kucera in 1982 found that having a vocabulary size of 2,000 word families is sufficient to cover nearly 80% of a written English text.

To understand dialogue in a movie or on TV, Professor Webb asserts that you need to know 3,000 of the most common word families. A similar assertion has been made by famous linguist Paul Nation, who defines 3,000 as the reasonable threshold of high-frequency words needed by a second-language learner.

With over 5,000 flashcards of verbs, nouns, and adjectives, as well as detailed grammar lessons, this book aims at getting you to that level where you can converse, understand, and speak French in everyday settings.

A lot of Anki cards are available online. Some are free, and many others are on the costlier side. However, the issue with many of the available products is that they simply do not have progressive guidelines that go hand-in-hand with the cards. After all, memorization is different from knowledge acquisition, which requires an understanding of the material you are learning. We attempt to solve this missing piece of the puzzle by providing the proper introduction, learning progression, and grammar knowledge to make sense of the information you are trying to memorize.

We truly hope that many learners will find this technique and this book useful and that learning French and other languages will find its way to as many people as possible to help us understand and recognize each other in a way that serves humanity as a whole.

HOW TO USE THIS BOOK

First and foremost, make sure that you read Chapter II of this book following this introduction. This chapter will help you set up Anki on your desktop computer and mobile device(s). It is essential that you do that successfully to gain the maximum benefit of this book. The coupon code to obtain the flashcards for Level I, available for free for a limited time, can be found in **Appendix A**. Once you download the cards and back them up with the Anki account you create, the cards do not expire.

As you go through each level's introductory topics and grammar, we recommend that you use this book to read the levels and lessons in the order that they are presented. You can, of course, go quickly over the lessons that you find familiar. Nevertheless, we do not recommend that you skip any lesson. The best way to study using this book is to start with reading Level I, Lesson 1 in the book, then go to your Anki app and activate the cards of that lesson. If the lesson is easy compared to your level, you will be able to answer most of the cards as *easy*. As a result, you will see these cards less often in the future as they *fade away* in the memory of the app.

There may be some lessons that you find useful to return to for further review or reference. We try to point these out throughout the book. The appendix also contains some cheat sheets that summarize some of these rules. You can use those if you find them useful. The Anki app will help you through this process because it will keep repeating the concepts that slip your memory.

In the vocabulary-building section, we cover basic verbs and adjectives; then, we go over nouns from different categories. The vocabulary-building section of each level in this book is meant to serve as a reference. The Anki flashcards are preferred to take away the dull and boring part of that process.

Finally, in the appendix, you will find two useful cheat sheets that give you an overall perspective of most moods and verb tenses in French. The first cheat sheet is the Verb Conjugation Chart, which is structured as a comprehensive reference for the reader. The second sheet dives deeper into the irregular verbs of each tense where necessary.

We recommend that you keep these two sheets handy by printing them out or having them available separately on your desk or electronic device.

II. Setting Up Anki

This is an important chapter that you should NOT skip if you want to use the Anki flashcards that accompany the book, which is highly recommended for your maximum benefit.

In this chapter, we cover how to download the Anki software, import the ADROS VERSE EDUCATION French Anki package, and activate the cards associated with the lessons in the book as you read through it.

If you prefer video instructions, go to our YouTube page at https://www.youtube.com/watch?v=kLlWwhFmMHM or simply search for **ADROS VERSE EDUCATION** channel on YouTube and look for the title: **Setting up Anki and Importing the ADROS VERSE Package - All Languages**.

The video in the link above goes through the same steps explained in this chapter.

DOWNLOAD ANKI SOFTWARE

The first step is to download the latest version of Anki compatible with your desktop, Android, or iOS device(s). You can download Anki on different devices and synchronize all of them to the latest study review that you have completed. It is highly recommended that you download a desktop version first to use it as a master copy and then synchronize any other mobile devices you have. However, you can choose to use Anki on your mobile device only.

Windows Desktop

1. Go to https://apps.ankiweb.net/ and download the latest Anki version for Windows. The procedure is similar for Mac and Linux if you use a different operating system.
2. Run the ".exe" file, and open the program by double-clicking on the Anki icon.

3. A default window will open under the username "**User 1**." It is recommended that you create an account to have a backup of your data in the cloud and synchronize it with other devices. To create an account, click on "**Sync**." A window that says "**Account Required**" will pop up. Click on "**Sign Up**." This will take you to a web page where you can complete the signup process.

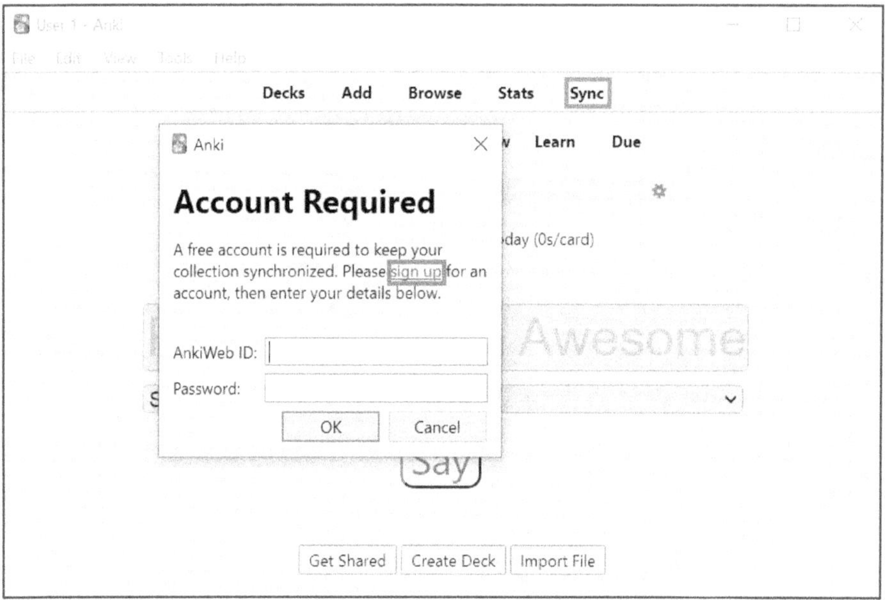

Android or iOS

1. If you have an Android device, go to "**Google Play**" and download "**AnkiDroid Flashcards**," available for free. If you have an iOS device, go to "**Apple Store**" and download "**AnkiMobile Flashcards**." Unfortunately, at the time of writing this book, the app is not free and is sold by "**Apple Store**" for $24.99. Alternatively, you can choose to use the desktop version for free.

2. Open the app from your mobile device.

3. If you have created an account on desktop Anki, you can simply synchronize to your account.

   ❖ On Android: Tap the three horizontal lines at the top left of the screen. Then, select **Settings** > **General Settings** >

AnkiWeb account. Enter the same email from the account you created on desktop Anki.

❖ On iOS: Tap "**Synchronize**" at the bottom right of the screen and enter the same email from the account you created on desktop Anki.

4. If you have not created an account on desktop Anki, you can continue to use Anki on your mobile device without creating an account. However, you will not have any backup online if you lose the data on your phone.

DOWNLOAD & IMPORT THE FRENCH ANKI PACKAGE

After downloading the Anki software on your device, you need to download the Anki package (.apkg) created specifically for this book.

Windows Desktop

1. Go to https://www.adrosverse.com/books-and-flashcards/, and download the "**French: Level I - Basic**" package. At the checkout, use the discount code provided to you in **Appendix A**. If you purchased the book, you should get the Level I Anki package for FREE for a limited time. Once you download the cards, the cards do not expire.
2. After downloading the package, take note of the folder in which it was downloaded.
3. Go to your Anki app, and in the menu bar, go to "**File**," then select "**Import**" from the list of options and navigate to where the package was downloaded.

4. If you have not done so already, you can still create an account to save a backup copy online and synchronize it with other devices by clicking on the **"Sync"** button; this is highly recommended.

Android or iOS

If you have created an account on a desktop device, you only need to log in to your account on the mobile Anki app and synchronize it with the backup copy online.

If you want to continue without creating an account, you can still download and import the package on Android. This is a little more difficult on iOS because you may need to create a download link.

ACTIVATE CARDS

As you successfully import the Anki package with the lessons, you may realize that all the cards are suspended. This is done intentionally because you do not want to be presented with cards from all levels before you even start reading the book.

You are expected to start reading Level 1, Lesson 1. After you finish, you want to activate or *unsuspend* the cards associated with that lesson. To do this, follow the simple steps described here.

Windows Desktop

1. On the main Anki page where decks are presented, click on **"Browse."**

2. Highlight Lesson 1 from the menu on the left.

3. Highlight all the cards (shown on the right) in Lesson 1 using CTRL+A. Alternatively, you can click on **Edit > Select All**.

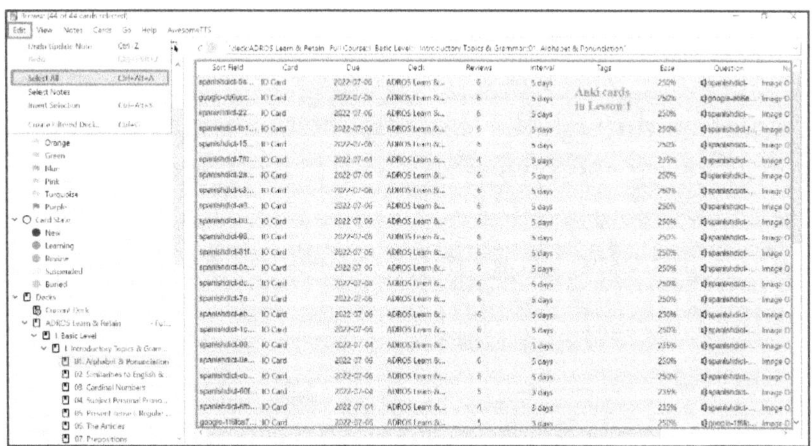

4. After highlighting all the cards from Lesson 1, activate them by clicking on **Cards > Toggle Suspend** to unsuspend the cards.

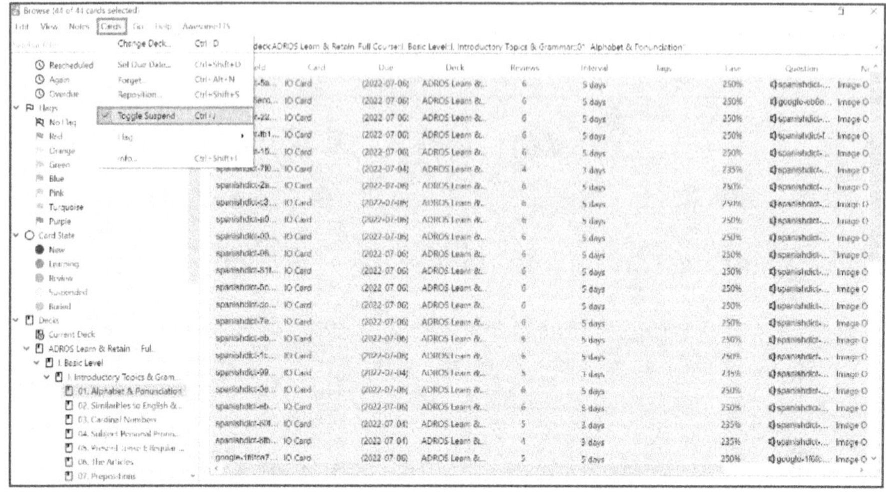

5. Go back to the decks page. You will notice now that there are a few cards that are due from Lesson 1.

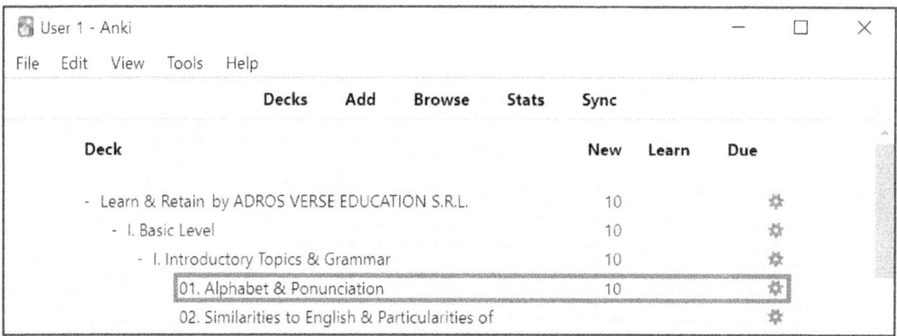

6. If you read through the lesson in the book and are ready, you can start studying and reviewing the cards by clicking on the deck, as highlighted above.

7. On the next page, click on the **"Study Now"** button.

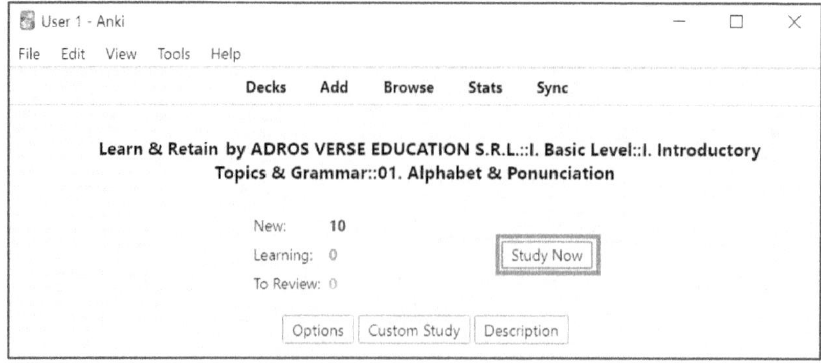

8. The first card will appear, and you will test your knowledge of the information presented on the card. Notice that you may see a different card than the one shown below. That is okay.

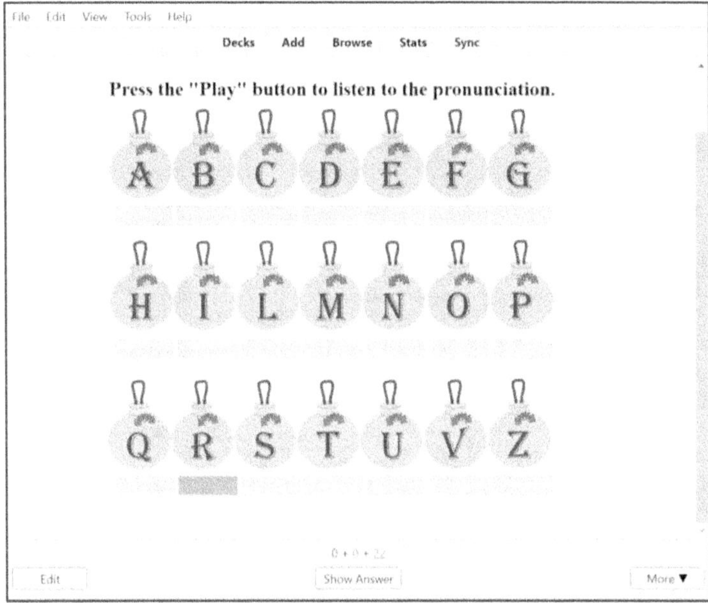

9. Once you are satisfied with your answer, click on the "**Show Answer**" button at the bottom of the page. The answer will appear with four options: "**Again**," "**Hard**," "**Good**," and "**Easy**." You will select the button that represents the difficulty you encountered in answering the card. This will determine how frequently you see the card in the future.

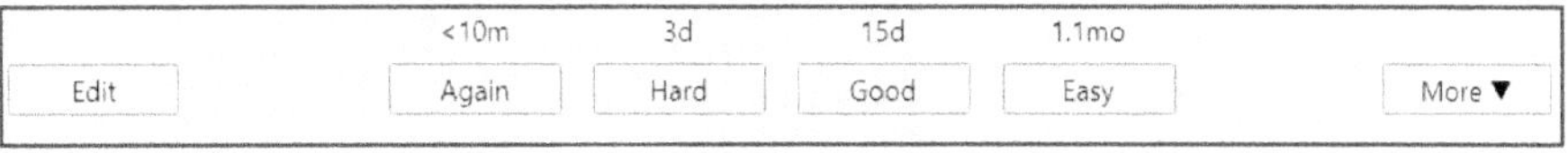

10. The next card will be shown after each answer until you finish all the cards due for the day.

Android

If you have activated the cards from the desktop app, you simply need to synchronize your phone version to see them activated. If you want to activate the cards from your mobile device, follow the steps below:

1. On the main AnkiDroid app page, where decks are presented, tap the three horizontal lines at the top left of the page. You will be presented with a list of options. Select **"Card browser."**

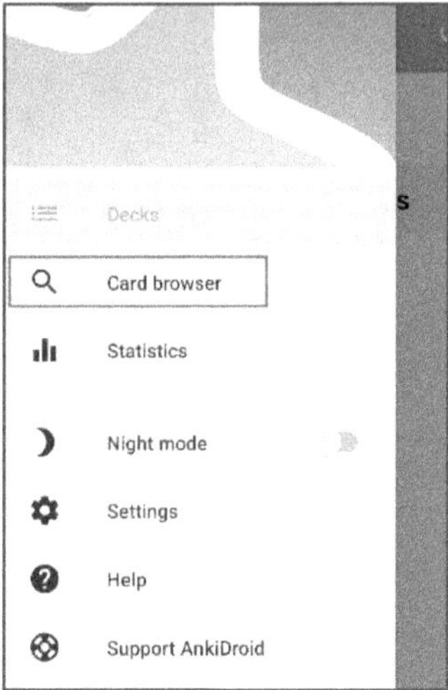

2. Tap the drop-down menu at the top and select Lesson 1 of Level I.

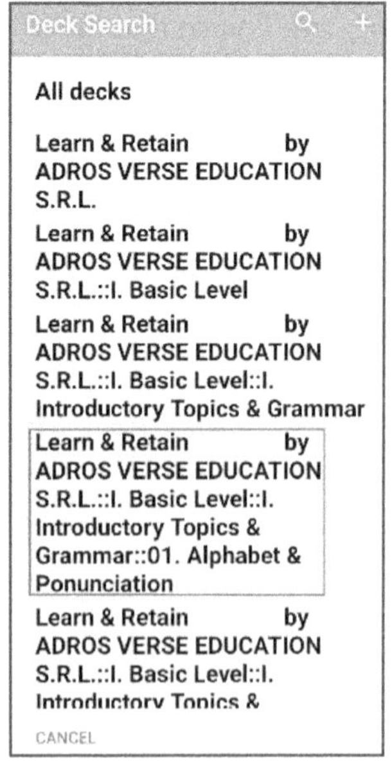

3. A list of cards will appear. Tap the three dots at the top right corner and select **"Select all"** to highlight all the cards.

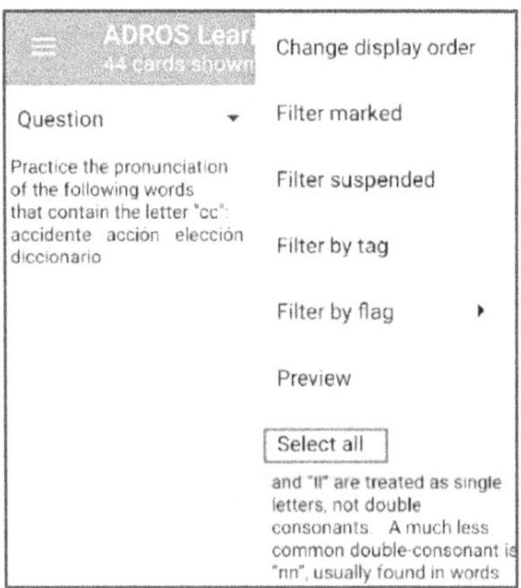

4. Tap the three dots at the top right corner again and select **"Unsuspend cards"** to activate all the cards in the lesson. If you make a mistake, go back to step 2, select all decks, select all cards, and suspend them. Then unsuspend only Lesson 1 of Level I.Go back to the main page where the decks are presented. You will notice now that there are a few cards that are due from Lesson 1.

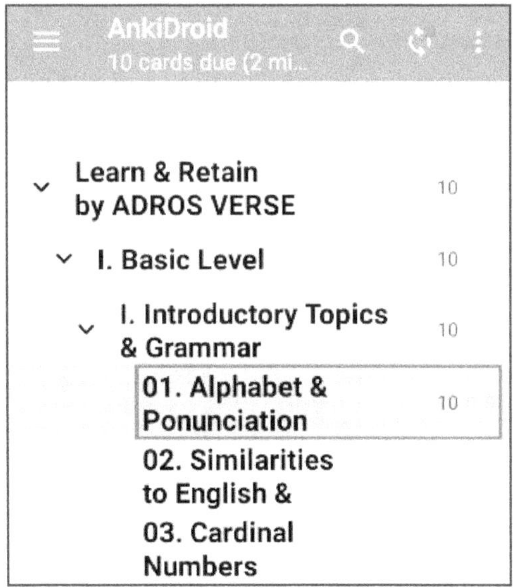

5. If you read through the lesson in the book and are ready, you can start studying and reviewing the cards by tapping on the deck, as highlighted above.

6. The first card will appear, and you will test your knowledge of the information presented on the card. Notice that you may see a different card than the one shown below. That is okay.

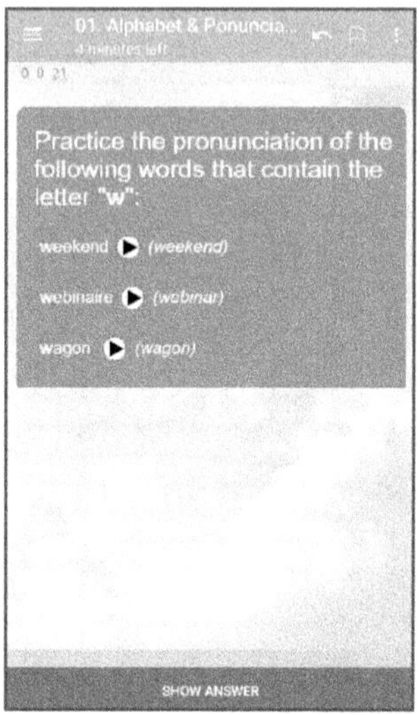

7. Once you have thought your answer through, tap the "**Show Answer**" button at the bottom of the page. The answer will appear with four options: "**Again**," "**Hard**," "**Good**," and "**Easy**." You will select the button that represents the difficulty you encountered in answering the card. This will determine how frequently you see the card in the future.

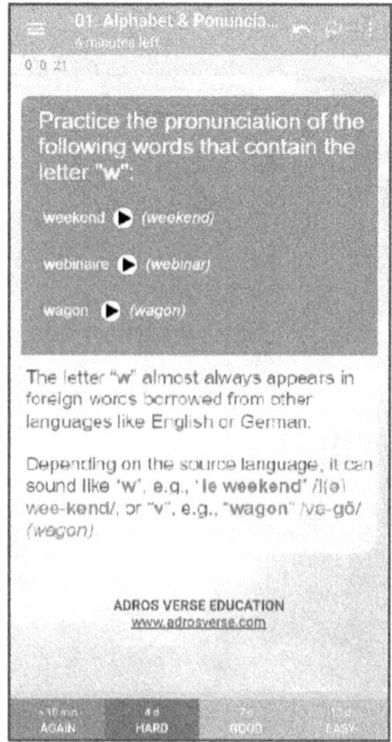

8. The next card will be shown after each answer until you finish all the cards due for today.

IMPORTANT:

If the cards appear too small or too large on your mobile device, as shown below, for example:

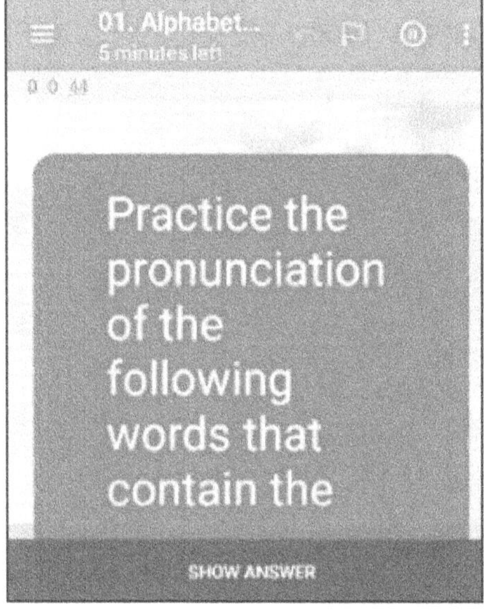

Tap on the three horizontal lines on the top left, then tap on: **Settings > Reviewing > Card Zoom**, and adjust the zoom until the font and card size fit your needs.

iOS

For iOS, replace the first four steps in the Android instructions with the following:

1. On the main AnkiMobile app page, where decks are presented, tap on Lesson 1 from Level I. You will be presented with the first card.

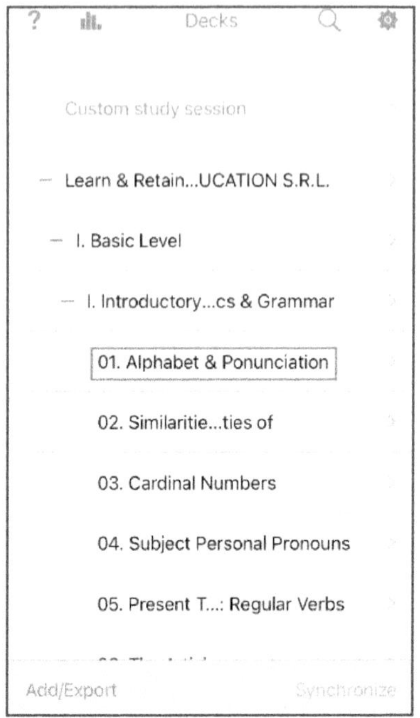

2. Tap on "**Browse**" at the top right of the screen.

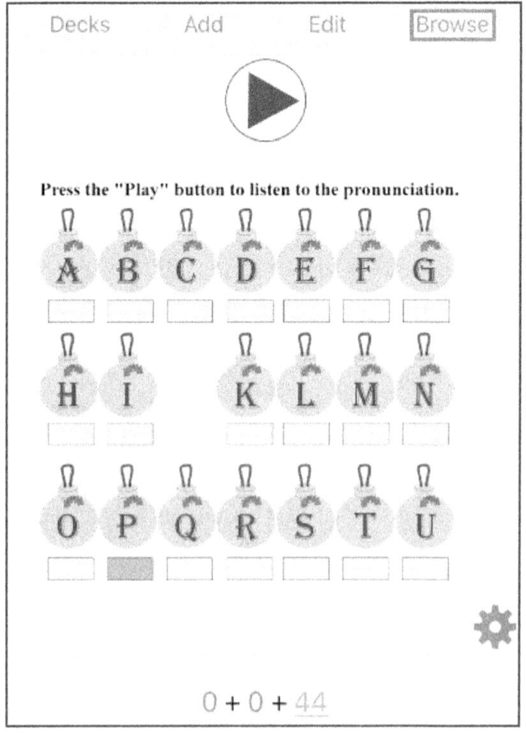

3. Tap on "**Select**" at the top right of the screen, then tap on "**Select All**."

4. Tap on "**Actions**," and from the drop-down menu, tap on "**Toggle Suspend**" to activate the cards in this lesson.

Follow the same remaining steps from 5 to 9 in the Android instructions.

MORE SETTINGS

You can always tweak your Anki settings based on how often you forget your cards. These settings can be accessed by clicking on the settings icon on your deck page, as shown below.

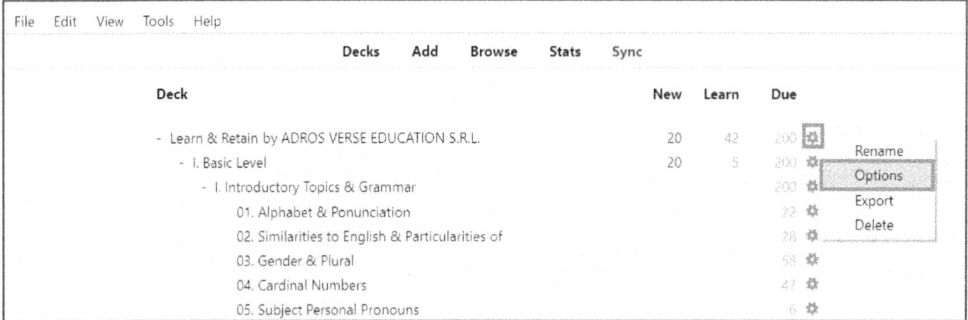

We recommend that you switch off the automatic audio play and keep the other default settings. However, feel free to experiment with the settings for a better personal experience.

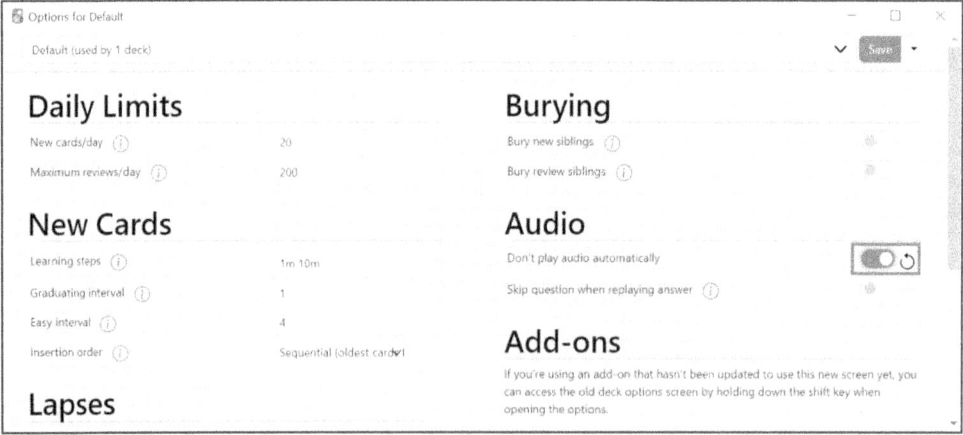

You can add your custom cards and even decks. To add a note (that is an Anki card), go to your **"Browse"** page and click on **Notes** > **Add Notes**.

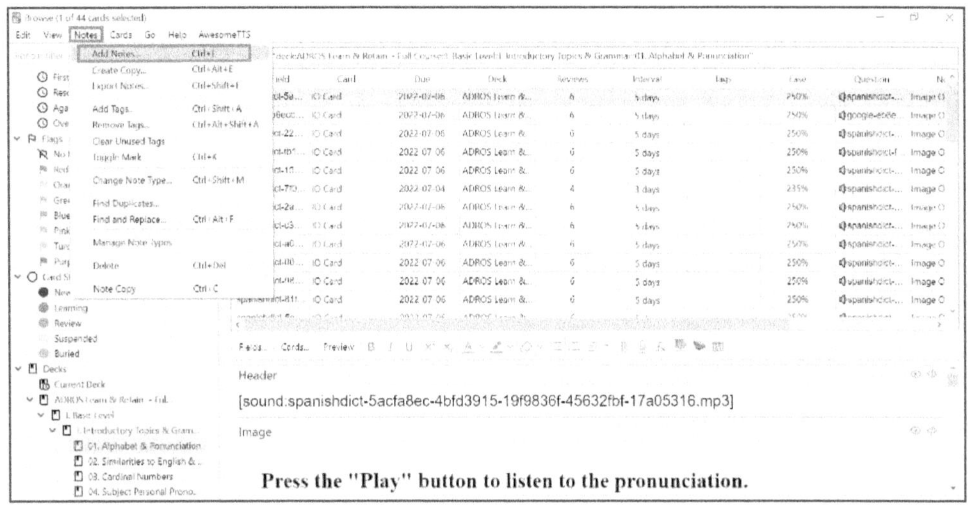

You can choose your preferred note type and add it to your learning deck.

It is not a requirement to know how to use Anki beyond the basics that we have covered in this introduction. However, if you are interested, we encourage you to learn from the plethora of resources online that teach you how to create and edit decks and notes on Anki.

I. Introductory Topics & Grammar

Start your journey with French by familiarizing yourself with the introductory topics in this section. We will cover some grammar and basic knowledge that you need to equip yourself with to make the learning process easier, such as the alphabet, numbers, etc.

Do not worry if you are not able to absorb all of the information. Your Anki cards will help you memorize the material in a non-boring way until you master what you have learned. Ensure that you did not skip the introductory Chapter II of this book on setting up Anki.

1. ALPHABET & PRONUNCIATION

Luckily, French uses the Latin letters used in English with only a few differences in pronunciation. French is generally not a phonetic language, meaning that what you read is not always what you hear. However, there are some rules that can help you guess the correct pronunciation with a good success rate.

There are 26 letters (six vowels and 20 consonants) in the French alphabet, which are identical to the letters in the English alphabet except in their pronunciation

Start with the French alphabet in the table below, and use your Anki cards to anchor what you learned via spaced-repetition exercises.

French Letter		English Pronunciation	Notes
A	a	ah	like "**a**" in "father"
B	b	be	equivalent to English "**b**"
C	c	se	sounds like English "**k**," except: 1. before "**e**," "**i**," or "**y**," it sounds like "**s**" 2. if written with a cedilla "**ç**," it sounds like "**s**" 3. before "**h**," "**ch**" sounds like "**sh**" in "**sheep**"
D	d	de	equivalent to English "**d**"
E	e	ə	like "**u**" in "**burn**" or "**i**" in "**girl**," but much shorter

F	f	ef	equivalent to English "**f**"
G	g	je	sounds like "**g**" in "**g**ab," and like "**j**" in "**j**ob" only before "**e**," "**i**," or "**y**"
H	h	ash	silent letter like "**h**" in "**h**our"
I	i	ee	like "**ee**" in "s**ee**" or "**i**" in "mar**i**ne"
J	j	jee	equivalent to English "**j**"
K	k	ka	equivalent to English "**k**"
L	l	el	equivalent to English "**l**," but softer
M	m	em	equivalent to English "**m**"
N	n	en	equivalent to English "**n**"
O	o	o	equivalent to English "**o**" but shorter
P	p	pe	equivalent to English "**p**"
Q	q	kμ	almost always followed by a mute "**u**" to form "**qu**" which sounds like "**k**," e.g., "**qui**," pronounced "**kee**"
R	r	eя	equivalent to English "**r**" but rolled using the back of the tongue near the throat to form the distinctive French "**r**" sound
S	s	es	can sound like English "**s**" or "**z**"
T	t	te	like "**t**" in "**t**able" but strongly pronounced
U	u	μ	This sound does not exist in English. Make your lips round as if you want to say "**o**" and say "**ee**" instead
V	v	ve	equivalent to English "**v**"
W	w	dooblə ve	like "**w**" in "**w**eek" or "**v**" in "**v**ideo," depending on the origin of the borrowed word
X	x	eeks	like "**x**" in "fi**x**" or "**x**" in "e**x**act," and in rare cases, like "**s**" in "**s**ea"
Y	y	ee gяek	pronounced exactly like French "**i**" when on its own or before a consonant and like "**y**" in "**y**ou" when it is in front of a vowel
Z	z	zed	equivalent to English "**z**"

One main challenge in French is mastering the different vowel sounds, some of which are formed from compound vowels and do not have equivalent sounds in English.

Another challenge is the silent consonant(s) at the end of most French words. This can be confusing to French learners in the beginning. We will discuss some general rules that will help us correctly guess the pronunciation in most cases.

Throughout the book, we will use slash marks "/" to mark the pronunciation of some words, and we will highlight the stressed syllable in bold in case of multi-syllable words, e.g., "**parler**" /paя-**le**/ *(to speak)*.

Vowels

The letters "**a**," "**u**," "**o**," "**e**," "**i**," and "**y**" are the vowel letters in French. There are two types of vowels in French: oral vowels and nasal vowels. Both oral and nasal vowels can have a combination of vowel letters.

1. Oral Vowels

The vowels "**a**," "**u**," and "**o**" are considered *hard* vowels, whereas "**e**," "**i**," and "**y**" are considered *soft* vowels. When soft vowels come after letters like "**c**" and "**g**," they dictate the pronunciation of that letter to be hard or soft. We will discuss this in detail in the next section on consonants.

The six vowel letters in French have a slightly different pronunciation in French than in English. Notice that we use different symbols from the standard International Phonetic Alphabet (IPA) for simplicity.

Let us start with the main six vowels in French:

a /a/	"**pa**rler" /paя-**le**/ *(to speak)*	always sounds like "**a**" in "father"
u /µ/	"**mur**" /mµя/ *(wall)*	This sound does not exist in English. Make your lips round as if you want to say "**o**" and say "**ee**" instead
o /o/	"**corps**" /coя/ *(body)* - open "**trop**" /тяo/ *(very)* - closed	1. closed: like "**o**" in "**go**" but without the final "**w**" sound 2. open: like "**o**" in "**cop**" but shorter
e /ə/, /e/	"**le**" /lə/ *(the)* - schwa "**elle**" /el/ *(she)* - open "**aller**" /a-**le**/ *(to go)* - closed	1. like a *schwa* sound in English but more rounded, and sometimes ignored 2. closed: like "**ay**" in "**say**" but without the final "**y**" sound, sometimes spelled "**é**" 3. open: like "**e**" in "**bed**," sometimes spelled "**è**" or "**ê**"
i /ee/	"**gi**rafe" /jee-яaf/ *(giraffe)*	like "**ee**" in "**see**" or "**i**" in "**marine**"
y /ee/	"**cy**cle" /seekl/ *(cycle)*	like "**ee**" in "**see**" or "**i**" in "**marine**"

The letter "**o**" has a closed sound and open sound. The closed "**o**" sound is often used when the "**o**" is the final sound of a word, e.g., "**trop**" /тяo/ *(too much)*; is followed by a "**z**" sound, e.g., "**rose**" /яoz/ *(pink)*; or has a circumflex, e.g., "**hôpital**" /o-pee-**tal**/ *(hospital)*. Otherwise, the open short sound is used. The open sound is similar to the "**o**" in "**cop**" but shorter, e.g., "**corps**" /coя/ *(body)*.

The letter "**e**" can have one of three sounds:

- Schwa sound

This sound is similar to the English schwa[1] but more rounded. This sound is often encountered at the end of single-syllable words, such as "**le**" /lə/ *(the)*, "**te**" /tə/ *(you)*, etc. In multi-syllable words, the schwa pronunciation is *sometimes* optional and can be omitted, e.g., "**devoirs**" /d(ə)v-**waя**/ *(homework)*, "**samedi**" /sam(ə)-**dee**/ *(Saturday)*, "**acheter**" /a-sh(ə)-**te**/ *(to buy)*, etc.

- Closed sound

The closed "**e**" sound is similar to the "**ay**" sound in *"say"* but without the final "**y**" sound. This sound is often encountered when the syllable sound ends in a *vowel*. For example, the last syllable in the verb "**aller**" /a-**le**/ *(to go)* has the *sound* "**le**," which is a vowel sound even though the spelling of the syllable ends in the consonant "**r**." If the "**e**" has an acute accent, it is also pronounced with a closed "**e**" sound, e.g., "**clé**" /kle/ *(key)*, "**désolé**" /de-zo-**le**/ *(sorry)*, etc.

- Open sound

The open "**e**" sound is similar to the "**e**" in *"bed"* or *"set."* This sound is often encountered when the syllable sound ends in a *consonant* sound, e.g., "**sept**" /s<u>e</u>t/ *(seven)*, "**elle**" /<u>e</u>l/ *(she)*, etc. If the "**e**" has a grave accent or a circumflex, it is pronounced with an open "**e**" sound, e.g., "**mère**" /m<u>e</u>я/ *(mother)*, "**prêt**" /pя<u>e</u>/ *(ready)*, etc. The

---

[1] A schwa sound in English is the relaxed unstressed vowel sound that we encounter in some pronunciations such as "**a**" in "**about**" or "**e**" in "**taken**."

circumflex often indicates that the original word had an "**s**" in the source language that was later dropped as the language developed.

In addition to the main six vowels, there are some compound vowel sounds that result from different combinations of the six vowels. Some are familiar and easy to grasp, such as:

ai /e/	"**faire**" /feя/ *(to do)* "**jamais**" /ja-**me**/ *(never)*	Similar to closed "**e**" sound (especially at verb ends), or open "**e**" sound (in most other cases)
au /o/	"**aussi**" /o-**see**/ *(also)* "**paume**" /pom/ *(palm)*	Similar to closed "**o**" sound
ei /e/	"**neige**" /nej/ *(snow)* "**peiner**" /pe-**ne**/ *(to struggle)*	Similar to closed "**e**" sound or open "**e**" sound
ua /ua/	"**nuage**" /noo-**aj**/ *(cloud)* "**gluante**" /gloo-**ant**/ *(sticky)*	This combination is pronounced as two different vowels, that is, "**oo-a**"
ue /we/	"**manuel**" /man-**wel**/ *(manual)* "**usuel**" /μz-**wel**/ *(usual)*	Exceptionally, the "**u**" is mute if preceded by "**q**" or "**g**," e.g., "**que**" /kə/ *(that/who)*
ui /wee/	"**pluie**" /plwee/ *(rain)* "**buisson**" /bwee-**sõ**/ *(bush)*	Exceptionally, the "**u**" is mute if preceded by "**q**" or "**g**," e.g., "**qui**" /kee/ *(that/who)*
ie /ye/	"**tiers**" /tyeя/ *(third)* "**fier**" /fyeя/ *(proud)*	Assuming it is not followed by a third vowel, e.g., "**ieu**" /yeu/
ia /ya/	"**fiable**" /fyabl/ *(reliable)* "**social**" /so-**syal**/ *(social)*	Assuming it is not followed by a third vowel, e.g., "**iau**" /yo/
ou /oo/	"**pour**" /pooя/ *(for)* "**rouge**" /яooj/ *(red)*	Pronounced like "**oo**" in "**food**," unless followed by a vowel, e.g., "**oue**" /we/

On the other hand, the following compound vowels are tricky and are often confusing to English learners:

eu /eu/	"**deux**" /deu/ *(two)* "**heure**" /euя/ *(hour)*	This sound does not exist in English. Make your lips round as if you want to say "**o**" and say "**e**" instead. Depending on whether the "**e**" sound is open or closed, the "**eu**" sound can have an open or closed sound as well.
œu /eu/	"**cœur**" /keuя/ *(heart)* "**œuf**" /euf/ *(egg)*	This vowel is treated like the "**eu**" vowel.
eau /o/	"**eau**" /o/ *(water)* "**beau**" /bo/ *(beautiful)*	This sounds like a closed "**o**."
ieu /yeu/	"**lieu**" /lyeu/ *(place)* "**mieux**" /myeu/ *(better)*	Combining the "**y**" sound with the "**eu**" sound.

iau /yo/	"**sociaux**" /so-**syo**/ *(social)* "**piauler**" /pyo-**le**/ *(peep)*	Found only in a few words.
oi /wa/	"**armoire**" /ая-**мвая**/ *(cabinet)* "**chinois**" /sheen-**wa**/ *(Chinese)*	Pronounced "**wa**" and not like the English "**oy**" sound.
oue /we/	"**ouest**" /west/ *(west)* "**jouer**" /jwe/ *(to play)*	An exception is at the end of a word when "**e**" is silent, e.g., "**boue**" /boo/ *(mud)*.
oui /wee/	"**oui**" /wee/ *(yes)* "**jouir**" /jweeя/ *(to enjoy)*	An exception is the letter combination "**ouil**" and "**ouille**," both pronounced "**ooy**," e.g., "**bouillir**" /boo-**yeeя**/ *(to boil)*.

Notice that when the "**o**" and "**e**" are combined into one symbol, called a ligature, "**œ**," they form a single sound. As we have seen, when followed by "**u**," the combination "**œu**" has a sound identical to "**eu**." This is the most common sound of the ligature "**œ**" in French. Here are four cases that produce the three possible sounds of the ligature "**œ**" in French:

œ + u /eu/	"**cœur**" /кеuя/ *(heart)* "**œuf**" /euf/ *(egg)*	Preceding "**u**," the "**œu**" combination sounds like "**eu**."
œ + il /eu/	"**œil**" /euy/ *(eye)* "**œillet**" /eu-**ye**/ *(eyelet)*	Preceding "**il**," the "**œil**" combination also sounds like "**eu**."
œ + st /e/ (open)	"**œstrogène**" /est-яо-**jen**/ *(estrogen)*	Preceding "**st**," the "**œ**" sounds like an open "**e**."
œ + consonant /e/ (closed)	"**œsophage**" /e-zo-**faj**/ *(esophagus)*	Preceding any other consonant, the "**œ**" sounds like a closed "**e**."

Finally, there is the *dieresis*, which can be found on "**e**," "**i**," or "**u**." It is used on the second vowel of a two-vowel combination to denote that the two vowels must be pronounced separately. For example, "**naïve**" is pronounced /na-**eev**/, not /**nev**/, despite the "**ai**" combination.

2. Nasal Vowels

A nasal pronunciation occurs in French often when a vowel precedes an "**n**" or "**m**," but not always. The nasal sound occurs when the "**n**" or "**m**" preceded by a vowel is at the end of a word or anywhere else in the word but followed by a consonant. To summarize:

at word end	*vowel* + "**n**" or "**m**"	nasal
anywhere else in a word	*vowel* + "**n**" or "**m**" + *consonant*	nasal
	vowel + "**n**" or "**m**" + *vowel*	not nasal

For example, the "**n**" in "**un**" *(a/an – masculine)* and "**anglais**" *(English)* is nasal, but the "**n**" in "**une**" *(a/an – feminine)* and "**reine**" *(queen)* is not nasal.

The three nasal vowel sounds in French are: nasal "**a**," nasal "**i**," and nasal "**o**." We refer to these three sounds throughout the book here using the symbols: "**ã**," "**ĩ**," and "**õ**." The three sounds occur in the following cases:

- The nasal sound "**õ**" occurs when "**o**" is followed by "**n**" or "**m**," i.e., "**on**" or "**om**."

- The nasal sound "**ã**" occurs when "**a**," "**e**," or "**ao**" is followed by "**n**" or "**m**," i.e., "**an**," "**am**," "**en**," "**em**," "**aon**," or "**aom**."

- The nasal sound "**ĩ**" occurs when "**i**," "**u**," "**y**," "**ai**," "**ei**," or "**ie**" is followed by "**n**" or "**m**," e.g., "**in**," "**im**," "**un**," "**um**," "**yn**," "**ym**," "**ain**," "**aim**," "**ein**," "**eim**," "**ien**," or "**iem**."

Here are some examples of words that contain each of the three nasal sounds:

	an/am		**en/em**		**aon/aom**	
ã	"blanc"	"ambre"	"encore"	"temps"	"faon"	"paon"
	/blã/	/ãbя/	/ã-koя/	/tã/	/fã/	/pã/
	(white)	*(amber)*	*(again)*	*(time)*	*(fawn)*	*(peacock)*
	in/im	**un/um**	**yn/ym**	**ain/aim**	**ien/iem**	**ein/eim**
ĩ	"vin"	"un"	"lynx"	"faim"	"chien"	"rein"
	/vĩ/	/ĩ/	/lĩks/	/fĩ/	/shyĩ/	/яĩ/
	(wine)	*(a/an)*	*(lynx)*	*(hunger)*	*(dog)*	*(kidney)*
	on/om					
õ	"bon"		"sombre"		"ombre"	
	/bõ/		/sõbя/		/õbя/	
	(good)		*(dark)*		*(shadow)*	

In the past, there used to be a distinction between the nasal sound from the combination "**un**" or "**um**" and the rest of nasal "ĩ" sounds. This is characterized by a fourth distinct nasal sound "œ̃." However, this sound is no longer in use in much of France and has been assimilated into the nasal "ĩ" sound.

Consonants

❖ The letter "**c**" in French is used to form the equivalents of the sounds "**k**" (*hard* "**c**") and "**s**" (*soft* "**c**") in English. The way this is achieved is as follows:

1. If the letter "**c**" is followed by "**e**," "**i**," or "**y**," it is considered a soft "**c**" and is pronounced like "*s*" in "*sea*," e.g., "**cinéma**" /see-ne-**ma**/ *(cinema)*.

2. If the letter "**c**" is written with a cedilla, i.e., "**ç**," it is considered a soft "**c**" and is pronounced like "*s*" in "*sea*," e.g., "**ça**" /sa/ *(this)*. The cedilla is always followed by a vowel other than "**e**," "**i**," or "**y**."

3. Otherwise, the letter "**c**" is considered a hard "**c**" and is pronounced like "*k*" in "*kit*," e.g., "**café**" /ka-**fe**/ *(coffee)*.

   Notice that an equivalent to the "**ch**" sound in English does not exist. The "**ch**" combination in French is pronounced like "*sh*" in "*sheep*." To summarize:

c	+	"**e**," "**i**," or "**y**"	soft "**c**"	"<u>**c**</u>inéma" /see-ne-**ma**/ *(cinema)*
ç	+	"**a**," "**o**," or "**u**"	soft "**c**"	"<u>**ç**</u>a" /sa/ *(this)*
c	+	"**h**"	"**sh**" sound	"<u>**c**</u>hat" /sha/ *(cat)*
c	+	any letter other than "**e**," "**i**," "**y**," or "**h**"	hard "**c**"	"<u>**c**</u>afé" /ka-**fe**/ *(coffee)*

❖ The letter "**g**" can also have a *hard* sound like "*g*" in "*gab*" or a *soft* sound like "*j*" in "*jam*." The basic rules are:

1. If the letter "**g**" is followed by "**e**," "**i**," or "**y**," it is considered a soft "**g**" and is pronounced like "*j*" in "*jam*," e.g., "**général**" /je-ne-**яal**/ *(general)*.

2. If the letter "**g**" is followed by "**n**," the combination "**gn**" is pronounced like "**ny**" in *"canyon,"* or "**lli**" in *"million,"* e.g., "**espagnol**" /es-pa-**nyol**/ *(Spanish)*.

3. If the letter "**g**" is not followed by "**e**," "**i**," "**y**," or "**n**," it is considered a hard "**g**" and is pronounced like "**g**" in *"gab,"* e.g., "**gare**" *(station)* is pronounced /гaя/.

Notice that the letter "**u**" is mute when it falls after the letter "**g**" to maintain the hard "**g**" pronunciation, e.g., "**guerre**" /гея/ *(war)*, "**guitare**" /gee-тaя/ *(guitar)*, etc.[1]

Similarly, to maintain the soft "**g**" pronunciation before an "**a**," "**o**," or a consonant, the letter "**g**" is followed by an "**e**." For example, "**nous mangeons**" /noo mã-**jõ**/ *(we eat)*.

To summarize:

g	+	"e," "i," or "y"	soft "g"	"**gérer**" /je-**яe**/ *(to manage)*
g	+	"n"	"ny" sound	"**oignon**" /o-**nyõ**/ *(onion)*
g	+	any letter other than "e," "i," "y," or "n"	hard "g"	"**gare**" /гaя/ *(train station)* "**gonfler**" /gõ-**fle**/ *(to swell)* "**grand**" /гяã/ *(large)*

❖ The letter "**h**" is generally not pronounced in French, unless it is part of the combination "**ch**" or "**ph**," which form the equivalent English sounds "**sh**" and "**f**," respectively.

Although the "**h**" is always not pronounced, there is a distinction between a *mute* "**h**" and *aspirated* "**h**." This simply goes back to the origin of the word. Words of Latin origin tend to have a mute "**h**," whereas words of Germanic origin tend to have an aspirated "**h**." The difference is subtle and only appears in a few cases such as contraction with the definite article, which will be discussed in **Lesson 7** of this level.

---

[1] There are only few exceptions in which the "**u**" is pronounced after the "**g**," such as: "**Uruguay**" /μ-яμ-**gwai**/, "**jaguar**" /ja-**gwaя**/, "**aiguille**" /e-**gμy**/ *(needle)*, and "**linguiste**" /lĩ-**gweest**/ *(linguist)*.

❖ The letter "**l**" is equivalent to the English *"l"* as in *"lake."* However, the "**l**" sound in French is much lighter since the back of the tongue is not raised against the palate. Exceptionally, there are two cases in which "**l**" sounds like *"y"* in *"yogurt."*

<u>Case #1</u>: The combination *vowel* + "**il**"

Examples include: "**bail**" /bey/ *(lease)*, "**œil**" /euy/ *(eye)*, "**soleil**" /so-**ley**/ *(sun)*, etc. Words ending in "-**uile**" are an exception, e.g., "**huile**" /ə-**weel**/ *(oil)*, "**tuile**" /t-**weel**/ *(tile)*, etc.

<u>Case #2</u>: The combination *vowel/consonant* + "**ill**"

If the combination "**ill**" is preceded by a *vowel*, then it falls under Case #1, e.g., "**fe<u>u</u>ille**" /feuy/ *(leaf)*, "**p<u>a</u>ille**" /pay/ *(straw)*, etc., and the "**ll**" is always pronounced like English "**y**."

If the combination "**ill**" is preceded by a *consonant*, the "**ll**" is pronounced like English "**y**" in most words and like simple "**l**" in some words. Here are some examples:

"**ll**" pronounced like "**y**"		"**ll**" pronounced like "**l**"	
fille[f]	*girl*	**ville**[f]	*city*
famille[f]	*family*	**tranquille**[m,f]	*calm*
vanille[f]	*vanilla*	**Lille**	*Lille (a city)*
cédille[f]	*cedilla (ç)*	**distiller**	*to distill*
Bastille[f]	*Bastille*	**osciller**	*to swing or oscillate*

In addition to the above examples, the "**ll**" in numbers such as "**mille**[m]" /meel/ *(thousand)*, "**million**[m]" /meel-**yõ**/ *(million)*, "**milliard**[m]" /meel-**yaя**/ *(billion)*, and "**billion**[m]" /beel-**yõ**/ *(trillion)*, is pronounced like "**l**."

Finally, if the "**ll**" is preceded by a vowel other than "**i**," it is pronounced like "**l**," e.g., "**salle**" /sal/ *(room)*, "**belle**" /bel/ *(beautiful)*, "**folle**" /fol/ *(crazy)*, "**syllabe**" /see-**lab**/ *(syllable)*, etc.

❖ The letter "**q**" is almost always followed by the letter "**u**" and sounds like "**k**," e.g., "**qui**" /kee/ *(who/that)*. There are only a few exceptions in which the "**q**" is not followed by "**u**," such as "**cinq**" /sĩk/ *(five)*, "**coq**" /kok/ *(rooster)*. In only a few words, the "**qu**" is pronounced like the English "**kw**" sound, e.g., "**équateur**" /ek-wa-**теия**/ *(equator)*.

❖ The letter "**s**" can sound like English "**s**" or "**z**." If the "**s**" falls between two vowels, it is often pronounced like English "**z**," e.g., "**ro**s**e**" /яoz/ *(pink)*. In most other cases, it is pronounced like the English "**s**" in *"start,"* e.g., "**salut**" /sa-lµ/ *(hi)*.

❖ The letter "**w**" almost always appears in foreign words borrowed from other languages like English or German. Depending on the source language, it can sound like "**w**," e.g., "**le weekend**" /l(ə) wee-**kend**/, or "**v**," e.g., "**wagon**" /va-**gõ**/ *(wagon)*.

❖ The letter "**x**" has a "**ks**" sound like the "**x**" in *fix* or a "**gz**" sound like the "**x**" in *exam.* The basic rules are:

1. If the letter "**x**" falls between two vowel sounds or at the beginning of a word, it often has a "**gz**" sound, e.g., "**e**x**amen**" /e-gza-**mã**/ *(exam)*, "**x**ylophone" /gzee-lo-**fon**/ *(xylophone)*, etc.

2. Only at the end of the numbers "**si**x" /sees/ *(six)* and "**di**x" /dees/ *(ten)* the final "**x**" is pronounced like "**s**."

3. In most other cases, the "**x**" has a "**ks**" sound, e.g., "**taxe**" /taks/ *(tax)*.

❖ The letter "**y**" is considered a semi-vowel in one case, that is, when it precedes another vowel. In this case, it is pronounced like English "**y**," e.g., "**yeux**" /yeu/ *(eyes)*, "**yaourt**" /ya-**ooяt**/ *(yogurt)*, etc. In all other cases, when it precedes a consonant or on its own, it is considered a vowel and is treated exactly like the vowel "**i**," e.g., "**y**" /ee/ *(there)*, "**cyclisme**" /seek-**leezm**/ *(cycling)*, "**Yves**" /eev/ *(Yves)*, etc.

❖ The final "**-tion**" in many French words is pronounced /-syõ/, e.g., "**nation**" /na-**syõ**/ *(nation)*, "**direction**" /dee-яek-**syõ**/ *(direction)*, "**relation**" /яe-la-**syõ**/ *(relation)*, etc.

❖ In most cases, other than "**ll**," double consonants generally do not change the pronunciation, e.g., "**annuler**" /a-nμ-**le**/ *(to cancel)*, "**essai**" /e-**se**/ *(essay)*, etc.

Silent Final Consonants

We have encountered the silent "**h**" sound in French, e.g., "**heure**" /euя/ *(hour)*. In addition, we saw how the letter "**e**" can be silent in many words, e.g., "**acheter**" /a-sh(ə)-**te**/ *(to buy)*. In addition, the final "**e**" in most multi-syllable words tends to be silent unless it is accented, e.g., "**sucre**" /sμkя/ *(sugar)*, "**père**" /pея/ *(father)*, etc.

You may have also noticed that the final consonant(s) is(are) often silent in many French words, e.g., "**trop**" /tяo/ *(too much)*, "**temp**" /tã/ *(time)*, etc. The general rule is to assume that the final consonant is silent. However, there are many exceptions to this rule. The following notes can help you determine when to treat the final consonant of a French word as silent or pronounce it:

1. The letters "**j**," "**v**," and "**w**" are seldom found in French except in some foreign names, in which case they are likely pronounced.
2. The letters "**b**," "**k**," and "**q**" are found at the end of very few words in French. In most of these words, they are pronounced, e.g., "**club**" /klμb/ *(club)*, "**biftek**" /beef-**tek**/ *(steak)*, "**cinq**" /sĩk/ *(five)*, "**coq**" /kok/ *(rooster)*. One notable exception is "**plomb**" /plõ/ *(lead)*.
3. The letter "**g**" is generally pronounced when it is a final consonant of an English loanword, e.g., "**blog**" /blog/, "**iceberg**" /ayz-**beяg**/, "**parking**" /paя-**keeng**/, "**meeting**" /mee-**teeng**/, etc. The main exception of this rule is when it forms the nasal sound "**ng**" in non-"**-ing**" suffixes, e.g., "**long**" /lõ/ *(long)*, "**sang**" /sã/ *(blood)*, etc.

4. The letters "**n**" and "**m**" often result in a nasal sound when they come at the end of a word, e.g., "**un**" /ĩ/ *(a/ an)*, "**balcon**" /bal-kõ/ *(balcony)*, "**nom**" /nõ/ *(name)*, "**parfum**" /pая-fĩ/ *(perfume)*, etc. There are some notable exceptions such as: "**abdomen**" /ab-do-**men**/ *(abdomen)*, "**Amen**" /a-**men**/ *(Amen)*, "**forum**" /fo-яµm/ *(forum)*, and "**cadmium**" /cad-**myµm**/ *(cadmium)*.

5. The final consonants "**c**," "**r**," "**f**," and "**l**" tend to be *pronounced* especially in short words of one or two syllables. The four letters are often remembered using the word "**CaReFuL**." Here are some examples and exceptions for each case:

	Pronounced (Often)	Silent (Exceptions)
c	"**avec**" *(with)*, "**bloc**" *(block)*, "**sac**" *(bag)*, "**truc**" *(trick)*	"**estomac**" *(stomach)*, "**porc**" *(pork)*, "**blanc**" *(white)*, "**tronc**" *(trunk)*
r	"**cher**" *(expensive)*, "**clair**" *(clear)*, "**fier**" *(proud)*, "**mer**" *(sea)*	Infinitive of "-er" verbs, e.g., "**parler**" *(to speak)*
f	"**actif**" *(active)*, "**chef**" *(chef)*, "**neuf**" *(nine)*, "**œuf**" *(egg)*, "**soif**" *(thirst)*	"**clef**" *(key)*, "**nerf**" *(nerve)*
l	"**avril**" *(April)*, "**bol**" *(bowl)*, "**hôtel**" *(hotel)*, "**il**" *(he)*, "**nul**" *(nul)*	"**gentil**" *(kind)*, "**outil**" *(tool)*, *vowel* + "**il**": "**accueil**" *(welcome)*, "**œil**" *(eye)*

6. The final consonants "**d**," "**p**," "**s**," "**t**," "**x**," and "**z**" are often *silent* with a few exceptions. Here are some examples and exceptions for each case:

	Silent (Often)	Pronounced (Exceptions)
d	"**canard**" *(duck)*, "**chaud**" *(hot)*, "**froid**" *(cold)*, "**grand**" *(big)*,	"**sud**" *(south)*, proper names: "**David**", "**Alfred**", etc.
p	"**beaucoup**" *(a lot)*, "**champ**" *(field)*, "**drap**" *(sheet)*, "**loup**" *(wolf)*	"**cap**" *(cape)*, "**slip**" *(underpants)*
s	"**bas**" *(down)*, "**les**" *(the)*, "**nous**" *(we)*, "**temps**" *(time)*, "**trois**" *(three)*	"**autobus**" *(bus)*, "**fils**" *(son)*, "**ours**" *(bear)*, "**tennis**" *(tennis)*
t	"**abricot**" *(apricot)*, "**et**" *(and)*, "**minuit**" *(midnight)*, "**petit**" *(small)*, "**poulet**" *(chicken)*, "**salut**" *(hi)*	"**brut**" *(raw)*, "**est**" *(east)*, "**ouest**" *(west)*, -**ct** ending: e.g., "**direct**" *(direct)*, -**pt** ending: e.g., "**sept**" *(seven)*
x	"**choix**" *(choice)*, "**deux**" *(two)*, "**époux**" *(spouse)*, "**prix**" *(price)*	"**six**" *(six)*, "**dix**" *(ten)*, "**index**" *(index)*
z	"**chez**" *(at the place of)*, "**riz**" *(rice)*, "**parlez**" *(you speak)*	"**gaz**" *(gas)*

7. As we will learn in **Lesson 6** of this level, the third-person plural
   verb conjugation suffix "**-ent**" in the present indicative tense is
   always *silent*, e.g., "**ils parlent**" /eel paʀl/ *(they speak)*.

Liaison

A liaison occurs when a word that normally ends with a silent
consonant is followed by a vowel or a mute "**h**" (but not an aspirated
"**h**"). In this case, the final consonant is pronounced. For example,
the word "**trois**" *(three)* on its own is pronounced /tʀwa/, where the
final "**s**" is silent. However, in the phrase "**trois amis**" /tʀwaz a-
mee/ *(three friends)*, the final "**s**" in "**trois**" is pronounced as a "**z**"
sound. Here are some more liaison examples:

les /le/ *(the - plural)*	**les amis** /lez a-**mee**/ *(the friends)*
un /ĩ/ *(a/ an)*	**un homme** /ĩn om/ *(a man)*
vous /voo/ *(you)*	**vous avez** /vooz a-**ve**/ *(you have)*
très /tʀe/ *(very)*	**très utile** /tʀez ɥ-**teel**/ *(very useful)*
Je suis /j(ə) swee/ *(I am/ have)*	**Je suis allé** /j(ə) sweez a-**le**/ *(I have gone)*
Il est /eel e/ *(He is)*	**Il est ici** /eel et ee-**see**/ *(He is here)*

There are a few cases in which a liaison is prohibited. A liaison is
prohibited *before* the following:

1. An aspirated "**h**," e.g., "**les héros**" /le e-ʀo/ *(the heroes)*, "**en haut**"
   /ã o/ *(up or on top)*, etc.
2. The words "**oui**" *(yes)* and "**onze**" *(eleven)*, e.g., "**les onze ans**" /le
   õz ã/ *(the eleven years)*.

A liaison is generally avoided or prohibited *after* the following:

1. The conjunction "**et**" *(and)*, e.g., "**adultes et enfants**" /a-dɥlt e
   ã-**fã**/ *(adults and children)*, "**fort et utile**" /foʀ e ɥ-**teel**/ *(strong and
   useful)*, etc.
2. The word "**toujours**" *(always)*, e.g., "**toujours ici**" /too-jooʀ ee-
   see/ *(always here)*.
3. Singular nouns, e.g., "**éléphant énorme**" /e-le-fã e-**noʀm**/ *(huge
   elephant)*, "**chat amical**" /sha a-mee-**kal**/ *(friendly cat)*, etc.
4. Proper nouns, e.g., "**Robert est là**" /ʀo-beʀ e la/ *(Robert is there)*.

Understanding all liaison cases can be complicated and may require some deep linguistic knowledge. Nevertheless, you simply need to recognize it when applied in normal speech. The above cases provide a good starting point and summary on the uses of liaisons.

Syllable Stress in French

In English, the stress can fall on any syllable in an individual word, e.g., "police" /po-**lees**/, "policy" /**po**-li-si/, where the stressed syllable is in bold. In French, the stress always falls on the last syllable of the word. Here are some examples of French words:

"police"	"politque"	"aliment"	"téléphone"
/po-**lees**/	/po-lee-**teek**/	/a-lee-**mã**/	/te-le-**fon**/
(police)	*(policy)*	*(food)*	*(phone)*

If the words are strung together to form a phrase, the stress often falls on the last syllable of the phrase, for example:

une mai**son** /ɲn me-**zõ**/	a house
une petite mai**son** /ɲn p(ə)-teet me-**zõ**/	a small house
une petite maison **blanche** /ɲn p(ə)-teet me-zõ **blãsh**/	a small white house
une belle petite maison **blanche** /ɲn bel p(ə)-teet me-zõ **blãsh**/	a small beautiful white house

2. SIMILARITIES TO ENGLISH & PARTICULARITIES OF THE FRENCH LANGUAGE

English is considered a Germanic language, whereas French is a Romance language. Yet, they share a substantial amount of vocabulary. The main reason is attributed to the Norman Conquest of England in the eleventh century, as a result of which the English language borrowed a lot of French words. French Prime Minister Georges Clemenceau (1841-1929) famously claimed that "English is just badly pronounced French." This is why the US Foreign Service Institute (FSI), which provides language training to diplomats and government employees, ranks French in the easiest language learning category for English speakers.

English Cognates

History aside, we can definitely capitalize on this connection. There are a lot of English cognates in the French language. Moreover, since English has become a universal language, some English words have obviously found their way into many languages, including French.

Although cognates will often have the same meaning in French and English, it is important to note that this is not always the case, as languages have evolved separately. For example, the French word "**déception**" means *disappointment* or *disillusion*, not *"deception"* as you may have guessed. That would be "**tromperie**." Similarly, the word "**location**" in French means *"rental"* and not *"location."* That being said, recognizing English cognates is a powerful tool that can enhance the French vocabulary of any English-speaking learner. We will include some English cognates in our vocabulary-building section at the end of each level to help give your French vocabulary a jump start.

As we delve into the English cognates, do not feel overwhelmed with the vocabulary. You are not expected to memorize all of the cognates at this basic level. It is only meant to give you an idea of the similarities to English and help provide a sense of the French language based on prior knowledge of English.

Here, we list some parallels between English and French words that will make you realize how many French words you already know or perhaps are able to guess correctly.

It is also important to note that these are not considered strict rules, but rather useful guidelines to make learning French easier for English speakers.

1. Many English words ending in *"-ile"* end in "**-ile**" in French, e.g., "**fragile**" *(fragile)* "**automobile**" *(automobile)*, "**hostile**" *(hostile)*.

2. Many English words ending in *"-or"* end in "-**eur**" (masculine) or "-**eure**" (feminine) in French, e.g., "**coul<u>eur</u>**," "**err<u>eur</u>**," "**supéri<u>eur</u>**(e)."

3. Many English words ending in *"-ble"* end in "-**ble**" in French, e.g., "**possi<u>ble</u>**," "**terri<u>ble</u>**," "**varia<u>ble</u>**."

4. Many English words ending in *"-al"* end in "-**al**" (masculine) or "-**ale**" (feminine) in French, e.g., "**anim<u>al</u>**," "**centr<u>al</u>**(e)," "**fin<u>al</u>**(e)."

5. Some English words ending in *"-al"* end in "-**el**" (masculine) or "-**elle**" (feminine) in French, e.g., "**personn<u>el</u>**(le)," "**industri<u>el</u>**(le)," "**ré<u>el</u>**(le)."

6. Some English words ending in *"-cal"* break the above two *"-al"* ending rules and end in "-**que**" in French, e.g., "**criti<u>que</u>**," "**physi<u>que</u>**," "**politi<u>que</u>**."

7. Many English words ending in *"-ic"* end in "-**ique**" in French, e.g., "**démocrat<u>ique</u>**," "**mécan<u>ique</u>**," "**plast<u>ique</u>**."

8. Many English words ending in *"-ant"* end in "-**ant**" (masculine) or "-**ante**" (feminine) in French, respectively, e.g., "**ignor<u>ant</u>**(e)," "**import<u>ant</u>**(e)."

9. Many English words ending in *"-ent"* end in "-**ent**" (masculine) or "-**ente**" (feminine) in French, respectively, e.g., "**différ<u>ent</u>**(e)," "**intellig<u>ent</u>**(e)."

10. Many English words ending in *"-ment"* end in "-**ment**" in French, e.g., "**doc<u>ument</u>**," "**suppl<u>ément</u>**," "**mon<u>ument</u>**."

11. Many English words ending in *"-ist"* end in "-**iste**" in French, e.g., "**pian<u>iste</u>**," "**art<u>iste</u>**," "**dent<u>iste</u>**."

12. Many English words ending in *"-am"* end in "-**amme**" in French, e.g., "**progr<u>amme</u>**," "**diagr<u>amme</u>**."

13. Many English words ending in *"-em"* end in "-**ème**" in French, e.g., "**probl<u>ème</u>**," "**syst<u>ème</u>**."

14. Many English words ending in *"-ous"* end in "-**eux**" (masculine) or "-**euse**" (feminine) in French, e.g., "**fam<u>eux</u>/fam<u>euse</u>**," "**relig<u>ieux</u>/relig<u>ieuse</u>**," "**cur<u>ieux</u>/cur<u>ieuse</u>**."

15. Many English words ending in *"-ary"* end in "-**aire**" in French, e.g., "**anivers<u>aire</u>**," "**imagin<u>aire</u>**," "**itiner<u>aire</u>**."

16. Many English words ending in *"-tion"* end in "-**tion**" /syõ/ in French, e.g., "**condi<u>tion</u>**," "**educa<u>tion</u>**," "**na<u>tion</u>**," "**situa<u>tion</u>**."

17. Many English words ending in *"-tional"* end in "-**tionnel**" /syo-**nel**/ (masculine) or "-**tionnelle**" /syo-**nel**/ (feminine) in French, e.g., "**condi<u>tionnel</u>(le)**," "**tradi<u>tionnel</u>(le)**."

18. Many English words ending in *"-tial"* end in "-**tiel**" /syel/ (masculine) or "-**tielle**" /syel/ (feminine) in French, e.g., "**poten<u>tiel</u>(le)**," "**par<u>tiel</u>(le)**."

19. Many English words ending in *"-ce"* end in "-**ce**" in French, e.g., "**différen<u>ce</u>**," "**importan<u>ce</u>**," "**violen<u>ce</u>**."

20. Many English words ending in *"-cy"* end in "-**tie**" or "-**ce**" in French, e.g., "**agen<u>ce</u>**," "**<u>d</u>émocra<u>tie</u>**," "**urgen<u>ce</u>**."

21. Many English words ending in *"-ty"* end in "-**té**" in French, e.g., "**<u>é</u>lectrici<u>té</u>**," "**universi<u>té</u>**," "**possibili<u>té</u>**."

22. Some English words ending in *"-ly"* end in "-**ment**" in French, e.g., "**normale<u>ment</u>**," "**naturelle<u>ment</u>**," "**totale<u>ment</u>**."

23. Many English nouns ending in *"-phy"* end in "-**phie**" in French, e.g., "**géogra<u>phie</u>**," "**photogra<u>phie</u>**," "**philoso<u>phie</u>**."

24. Many English words ending in *"-sion"* end in "-**sion**" in French, e.g., "**conclu<u>sion</u>**," "**conver<u>sion</u>**," "**ver<u>sion</u>**."

25. Many English words ending in *"-ism"* end in "-**isme**" in French, e.g., "**organ<u>isme</u>**," "**patriot<u>isme</u>**," "**commun<u>isme</u>**."

26. Many English words ending in *"-id"* end in "-**ide**" in French, e.g., "**flu<u>ide</u>**," "**liqu<u>ide</u>**," "**tim<u>ide</u>**."

27. Many English words ending in *"-ive"* end in "-**if**" (masculine) or "-**ive**" (feminine) in French, e.g., "**défini<u>tif</u>/défini<u>tive</u>**," "**ac<u>tif</u>/ac<u>tive</u>**," "**néga<u>tif</u>/néga<u>tive</u>**."

28. Many English verbs ending in *"-fy"* end in "-**fier**" in French, e.g., "**classi<u>fier</u>**," "**modi<u>fier</u>**," "**véri<u>fier</u>**."

29. Many English verbs ending in *"-cate"* end in "-**quer**" in French, e.g., "**compli<u>quer</u>**," "**édu<u>quer</u>**," "**indi<u>quer</u>**."

A summary of the above rules is given in the table below:

English	French	Examples
-ile	-ile	agile, automobile, fragile, hostile
-or	-eur -eure	couleur, erreur, intérieur, inventeur, supérieur
-ble	-ble	inévitabile, noble, notable, possible, probable, terrible
-al	-al -ale	animal, canal, central, final, local, social
-al	-el -elle	réel, personnel, industriel
-cal	-que	critique, physique, logique, magique, mécanique
-ic	-ique	démocratique, diabétique, fantastique, plastique
-ant	-ant -ante	élégant, ignorant, important, tolérant
-ent	-ent -ente	client, compétent, continent, différent, intelligent
-ment	-ment	document, élément, monument, parlement
-ist	-iste	artiste, communiste, dentiste, pianiste, touriste
-am	-amme	calligramme, diagramme, programme, télégramme
-em	-ème	emblème, poème, problème, sistème
-ous	-eux -euse	curieux, furieux, mystérieux, nerveux, religieux
-ary	-aire	anniversaire, contraire, culinaire, dictionnaire, imaginaire, itinéraire, salaire
-tion	-tion	condition, édition, nation, notion, situation
-tional	-tionnel -tionnelle	additionnel, rationnel, traditionnel, conditionnel
-tial	-tiel -tielle	confidentiel, essentiel, partiel, potentiel, résidentiel
-ce	-ce	différence, évidence, violence, importance, élégance

-cy	-ce -tie	agence, démocratie, aristocratie, urgence, clémence
-ty	-té	autorité, cavité, dignité, identité, possibilité, unité
-ly	-ment	naturellement, normalement, probablement, totalement
-phy	-phie	cinématographie, philosophie, photographie, géographie
-sion	-sion	compassion, conclusion, conversion, décision, discussion, occasion, version
-ism	-isme	astigmatisme, communisme, idéalisme, organisme
-id	-ide	avide, splendide, fluide, liquide, lucide, placide, rapide, solide, timide, valide
-ive	-if -ive	actif, adhésif, additif, attractif, décisif, définitif, positif, négatif
-fy	-fier	certifier, glorifier, justifier, modifier, notifier, vérifier
-cate	-quer	compliquer, éduquer, impliquer, indiquer

As mentioned earlier, there are some *false cognates*. It can be useful to be familiar with these false friends to avoid some embarrassing errors. Below is a list of some of the most common ones:

French Word	Meaning in English	English Cognate	Meaning of cognate in French
attendre	*to wait*	attend	**assister à**
blessé	*hurt or injured*	blessed	**béni**
coin	*corner*	coin	**pièce de monnaie**
déception	*disappointment*	deception	**tromperie**
librairie	*book store*	library	**bibliothèque**
location	*rental*	location	**localization**
monnaie	*change (money)*	money	**argent**
prune	*plum*	prune	**pruneau**
raisin	*grape*	raisin	**raisin sec**

Negation

To form the negation in French, we add "**ne**" in front of the verb (and before any object pronoun before the verb) and "**pas**" after the verb, e.g., "**Je <u>ne</u> joue <u>pas</u> au football**" *(I don't play soccer)*, "**Je <u>ne</u> le veux <u>pas</u>**" *(I don't want it)*, etc.

We can have a double negative in French without changing the meaning to affirmative, e.g., "**Je <u>ne</u> le fais <u>jamais</u>**" (*I <u>never</u> do it*). Notice that when another negation word is used, e.g., "**jamais**" *(never)*, "**rien**" *(nothing/anything)*, "**personne**" *(nobody/anybody)*, "**plus**" *(anymore)*, etc., it often replaces "**pas**" following the verb to form the negative. Here are some examples:

Je **n'**ai **rien** fait de mal.	*I didn't do* **anything** *wrong.*
Je **ne** vois **personne** ici.	*I don't see* **anybody** *here.*
Il **ne** répond **plus**.	*He doesn't respond* **anymore.**

Notice that "**ne**" is contracted to "**n'**" before a vowel or a mute "**h.**" If a compound tense (a tense that uses an auxiliary verb) is used, the "**ne … pas**," or a similar negative construction like the aforementioned examples, is placed around the first verb, that is, the auxiliary verb, e.g., "**Je n'<u>ai</u> pas <u>mangé</u>**" (*I <u>have</u> not <u>eaten</u>*).

Written Accents

In French, there are five written accents: acute (´), grave (`), circumflex (ˆ), dieresis (¨), and cedilla (¸). Let us discuss each in more detail:

1. Acute (´): This can be found only on the letter "**e.**" It indicates a closed "**e**" sound. In some cases, especially at the beginning of some words, it may indicate that the word starts with "**s**" in the original Latin spelling, e.g., "**école**" *(school)*, "**état**" *(state)*, "**étudier**" *(to study)*, etc.

2. Grave (`): The grave accent is often found on the letters "**a**" and "**e**," and in only one case on the letter "**u**," that is "**où**" *(where)*. If it appears on the letter "**e**," it indicates an open "**e**" sound.

   Another use of the grave accent in French is to distinguish between the meaning of monosyllabic words that would otherwise be written in the same manner. For example, "**a**" is used as a third-person singular form of the verb *"to have,"* whereas "**à**" is a preposition that often means *"at"* or *"in."* Similarly, "**la**" is used as a feminine singular definite article meaning *"the,"* whereas *"*là*"* means *"there."*

3. Circumflex (ˆ): The pointy hat-like accent can be used with any of the five vowels: "**a**," "**e**," "**i**," "**o**," or "**u**." When used with "**o**," it denotes closed "**o**" sound, whereas it denotes an open sound when used with "**a**" or "**e**." In many cases, the circumflex can point to an "**s**" that was dropped after the circumflex letter from the original source language, e.g., "**forêt**" *(forest)*, "**hôpital**" *(hospital)*, "**côte**" *(coast)*, "**pâté**" *(paste)*, "**rôtir**" *(to roast)*, etc.

   Similar to the grave accent, the circumflex is sometimes used to distinguish between the meaning of monosyllabic words that would otherwise be written in the same manner. For example, "**sur**" is a preposition meaning *"above,"* whereas "**sûr**" is an adjective meaning *"sure"* or *"certain."* Similarly, "**mur**" means *"wall,"* whereas "**mûr**" means *"ripe"* or *"mature."*

4. Dieresis (¨): The dieresis is a special accent that is often used on the second vowel of a two-vowel combination to denote that the two vowels must be pronounced separately. The dieresis is often found on the letter "**e**" or "**i**," and in rare cases on the letter "**u**." For example, "**naïve**" *(naïve)* is pronounced /na-**eev**/, not /**nev**/, despite the "**ai**" combination. Similarly, "**Noël**" *(Christmas)* is pronounced /no-**el**/, not /**neul**/, despite the "**oe**" combination.

5. Cedilla (¸): This accent is used uniquely with the letter "**c**" to denote a soft "**s**" sound even though the letter is followed by "**a**," "**o**," or "**u**," e.g., "**français**" *(French)*, "**garçon**" *(boy)*, "**ça**" *(this)*, "**leçon**" *(lesson)*, "**reçu**" *(receipt)*, "**façon**" *(way or method)*, and "**façade**" *(façade)*.

Punctuation

In general, French punctuation marks are used the same way as in English. For instance, interrogation and exclamation marks are used in French at the end of a question or exclamation, such as "**Comment vas-tu?**" *(How are you?)* and "**Quel dommage!**" *(What a pity!).*

Punctuation is also important to distinguish a question from a statement. For instance, the sentence "**Tu parles français**" *(You speak French)* is a statement. Adding a question mark to the end of the sentence "**Tu parles français?**" makes it a question. This is how many questions are informally formed in French. Obviously, the voice intonation needs to change in the spoken language.

Another more formal way to form a "**oui**" *(yes)* or "**non**" *(no)* question from a statement is to place the phrase "**Est-ce que**" before the statement, e.g., "**Est-ce que tu parles français?**" *(Do you speak French?)*. The introductory phrase "**Est-ce que…**" translates literally as *"Is it that …"*

A third way to form a "**oui**" *(yes)* or "**non**" *(no)* question from a statement is called *inversion*. The subject pronoun and the verb are inverted and a hyphen is placed in between, e.g., "**Parles-tu français?**" *(Do you speak French?)*. This method is more common in written language. Notice that inversion requires a subject pronoun such as "**je**" *(I)*, "**tu**" *(you)*, or "**il/elle**" *(he/she/it)*. If the subject is a noun instead of a subject pronoun, the subject is maintained and repeated using the proper subject pronoun, e.g., "**<u>Le café</u>, est-<u>il</u> chaud**" *(Is the coffee hot?)*. If a verb that ends in a vowel precedes "**il/elle**" *(he/she/it)* or "**on**" *(we/one)*, the letter "**t**" must be added before the subject pronoun that begins with a vowel, e.g., "**Parle-<u>t</u>-il français?**" *(Does he speak French?)*.

Finally, contractions in French are always mandatory whether they are in the form of using the apostrophe, such as "**l'eau**" *(the water)* and "**j'ai**" *(I have)*, or in the case of compound articles, such as "**au**" (= "**à**" + "**le**") and "**des**" (= "**de**" + "**les**"). We will cover more on the definite articles and prepositions in the lessons to come.

Abbreviations

The concepts behind the formation of acronyms and abbreviations in French are very similar to those in English. For more detail and a list of common abbreviations in French, interested readers can refer to **Appendix C** at the end of this book.

Capitalization

The words in French are capitalized in cases almost identical to those in English, with a few notable exceptions that are not capitalized in French, mainly:

❖ Adjectives of nationalities and languages, e.g., **"français"** (*French*), **"canadien"** (*Canadian*), **"espagnol"** (*Spanish*), etc.

❖ Days and months, e.g., **"mardi"** (*Tuesday*), **"janvier"** (*January*), **"juillet"** (*July*), etc.

It is also worth noting that all letter of the alphabet are masculine in French. For example, when referring to a letter in French, one may say: **le "n" dans "animal"** (*the "n" in "animal"*), referring to the letter "n" using the masculine article **"le."** The word **"letter"** (*letter*) itself, however, is feminine; thus, we could also say: **la lettre "n" dans "animal"** (*the letter "n" in "animal"*). We will learn more about masculine and feminine nouns and adjectives in the next lesson.

3. GENDER AND PLURAL

Each noun and adjective in French has a gender. Nouns and adjectives in French have only two genders: *masculine* and *feminine*. There is no neuter gender. Throughout the book, we use the superscripts ^{m} and ^{f} to refer to masculine and feminine genders, respectively.

The adjective follows the noun it describes in gender and number. The only certain way to determine the gender of a noun is by looking it up in a dictionary. Nevertheless, there are some general rules that can help you be right most of the time. Remember, however, that these are general rules, and there are many exceptions.

Gender of a Noun

The main rule is that a noun that ends with "-**e**" or "-**ion**" is likely feminine, except for nouns ending in "-**ge**" or "-**isme**," which arc likely masculine even though they end with "-**e**." Any other noun in French that does not end with "-**e**" is likely, but not certainly, masculine.

Of course, there will be some obvious masculine and feminine nouns. For instance, we know that "**homme**" *(man)* and "**prince**" *(prince)* are masculine regardless of the above rule.

Let us look at some examples of nouns that follow the general rule as well as some exceptions:

Gender	Ending	Nouns that follow the rule	Exceptions
feminine	-e	couverture *(blanket)*, fenêtre *(window)*, plante *(plant)*	spectacle *(spectacle)*, stade *(stadium)*, silence *(silence)*, incendie *(fire)*
	-ion	destination *(destination)*, nation *(nation)*, production *(production)*	avion *(plane)*, camion *(truck)*
masculine	-ge	âge *(age)*, garage *(garage)*, nuage *(cloud)*, stage *(internship)*, orage *(thunderstorm)*, village *(village)*, siège *(seat)*, piège *(trap)*, liège *(cork)*, collège *(college)*	cage *(cage)*, page *(page)*, plage *(beach)*, image *(image)*, rage *(rage)*
	-isme	cyclisme *(cycling)*, prisme, schisme, tourisme *(tourism)*	-
masculine	Other	bureau *(office)*, papier *(paper)*, journal *(newspaper)*, bras *(arm)*, changement *(change)*, lit *(bed)*	eau *(water)*, peau *(skin)*, souris *(mouse)*

Some words have a different meaning when used in the masculine form versus when used in the feminine form. For example:

livre[m]	*book*	**livre**[f]	*pound*
mode[m]	*mode, way or method*	**mode**[f]	*fashion*
capitale[m]	*capital (money)*	**capitale**[f]	*capital (city)*
tour[m]	*tour*	**tour**[f]	*tower*
mémoire[m]	*report*	**mémoire**[f]	*memory*
poste[m]	*job*	**poste**[f]	*post office*
vase[m]	*vase*	**vase**[f]	*mud*

Notice that many words that end in "**-me**" and originate from *Greek* are masculine, for example:

problème^m	*problem*	**drame**^m	*drama*
système^m	*system*	**dilemme**^m	*dilemma*
thème^m	*topic or theme*	**diagramme**^m	*diagram*
diplôme^m	*diploma*	**poème**^m	*poem*

This exception does not apply to words that do *not* originate from *Greek*, such as "**forme**" *(form)* and "**plateforme**" *(platform)*, which are feminine.

In addition, there are many foreign nouns that have made inroads into the French life and dictionary such as "**sport**" and "**Internet**." In general, the majority of these nouns are masculine.

Some nouns that refer to people can be masculine or feminine. The most common pattern to form the feminine noun from a masculine noun is to add an "**e**" at the end, for example:

étudiant^m	*student*	**étudiante**^f	*student*
ingénieur^m	*engineer*	**ingénieure**^f	*engineer*

Nouns that end with a vowel followed by "**n**" or "**t**" often double the last consonant and add an "**e**" at the end, for example:

lion^m	*lion*	**lionne**^f	*lioness*
chat^m	*cat*	**chatte**^f	*cat*

Nevertheless, this is not the only gender pattern in French. Other patterns include:

-teur/-trice	*actor/actress*	**acteur**^m	**actrice**^f
	director	**directeur**^m	**directrice**^f
-eur/-euse	*hair dresser*	**coiffeur**^m	**coiffeuse**^f
	waiter/waitress	**serveur**^m	**serveuse**^f
-e/-esse	*poet*	**poète**^m	**poétesse**^f
	host/hostess	**hôte**^m	**hôtesse**^f

Most nouns that end in "**-iste**," "**-yste**," or "**-naire**" can refer to masculine or feminine people performing a role or profession, for example:

dentiste[m,f]	*dentist*	**analyste**[m,f]	*analyst*
artiste[m,f]	*artist*	**pianiste**[m,f]	*pianist*
vétérinaire[m,f]	*veterinary*	**partenaire**[m,f]	*partner*
millionaire[m,f]	*millionaire*	**révolutionnaire**[m,f]	*revolutionary*

Others may only have one form (masculine or feminine) regardless of the gender of the person that the noun refers to, for example:

personne[f]	*person*	**victime**[f]	*victim*
professeur[m]	*teacher*	**médecin**[m]	*doctor*
écrivain[m]	*writer*	**juge**[m]	*judge*

It is also commonly acceptable to add the word "**femme**" *(woman)* to describe a female with a non-form changing masculine noun, e.g., "**une femme médecin**" *(a female doctor)*.

In general, most countries ending with "-e" are *feminine*, e.g., "**la France**" *(France)*. Exceptionally, the following six countries end with "-e" but are *masculine*:

Mexique[m]	*Mexico*	**Belize**[m]	*Belize*
Cambodge[m]	*Cambodia*	**Mozambique**[m]	*Mozambique*
Zimbabwe[m]	*Zimbabwe*	**Suriname**[m]	*Surinam*

Most other countries that do not end in "-e" are masculine. Here are some examples:

Maroc[m]	*Morocco*	**Iran**[m]	*Iran*
Canada[m]	*Canada*	**Portugal**[m]	*Portugal*

Notice that most countries are often preceded by a definite article, while only a few cannot be used by a definite article, such as:

Bahreïn[m]	*Bahrain*	**Chypre**[f]	*Cyprus*
Singapour[m]	*Singapore*	**Haïti**[m]	*Haiti*
Cuba[m]	*Cuba*	**Sri Lanka**[m]	*Sri Lanka*
Malte[f]	*Malta*	**Monaco**[m]	*Monaco*

Some countries are always in plural form, such as:

États-Unis[m]	*United States*	**Pays-Bas**[m]	*Netherlands*
Philippines[f]	*Philippines*	**Bahamas**[m]	*Bahamas*

Gender of an Adjective

An adjective follows the noun it describes in gender and number. For the purpose of brevity throughout the book, we often refer only to the masculine singular form of an adjective. We trust that by learning some basic rules, you will be able to guess the feminine and plural forms most of the time.

Adjectives in French, unlike in English, come after the noun they describe, for example, **"bâtiment historique"** *(historic building)*. There are some exceptions to this rule, for example, **"grande ville"** *(big or great city)*. Many adjectives that come before the noun are *indefinite adjectives*, which will be covered in **Level III, Lesson 3**.

Most adjectives form the feminine singular by adding a final "**-e**" to the masculine singular form. However, there are many exceptions that follow different patterns. The following are the most common patterns:

1. Adjectives ending in "-eux"

The feminine form of masculine adjectives ending in "**-eux**" is often obtained by changing the final "**-eux**" to "**-euse**":

happy	**heureux**[m]	**heureuse**[f]
joyful	**joyeux**[m]	**joyeuse**[f]
serious	**sérieux**[m]	**sérieuse**[f]
curious	**curieux**[m]	**curieuse**[f]
nervous	**nerveux**[m]	**nerveuse**[f]
religious	**religieux**[m]	**religieuse**[f]

2. Adjectives ending in "-é"

The feminine form of masculine adjectives ending in "**-é**" is often obtained by adding an extra "**-e**":

tired	**fatigué**[m]	**fatiguée**[f]
busy	**occupé**[m]	**occupée**[f]
complicated	**compliqué**[m]	**compliquée**[f]
salty	**salé**[m]	**salée**[f]

3. Adjectives ending in a silent "-e"

The feminine form of masculine adjectives ending in a silent "**-e**" is the same, for example:

clean	propre[m]	propre[f]
comfortable	confortable[m]	confortable[f]
dirty	sale[m]	sale[f]
easy	facile[m]	facile[f]
empty	vide[m]	vide[f]
funny	drôle[m]	drôle[f]
honest	honnête[m]	honnête[f]
poor	pauvre[m]	pauvre[f]
pleasant	aimable[m]	aimable[f]
sad	triste[m]	triste[f]
weak	faible[m]	faible[f]

4. Adjectives ending in "**-f**"

The feminine form of masculine adjectives ending in "**-f**" is often obtained by changing the final "**-f**" to "**-ve**":

active	actif[m]	active[f]
attractive	attractif[m]	attractive[f]
decisive	décisif[m]	décisive[f]
positive	positif[m]	positive[f]
negative	négatif[m]	négative[f]
widower/widow	veuf[m]	veuve[f]

5. Adjectives ending in a consonant "**l**," "**n**," or "**s**"

The feminine form of many masculine adjectives ending in the consonant "**l**," "**n**," or "**s**" is obtained by adding an "**-e**" to the end of the word and doubling the consonant before the final "**-e**":

cruel	cruel[m]	cruelle[f]
European	européen[m]	européenne[f]
fat	gros[m]	grosse[f]
former, old, or ancient	ancien[m]	ancienne[f]
good	bon[m]	bonne[f]
kind or nice	gentil[m]	gentille[f]
low	bas[m]	basse[f]

Finally, there are some irregular adjectives that do not follow any pattern and must simply be memorized. Here are some examples:

beautiful	**beau**[m]	**belle**[f]
dry	**sec**[m]	**seche**[f]
false	**faux**[m]	**fausse**[f]
favorite	**favori**[m]	**favorite**[f]
frank	**franc**[m]	**franche**[f]
fresh	**frais**[m]	**fraîche**[f]
long	**long**[m]	**longue**[f]
new	**nouveau**[m]	**nouvelle**[f]
old	**vieux**[m]	**vieille**[f]
public	**public**[m]	**publique**[f]
soft / sweet	**doux**[m]	**douce**[f]
white	**blanc**[m]	**blanche**[f]

Among the above irregular adjectives, there are three adjectives that change form only if they come before a *masculine* noun that starts with a vowel or mute "**h**." The three adjectives are: "**beau**" *(beautiful)*, "**nouveau**" *(new)*, and "**vieux**" *(old)*. Here are some examples:

beau[m] *(beautiful)*	**beau pays** *(beautiful country)*	**bel <u>a</u>nimal** *(beautiful animal)*
nouveau[m] *(new)*	**nouveau livre** *(new book)*	**nouvel <u>a</u>mi** *(new friend)*
vieux[m] *(old)*	**vieux port** *(old port)*	**vieil <u>h</u>omme** *(old man)*

If the noun is feminine or the adjective is placed after the noun, the change of form is not applied even if the noun starts with a vowel or a mute "**h**," e.g., "**Cet animal est beau**" *(This animal is beautiful)*, "**nouvelle année**" *(new year)*, etc.

Forming the Plural of a Noun or Adjective

Forming the plural of a singular noun or adjective is often straightforward and resembles the English common way of adding an "**-s**" at the end of a word. Here are some examples:

livre[m]	*book*	**livres**[m]	*books*
chat[m]	*cat*	**chats**[m]	*cats*
téléphone[m]	*phone*	**téléphones**[m]	*phones*
balle[f]	*ball*	**balles**[f]	*balls*
maison[f]	*house*	**maisons**[f]	*houses*

However, there are four main categories of nouns that do not follow the above simple rule to form the plural:

1. Nouns ending in "-s," "-x," or "-z"

The majority of nouns under this category do not change form in the plural, for example:

bras[m]	*arm*	**bras**[m]	*arms*
choix[f]	*choice*	**choix**[f]	*choices*
gaz[m]	*gas*	**gaz**[m]	*gasses*

2. Nouns ending in "-au" or "-eu"

Nouns ending in "-au" or "-eu" add an "-x" to the ending to form the plural, for example:

chapeau[m]	*hat*	**chapeaux**[m]	*hats*
rideau[m]	*curtain*	**rideaux**[m]	*curtains*
feu[m]	*fire*	**feux**[m]	*fires*
lieu[m]	*place*	**lieux**[m]	*places*

A notable exception is "**pneu**[m]" *(tire)*, whose plural is "**pneus**."

3. Nouns ending in "-ail" or "-al"

Nouns ending in "-ail" or "-al" change the ending to "-aux" to form the plural, for example:

animal[m]	*animal*	**animaux**[m]	*animals*
cheval[m]	*horse*	**chevaux**[m]	*horses*
travail[m]	*work*	**travaux**[m]	*works*
corail[m]	*coral*	**coraux**[m]	*corals*

4. Some nouns ending in "-ou"

The following nouns ending in "-ou" add "-x" to the ending to form the plural. These words need to be memorized.

bijou[m]	*jewel*	**bijoux**[m]	*jewels*
caillou[m]	*pebble*	**cailloux**[m]	*pebbles*
chou[m]	*cabbage*	**choux**[m]	*cabbages*
genou[m]	*knee*	**genoux**[m]	*knees*
hibou[m]	*owl*	**hiboux**[m]	*owls*
pou[m]	*louse*	**poux**[m]	*louses*
joujou[m]	*toy*	**joujoux**[m]	*toys*

Although the categories above cover most irregular plurals. There are a few words that do not fall under any of these categories. For instance, the plural of "**l'œil**[m]" *(the eye)* is "**les yeux**" *(the eyes)*. Moreover, some words are only used in plural form such as "**ciseaux**[m]" *(scissors)* and "**lunettes**[f]" *(glasses)*.

To form the plural of an adjective, the general rule is to add an "**-s**" to the end of the adjective, e.g., "**petits**" is the plural of "**petit**" *(small)*, with the following exceptions:

1. If the adjective ends with "**-s**" or "**-x**," the plural form is the same as the singular, e.g., "**français**" is the plural of "**français**" *(French)*, and "**heureux**" is the plural of "**heureux**" *(happy)*.
2. If the adjective ends with "**-al**" or "**-eau**," the plural form ends in "**-aux**," e.g., "**principaux**" is the plural of "**principal**" *(main or principal)*, and "**nouveaux**" is the plural of "**nouveau**" *(new)*.

4. CARDINAL NUMBERS

un, une	1	vingt et un	21	cent un	101
deux	2	vingt-deux	22	cent deux	102
trois	3	vingt-trois	23	deux cents	200
quatre	4	trente	30	trois cents	300
cinq	5	trente et un	31	quatre cents	400
six	6	trente-deux	32	cinq cents	500
sept	7	quarante	40	six cents	600
huit	8	quarante et un	41	sept cents	700
neuf	9	quarante-deux	42	huit cents	800
dix	10	cinquante	50	neuf cents	900
onze	11	cinquante et un	51	mille	1.000
douze	12	cinquante-deux	52	deux mille	2.000
treize	13	soixante	60	dix mille	10.000
quatorze	14	soixante-dix	70	cent mille	100.000
quinze	15	soixante et onze	71	cent mille un	100.001
seize	16	soixante-douze	72	un million	1.000.000
dix-sept	17	quatre-vingts	80	deux millions	2.000.000
dix-huit	18	quatre-vingt-dix	90	dix millions	10.000.000
dix-neuf	19	quatre-vingt-quinze	95	un milliard	1.000.000.000
vingt	20	cent	100	deux milliard	2.000.000.000

❖ The number "**0**" in French is "**zéro**," pronounced as "ze-яo."

❖ Notice the following regarding pronunciation:

1. In the number "**sept**" (7), the "**p**" is always silent, and the final "**t**" is always pronounced. Thus, "**sept**" is pronounced /set/.

2. The final "**f**" in "**neuf**" (9) is always pronounced.

3. The final letter is pronounced in "**cinq**" (5), "**six**" (6), "**huit**" (8), and "**dix**" (10), unless they are followed by a consonant. In this case, the final letter is mute. Some people pronounce the final "**q**" in "**cinq**" in all contexts.

❖ Notice that the number "**soixante-dix**" (70) is formed by combining "**soixante**" (60) and "**dix**" (10), and the number "**quatre-vingts**" (80) literally means *"four-twenties,"* i.e., 4 times 20.

❖ The numbers 21-99 are formed by combining the tens (**vingt, trente, quarante, … etc.**) and the units (**un, deux, trois, … etc.**) with a hyphen in the middle. The only exception is when the unit is "**un**" or "**onze**." In this case, the preposition "**et**" *(and)* is used, e.g., "**cinquante et un**" (51), "**soixante et onze**" (71).

❖ The word for *a hundred* in French is "**cent**." The multiples of a hundred (200-900) are formed by combining the cardinal number (**deux, trois, … etc.**) and the plural form "**cents**" to form (**deux cents, trois cents, … etc.**).

❖ The word for *a thousand* in French is "**mille**." The multiples of a thousand are formed by combining the cardinal number and "**mille**" to form (**deux mille, trois mille, … etc.**).

❖ We use a *comma* to separate *decimals* and a *period* to separate *thousands* in French. For instance, the number **2.155,25** in French is equivalent to *2,155.25* in English.

❖ Numbers of more than two digits in length are written separately. Unlike in English, the conjunction *"and"* is not used anywhere between units, tens, hundreds, thousands, etc., except before "un" and "onze," for example, **"deux cent trente-sept"** (237), **"quatre cent cinquante et un"** (451), **"cent soixante et onze"** (171), etc.

❖ To say *a billion* in French, we use **"milliard."** The word **"billion,"** in French, is *a trillion* in English.

❖ When describing items in millions or billions, one must add **"de,"** or **"d'"** before a vowel or a mute **"h,"** after **"million(s)"** or **"milliard(s),"** e.g., **"un million d'étudiants"** *(a million students)*, **"trois millions de livres"** *(three million books)*, **"deux milliards d'habitants"** *(two billion inhabitants)*, etc.

❖ Notice that, in French, we cannot use the English way of expressing years, as in *"nineteen seventy-three"* (1973); that is, saying **"dix-neuf soixante-treize"** is incorrect. The correct way is to say **"mille neuf cent soixante-treize."**

❖ The basic arithmetic operations in French are as follows:

+	plus	*plus*
-	moins	*minus*
×	fois	*times*
÷	divisé par	*divided by*
=	égalent/font	*equals*

5. SUBJECT PERSONAL PRONOUNS

Subject personal pronouns in French serve the same function as their English counterparts by pointing out who carries out the action described by the verb.

je	*I*	1st person singular
tu	*you (informal)*	2nd person singular
vous	*you (formal)*	2nd person singular
il/elle	*he/she/it*	3rd person singular
on	*one, we, they*	3rd person singular
nous	*we*	1st person plural
vous	*you*	2nd person singular formal *"you"* 2nd person plural formal/informal *"you"*
ils/elles	*they*	3rd person plural

❖ The special pronoun "**on**" can mean *"we," "one,"* or *"they,"* especially in passive constructions, e.g., "**On va à la plage aujourd'hui**" *(We go to the beach today)*, "**On parle français ici**" *(We/They speak French here)*, etc. Note that the pronoun "**on**" uses the third-person singular conjugation.

❖ There are two forms of the singular *"you"* in French; the first is the informal "**tu**," which is used with familiar people (e.g., child, relative, friend, peer, etc.), and the second is the formal "**vous**," which is used with older people and with people we are not familiar with to show respect.

❖ The pronoun "**vous**" is used for all second-person plural forms: formal and informal.

❖ The third-person singular pronouns "**il**" and "**elle**" are also used as the equivalent to the English subject pronoun *"it,"* when referring to a masculine or feminine object. When referring to a statement or a fact, the masculine pronoun "**il**" is often used, e.g., "**il est important**" *(it is important)*.

6. PRESENT INDICATIVE TENSE I

Verbs in their infinitive form in French have one of the three endings: "**-er**," "**-ir**," or "**-re**." When conjugated, these endings are replaced with different conjugation suffixes based on the subject. In English, verb conjugation in the present tense is quite simple. For example, the verb *"to break"* is conjugated as follows: *I/you/we/they break, he/she/it breaks.* Thus, there are only two conjugation forms of the verb *"to break"* in the simple present tense, which are *"break"* and *"breaks."* In French, it is a little more complicated. Regular verbs in the present indicative tense follow different conjugation rules as shown in the examples in the following table from each verb group: "**-er**," "**-ir**," and "**-re**." First, the stem is formed by removing the final "**-er**," "**-ir**," or "**-re**." Then, the conjugation ending is added depending on the personal pronoun.

	-er ending parler *(to speak)*	**-ir ending** finir *(to finish)*	**-re ending** vendre *(to sell)*
je	parle /paяl/	finis /fi-**ni**/	vends /vã/
tu	parles /paяl/	finis /fi-**ni**/	vends /vã/
il/elle/on	parle /paяl/	finit /fi-**ni**/	vend /vã/
nous	parlons /paя-**lõ**/	finissons /fi-ni-**sõ**/	vendons /vã-**dõ**/
vous	parlez /paя-**le**/	finissez /fi-ni-**se**/	vendez /vã-**de**/
ils/elles	parlent /paяl/	finissent /fi-**nis**/	vendent /vãd/

Notice that the conjugation suffixes of the singular forms in the table above are not pronounced. In other words, "**parle**" and "**parles**" are both pronounced the same i.e., /paяl/. Similarly, "**finis**" and "**finit**" are both pronounced the same, i.e., /fi-**ni**/. In addition, the third-person plural suffix "-**ent**" is never pronounced, e.g., "**parlent**" /paяl/, "**vendent**" / vãd /, etc.

Not all verbs are regular in the present indicative tense. For example, the verbs "**être**" /etя/ *(to be)*, "**avoir**" /av-**waя**/ *(to have)*, and "**aller**" /a-**le**/ *(to go)* are three important verbs in French used to form sentences and as auxiliary verbs. These verbs are completely irregular and are conjugated as follows:

	être *(to be)*		**avoir** *(to have)*		**aller** *(to go)*	
je/j'	suis	/swee/	ai	/e/	vais	/ve/
tu	es	/e/	as	/a/	vas	/va/
il/elle/on	est	/e/	a	/a/	va	/va/
nous	sommes	/som/	avons	/a-**võ**/	allons	/a-**lõ**/
vous	êtes	/et/	avez	/a-**ve**/	allez	/a-**le**/
ils/elles	sont	/sõ/	ont	/õ/	vont	/võ/

We will learn more about irregular verbs in the present indicative tense in **Level II, Lesson 2**.

It is important to note that the present tense we have discussed so far is also called the present *indicative* tense to distinguish it from the present *subjunctive* tense. The indicative and the subjunctive are two different moods. You do not have to worry about the difference for now. We will cover the subjunctive mood in more advanced lessons starting in **Level IV, Lesson 5**. As we progress with more advanced tenses in the levels to come, refer to **Appendix B** to use the provided verb conjugation chart as a cheat sheet to gain perspective on the different moods and tenses in French.

7. THE ARTICLES

In French, both definite and indefinite articles must agree with the noun they describe in gender and number.

Definite Articles

Below are the definite articles in French, equivalent to *"the"* in English:

	Singular	Plural
Before a **masculine** or **feminine** noun that begins with a vowel or a mute "**h**"	l'	
Before a **masculine** noun that does not begin with a vowel or a mute "**h**"	le	les
Before a **feminine** noun that does not begin with a vowel or a mute "**h**"	la	

If an adjective precedes the noun, the definite article is adjusted according to the beginning of the adjective. For example, "**l'ami**" means *"the friend,"* whereas "**le bon ami**" means *"the good friend."* Notice the change in the definite article from "**l'**" to "**le.**"

Notice that only a mute "**h**" takes the definite article "**l'**" in singular form, e.g., "**l'homme**" /lom/ *(the man)*, and a liaison is applied in plural form, i.e., "**les hommes**" /le<u>z</u>-om/ *(the men)*. On the other hand, an aspirated "**h**" takes the definite article "**le**" in singular form, e.g., "**le héros**" /lə e-яo/ *(the hero)*, and a liaison is prohibited in plural form, i.e., "**les héros**" /le e-яo/ *(the heroes)*, not /le<u>z</u> e-яo/.

Indefinite Articles

The singular definite articles "**un**" (masculine) and "**une**" (feminine) in French are equivalent to *"a"* or *"an"* in English, whereas "**des**" is used with plurals and often translated as *"some."* The table below summarizes the indefinite articles in French:

	Singular	Plural
Before a **masculine** noun	**un**	**des**
Before a **feminine** noun	**une**	

Use of the Definite Article in French versus English

There are cases in which French uses the definite article when it would be omitted in English, such as:

1. Abstract concepts or speaking in a general sense, e.g., "**La science est importante**" *(Science is important)*, "**Les animaux sont intelligents**" *(Animals are intelligent)*, etc.

2. Languages and nationalities, e.g., "**le français**" *(French)*, "**les allemands**" *(Germans)*, etc. Exceptionally, we drop the definite article in French when the language name is an object of some verbs, e.g., "**Je parle français**" *(I speak French)*, or after the preposition "**en**," e.g., "**écrit en français**" *(written in French)*.

3. Days of the week when referring to a repeated action or habit on the same day of every week, e.g., "**Je vais à la gym le jeudi**" *(I go to the gym on Thursdays)*. If we do not refer to a repeated action, we do not use the definite article, e.g., "**J'arrive lundi**" *(I arrive on Monday)*.

4. Body parts are often preceded with the definite instead of the possessive pronoun if the possessor is the same as the subject of the sentence, e.g., "**Il se lave la main**" *(He washes his hand)*, "**Je me brosse les cheveux**" *(I brush my hair)*, etc.

5. Before each noun in the case of multiple nouns, e.g., "**le père et la mère**" *(the father and mother)*, "**les chiens et les chats**" *(the dogs and cats)*, etc. Although you can use one definite article in English to refer to all nouns, the grammatically correct way in French is to repeat the definite article for each noun.

It is common to omit the definite article before the seasons of the year: "**en été**" *(in summer)*, "**en hiver**" *(in winter)*, and "**en automne**" *(in autumn)*, but we maintain the definite article in "**au printemps**" *(in spring)*.

8. Interrogative Pronouns & Adjectives

Interrogative pronouns are important tools that we use to form questions. If the interrogative pronoun is followed by a noun, it becomes an interrogative adjective, e.g., "**Quel bâtiment est le plus grand?**" *(Which building is the tallest?)*. In this case, the interrogative "**quel**" is considered an interrogative adjective. If it is not followed by a noun, "**quel**" becomes an interrogative pronoun, e.g., "**Quel est plus grand?**" *(Which is taller?)*.

Interrogative pronoun/adjective	English meaning	Examples
Que? Quoi?	*What?*	**Que** fais-tu? ***What** are you doing?*
Qui?	*Who/Whom?*	**Qui** a fait cela? ***Who** did this?*
À qui?	*Whose?*	**À qui** est ce livre? ***Whose** book is this?*
Comment?	*How?*	**Comment** as-tu fais cela? ***How** did you do it?*
Quel(s)? Quelle(s)?	*Which?*	**Quelles** sont tes clés? ***Which** ones are your keys?*
Combien?	*How much?* *How many?*	**Combien** coûte ce manteau? ***How** much does this coat cost?*
Quand?	*When?*	**Quand** veux-tu venir? ***When** do you want to come?*
Où?	*Where?*	**Où** es-tu en ce moment? ***Where** are you now?*
Pourquoi?	*Why?*	**Pourquoi** ne veux-tu pas manger? ***Why** don't you want to eat?*

❖ The interrogative "**quoi**" *(what)* is often used in familiar language, for example, "**C'est quoi?**" *(What is this?)* or "**Tu fais quoi?**" *(What are you doing?)*, or when a preposition is used with the verb, e.g., "**En quoi pouvez-vous m'aider?**" *(In what can you help me?)*, "**De quoi parles-tu?**" *(What are you talking about?)*, etc.

❖ The interrogative "**que**" has a longer form that is more formal and polite, which is "**qu'est-ce que**" /kes-kə/, e.g., "**Qu'est-ce que vous voudriez manger?**" *(What would you like to eat?)*. Notice that the subject always precedes the verb when **"qu'est-ce que"** is used.

❖ The interrogative adjective **"quel"** *(which)* has four forms depending on their gender and number: **"quel"** (masculine singular), **"quelle"** (feminine singular), **"quels"** (masculine plural), and **"quelles"** (feminine plural).

II. Vocabulary Building

This section contains some vocabulary that you will need to get you going at this basic level. As you go over it in the book, we recommend that you use the Anki flashcards to study and memorize the new vocabulary as a more efficient and less boring way of learning and reviewing the material.

1. VERBS I

Below is a list of the most common 40 verbs in French. You can start by adding them to your vocabulary to improve your comprehension of French speech and writing. Use the Anki flashcards created for this section to help you memorize the meaning of each verb in its proper context. We limit verb conjugation here to the infinitive and the regular present tense which are what we have learned so far.

English	French	Examples
arrive	arriver	Je prévois d'**arriver** en retard demain. *I expect to **arrive** late tomorrow.*
believe	croire	Je **crois** que mes parents ne viendront pas aujourd'hui. *I **believe** that my parents won't come today.*
call	appeler	Ma mère m'**appelle** toujours le soir. *My mom always **calls** me at night.*
can be able to	pouvoir	J'ai besoin de mes chaussures pour **pouvoir** courir. *I need my shoes to **be able to** run.*
change	changer	Tu dois **changer** ta routine quotidienne. *You have to **change** your daily routine.*
close	fermer	Je n'aime pas **fermer** les fenêtres l'après-midi. *I don't like to **close** the windows in the afternoon.*
come	venir	Je pense que mon frère ne veut pas **venir**. *I think that my brother doesn't want to **come**.*

create	créer	Les scientifiques **créent** toujours de nouvelles méthodes. *Scientists always **create** new methods.*
do make	faire	Nous voulons tout **faire** aujourd'hui. *We want to **do** everything today.*
drink	boire	Est-ce que tu veux **boire** de l'eau? *Do you want to **drink** water?*
eat	manger	Le vendredi, nous **mangeons** à 4 heures. *On Fridays, we **eat** at four o'clock.*
exit go out	sortir	Nous aimons **sortir** le week-end. *We like to **go out** on the weekend.*
explain	expliquer	Ce professeur **explique** très bien les leçons. *This teacher **explains** the lessons very well.*
finish end	finir terminer	Je m'attends à **finir** le roman très bientôt. *I expect to **finish** the novel very soon.*
give	donner	Ils **donnent** leur vie pour aider les autres. *They **give** their lives to help others.*
go	aller	Je ne veux pas **aller** à l'école demain. *I don't want to **go** to school tomorrow.*
have	avoir	Je veux **avoir** un bon travail. *I want to **have** a good job.*
learn	apprendre	Je veux **apprendre** l'histoire de la Turquie. *I want to **learn** about the history of Turkey.*
live	habiter vivre	Maria **habite** dans un petit quartier. *Maria **lives** in a small neighborhood.*
look watch	regarder	J'aime **regarder** de beaux paysages. *I like to **look** at beautiful scenes.*
love	aimer	J'**aime** le son des oiseaux. *I **love** the sound of birds.*
open	ouvrir	Les boulangeries n'**ouvrent** pas très tard. *Bakeries don't **open** very late.*
put	mettre	Tu dois **mettre** les vêtements dans l'armoire. *You must **put** the clothes in the wardrobe.*
read	lire	Je **lis** le français, mais je ne le parle pas bien. *I **read** French, but I don't speak it well.*
receive	recevoir	Nous **recevons** toujours des invités en été. *We always **receive** guests in the summer.*
say tell	dire	Il doit **dire** la vérité. *He must **tell** the truth.*
see	voir	J'aime **voir** ma mère tous les jours. *I like to **see** my mom every day.*
sleep	dormir	Il est plus sain de **dormir** tôt. *It is healthier to **sleep** early.*

English	French	Examples
speak talk	parler	Elle **parle** couramment trois langues. *She **speaks** three languages fluently.*
start	commencer	Nous pouvons **commencer** les cours à 8 heures du matin. *We can **start** classes at 8 a.m.*
study	étudier	Les garçons **étudient** avec leurs amis. *The boys **study** with their friends.*
take	prendre	Je préférerais **prendre** le bus la prochaine fois. *I'd prefer to **take** the bus next time.*
think	penser	Je ne veux pas **penser** à l'avenir maintenant. *I don't want to **think** of the future now.*
travel	voyager	Je voudrais **voyager** en Chine cette année. *I would like to **travel** to China this year.*
understand	comprendre	Je ne peux pas **comprendre** ce qu'il dit. *I can't **understand** what he's saying.*
use	utiliser	Nous n'**utilisons** pas le train dans cette partie du monde. *We don't **use** the train in this part of the world.*
walk	marcher [1]	Je **marche** toujours après avoir dîné. *I always **walk** after having dinner.*
want to	vouloir	Qu'est-ce qui vous pousse à **vouloir** être une meilleure personne? *What drives you to **want to** be a better person?*
work	travailler	Je **travaille** en tant que comptable. *I **work** as an accountant.*
write	écrire	Cet auteur **écrit** des romans divertissants. *This author **writes** entertaining novels.*

In addition to the above new verbs, we add 20 English cognates that are easy to memorize.

English	French	Examples
accept	accepter	Désolé! Je ne peux pas **accepter** votre invitation. *Sorry! I can't **accept** your invitation.*
calm	calmer	J'aime lire pour **calmer** mes nerfs. *I like to read to **calm** my nerves.*
circulate	circuler	L'air devrait **circuler** dans la pièce. *The air should **circulate** through the room.*
compensate	compenser	Je dois **compenser** d'être arrivé en retard. *I have to **compensate** for arriving late.*

---

[1] The verb "**marcher**" also means *"to function"* or *"to work,"* especially in informal conversation, e.g., "**Le téléphone marche**" *(The phone works)*, "**Ça marche pour toi?**" *(Does this work for you?)*, "**Ça ne marche pas**" *(It doesn't work)*, etc.

comprehend	comprendre	Je ne peux pas **comprendre** ces instructions. *I can't **comprehend** these instructions.*
confirm	confirmer	Pouvez-vous **confirmer** le numéro? *Can you **confirm** the number?*
continue	continuer	La rue **continue** jusqu'à la rivière. *The street **continues** to the river.*
copy	copier	Dans le passé, il était difficile de **copier** des livres. *In the past, it was hard to **copy** books.*
dance	danser	Je ne **danse** pas très bien. *I don't **dance** very well.*
decide	décider	Vous **décidez** vous-même quelle voiture vous voulez acheter. *You yourself **decide** which car you want to buy.*
depend	dépendre	Les résultats **dépendent** de nombreuses variables. *The results **depend** on many variables.*
enter	entrer [1]	Nous devons **entrer** dans le bâtiment tôt. *We must **enter** the building early.*
exist	exister	Beaucoup de langues **existent** dans le monde. *A lot of languages **exist** in the world.*
force	forcer	Tu ne devrais pas **forcer** la serrure. *You shouldn't **force** the lock.*
form	former	Les quatre pays **forment** une alliance. *The four countries **form** an alliance.*
insult	insulter	Il n'est pas poli d'**insulter** les autres personnes. *It is not polite to **insult** other people.*
observe	observer	La police **observe** ses mouvements. *The police **observe** his movements.*
organize	organiser	Je veux **organiser** un voyage ce mois-ci. *I want to **organize** a trip this month.*
repair	réparer	Vous devez **réparer** cette voiture. *You have to **repair** that car.*
verify check	vérifier	Les médecins **vérifient** les résultats après le test. *The doctors **verify** the results after the test.*

2. ADJECTIVES I

Below is a list of the most common 50 adjectives in French. Use the Anki cards created for this section to help you memorize the meaning

---

[1] Whereas the verb *"enter"* is not followed by a preposition in English, the verb **"entrer"** in French is often followed by **"dans"** *(in)*.

of each word in proper contexts. Notice that an adjective must agree with the noun in number and gender.

English	French	Examples
available	disponible	Le siège du passager est **disponible**. *The passenger's seat is **available**.*
bad	mauvais	Le service est **mauvais** ici. *The service is **bad** here.*
beautiful	beau^m belle^f	La vue est très **belle**. *The view is very **beautiful**.*
better	meilleur	J'espère toujours un **meilleur** lendemain. *I always hope for a **better** tomorrow.*
big	grand	Nos voisins ont une **grande** maison. *Our neighbors have a **large** house.*
boring	ennuyeux	Cette classe est très **ennuyeuse**. *This class is very **boring**.*
busy	occupé	Je suis très **occupé** ce week-end. *I'm very **busy** this weekend.*
cheap inexpensive	bon marché	Je cherche un vol **bon marché**. *I'm looking for a **cheap** flight.*
clean	propre	Ma salle de bains doit toujours être **propre**. *My bathroom must always be **clean**.*
closed	fermé	Le cinéma est **fermé** aujourd'hui. *The cinema is **closed** today.*
cold	froid	J'aime le café **froid**. *I like **cold** coffee.*
crazy	fou^m folle^f	Ce garçon est **fou**. *This boy is **crazy**.*
difficult	difficile	Le calcul des impôts peut être **difficile**. *Calculating taxes can be **difficult**.*
dirty	sale	C'est le panier à linge **sale**. *This is the **dirty** laundry basket.*
dry	sec	Cette région a un climat **sec**. *This region has a **dry** climate.*
easy	facile	Ce puzzle est très **facile**. *This puzzle is very **easy**.*
expensive	cher	Cette robe est très **chère**. *That dress is very **expensive**.*
fast	rapide	Cette voiture est très **rapide**. *This car is very **fast**.*
fun	amusant	Le voyage de demain va être **amusant**. *Tomorrow's trip is going to be **fun**.*

funny	**drôle**	Cet homme est très **drôle**. *This man is very **funny**.*
good	**bon**	C'est un **bon** livre. *This is a **good** book.*
happy	**heureux**	L'argent seul ne vous rend pas **heureux**. *Money alone doesn't make you **happy**.*
hard (inflexible)	**dur**	Ce plâtre ne me semble pas **dur**. *This plaster doesn't seem **hard** to me.*
high **tall**	**haut** **grand** [1]	Cet arbre est très **grand**. *This tree is very **tall**.*
hot	**chaud**	Le thé est très **chaud**. *The tea is very **hot**.*
much	**beaucoup**	Il reste encore **beaucoup** de travail à faire. *There is still **much** work to be done.*
many	**beaucoup**	Il y a **beaucoup** de maisons ici. *There are **many** houses here.*
new	**nouveau**[m] **nouvelle**[f]	C'est ma **nouvelle** voiture. *This is my **new** car.*
old	**vieux**	La maison de ma grand-mère est très **vieille**. *My grandmother's house is very **old**.*
open	**ouvert**	Le supermarché est déjà **ouvert**. *The supermarket is already **open**.*
poor	**pauvre**	Cet homme est **pauvre**. *This man is **poor**.*
quiet	**calme** **tranquille**	J'aime lire dans un endroit **calme**. *I like to read in a **quiet** place.*
ready	**prêt**	Je suis **prêt** pour les vacances. *I am **ready** for vacation.*
sad	**triste**	C'est un homme très **triste**. *He is a very **sad** man.*
same	**même**	J'ai deux chemises de la **même** couleur. *I have two shirts of the **same** color.*
short	**court** **petit** [1]	Mon frère est **petit**. *My brother is **short**.*
sick	**malade**	Je vais rendre visite à mon grand-père **malade**. *I'm going to visit my **sick** grandfather.*
slow	**lent**	Il est plus sain de manger à un rythme **lent**. *It's healthier to eat at a **slow** pace.*

---

[1] The direct translation of "**grand**" and "**petit**" is *"large"* and *"small,"* respectively. On the other hand, the direct translation of "**haut**" and "**court**" is *"high"* and *"short,"* respectively. However, only when we refer to the height of a person or an object, we use "**grand**" and "**petit**" to mean *"tall"* and *"short,"* and we do not use "**haut**" and "**court**," respectively.

small	**petit**	Carlo a un **petit** nez. *Carlo has a **small** nose.*
soft	**doux**	Ce pain est très **doux**. *This bread is very **soft**.*
strong	**fort**	Mon cheval est très **fort**. *My horse is very **strong**.*
sure **certain**	**sûr** **certain**	J'essaie toujours de répondre si je suis **certain**. *I always try to answer if I'm **certain**.*
sweet	**sucré** **doux**	Cette collation me semble trop **sucrée**. *This refreshment seems too **sweet** to me.*
tired	**fatigué**	Après le travail, je rentre chez moi **fatigué**. *After work, I get home **tired**.*
too much	**trop**	Je ne veux pas manger **trop** de sucre aujourd'hui. *I don't want to eat **too much** sugar today.*
ugly	**laid**	C'est une statue **laide**. *This is **ugly** statue.*
weak	**faible**	Il a un corps **faible** parce qu'il mange à peine. *He has a **weak** body because he hardly eats.*
wet	**mouillé**	Je n'aime pas me coucher avec les cheveux **mouillés**. *I don't like going to bed with my hair **wet**.*
worse	**pire**	Dans le **pire** des cas, vous annulez. *In the **worst** case, you cancel.*
young	**jeune**	Tu ne seras pas **jeune** pour toujours. *You won't be **young** forever.*

In addition to the above new adjectives, we add 30 more English cognates that are easy to memorize.

English	French	Examples
adult	**adulte**	La présente médication est destinée uniquement aux patients **adultes**. *This medication is for **adult** patients only.*
aggressive	**agressif**	Le chat de mon ami est très **agressif**. *My friend's cat is very **aggressive**.*
common	**commun** **courante**	Cette marque est très **courante** ici. *That brand is very **common** here.*
complete	**complet**	Le processus **complet** est très long. *The **complete** process is very long.*
complex	**complexe**	Cette structure est très **complexe**. *This structure is very **complex**.*
correct **right**	**correct**	Vous devez choisir le choix **correct**. *You must select the **right** option.*

diverse	diversifié	J'aime manger des aliments **diversifiés**. *I like to eat **diverse** foods.*
exact	exact	Je ne connais pas l'emplacement **exact**. *I don't know the **exact** location.*
excellent	excellent	Ses notes sont **excellentes**. *His grades are **excellent**.*
familiar	familier	Son visage me semble **familier**. *His face seems **familiar** to me.*
frank	franc	Il essaie d'être **franc** avec son père. *He tries to be **frank** with his father.*
global	**global** **mondial**	Internet facilite la communication **mondiale**. *The internet facilitates **global** communication.*
honest	honnête	J'ai besoin de ton opinion **honnête**. *I need your **honest** opinion.*
impatient	impatient	Il est une personne **impatiente**. *He is an **impatient** person.*
important	important	Je sauvegarde des fichiers **importants** ici. *I store **important** files here.*
intelligent	intelligent	Ma mère est très **intelligente**. *My mom is very **intelligent**.*
interesting	intéressant	Ce livre est très **intéressant**. *This book is very **interesting**.*
long	long	En été, les jours sont **longs**. *In the summer, the days are **long**.*
necessary	nécessaire	Il est **nécessaire** d'aller chez le médecin périodiquement. *It's **necessary** to go to the doctor periodically.*
patient	patient	Les mères sont **patientes** avec leurs enfants. *Mothers are **patient** with their children.*
personal	personnel	Ceci est mon journal **personnel**. *This is my **personal** diary.*
practical	pratique	Il est **pratique** d'avoir les choses organisées. *It's **practical** to have things organized.*
rare	rare	Il est très **rare** de trouver des pierres précieuses là-bas. *It's very **rare** to find precious stones there.*
real	réel	Évidemment, les monstres ne sont pas **réels**. *Obviously, monsters aren't **real**.*
rich	riche	Les personnes **riches** ont beaucoup d'argent. ***Rich** people have a lot of money.*
simple	simple	L'examen est très **simple**. *The exam is very **simple**.*
sincere	sincère	Il vaut mieux que vous soyez **sincère** à ce sujet. *It is better that you be **sincere** with this.*

special	spécial	Je vais préparer une recette **spéciale** pour toi. *I am going to prepare a **special** recipe for you.*
strict	strict	Mon voisin est **strict** avec ses enfants. *My neighbor is **strict** with his children.*
stupid	stupide	Ces erreurs me font me sentir **stupide**. *These errors make me feel **stupid**.*

3. COUNTRIES & NATIONALITIES I

A *country* in French is "**un pays**" /ĩ pe-**ye**/ and a *nationality* is "**une nationalité**." The following are some countries and nationalities (or demonyms) in French. Notice the extra "**e**" or "**ne**" needed sometimes to form the feminine form.

Africa	**Afrique**^f	*African*	**africain(e)**
Argentina	**Argentine**^f	*Argentinian*	**argentin(e)**
Asia	**Asie**^f	*Asian*	**asiatique**^{m,f}
Australia	**Australie**^f	*Australian*	**australien(ne)**
Brazil	**Brésil**^m	*Brazilian*	**brésilien(ne)**
Canada	**Canada**^m	*Canadian*	**canadien(ne)**
China	**Chine**^f	*Chinese*	**chinois(e)**
Colombia	**Colombie**^f	*Colombian*	**colombien(ne)**
Croatia	**Croatie**^f	*Croatian*	**croate**^{m,f}
Cuba	**Cuba**^m	*Cuban*	**cubain(e)**
Egypt	**Égypte**^f	*Egyptian*	**égyptien(ne)**
England	**Angleterre**^f	*English*	**anglais(e)**
Europe	**Europe**^f	*European*	**européen(ne)**
France	**France**^f	*French*	**français(e)**
Germany	**Allemagne**^f	*German*	**allemand(e)**
Iran	**Iran**^m	*Iranian*	**iranien(ne)**
Iraq	**Irak**^m	*Iraqi*	**irakien(ne)**
Italy	**Italie**^f	*Italian*	**italien(ne)**
Japan	**Japon**^m	*Japanese*	**japonais(e)**
Jordan	**Jordanie**^f	*Jordanian*	**jordanien(ne)**
Latin America	**Amérique latine**^f	*Latin American*	**latino-américain(e)**
Mexico	**Mexique**^m	*Mexican*	**mexicain(e)**
Morocco	**Maroc**^m	*Moroccan*	**marocain(e)**
Palestine	**Palestine**^f	*Palestinian*	**palestinien(ne)**
Panama	**Panama**^m	*Panamanian*	**panaméen(ne)**
Poland	**Pologne**^f	*Polish*	**polonais(e)**
Russia	**Russie**^f	*Russian*	**russe**^{m,f}

South America	**Amérique^f du Sud**	*South American*	**sud-américain(e)**
Spain	**Espagne^f**	*Spanish*	**espagnol(e)**
Turkey	**Turquie^f**	*Turkish*	**turc^m/turque^f**
Uruguay	**Uruguay^m**	*Uruguayan*	**uruguayen(ne)**

4. COLORS I

The word *"color"* in French is **"couleur"** /koo-леия/. Some of the basic colors in French are:

black	**noir(e)**	*orange*	**orange^{m,f}**
blue	**bleu(e)**	*purple*	**violet(te)** **pourpre^{m,f}**
brown	**marron^{m,f}** **brun(e)**	*red*	**rouge^{m,f}**
gray	**gris(e)**	*white*	**blanc^m** **blanche^f**
green	**vert(e)**	*yellow*	**jaune^{m,f}**

5. TIMES & SEASONS

A *day* in French is **"un jour,"** and a *week* is **"une semaine."** The *days of the week* or **"les jours de la semaine"** are:

Monday	**lundi**	*Friday*	**vendredi**
Tuesday	**mardi**	*Saturday*	**samedi**
Wednesday	**mercredi**	*Sunday*	**dimanche**
Thursday	**jeudi**	*weekend*	**fin^f de semaine** **weekend^m**

Today is **"aujourd'hui,"** and *tomorrow* is **"demain,"** followed by **"après-demain"** *(the day after tomorrow)*. *Yesterday* is **"hier,"** preceded by **"avant-hier"** *(the day before yesterday)*.

Tonight is **"ce soir"** (literally *this evening*) or **"cette nuit"** (literally *this night*), *last night* is **"hier soir"** (literally *yesterday evening*) or **"la nuit dernière,"** and *tomorrow night* is **"demain soir"** (literally *tomorrow evening*).

The main periods of the day are **"le matin"** *(morning)*, **"l'après-midi"** *(afternoon)*, and **"la nuit"** *(night)*. We generally use the preposition **"dans"** *(in)* or **"pendant"** *(during)* to describe actions or events taking place during the main periods of the day: **"dans/pendant le matin"** *(in the morning)*, **"dans/pendant l'après-midi"** *(in the afternoon)*, or **"dans/pendant la nuit"** *(at night)*.

A *month* in French is **"un mois"** and a *year* is **"un an."** A *decade* is **"une décennie,"** and a *century* is **"un siècle."**

The *months of the year* or **"les mois de l'année"** are:

January	**janvier**	*July*	**juillet**
February	**février**	*August*	**août**
March	**mars**	*September*	**septembre**
April	**avril**	*October*	**octobre**
May	**mai**	*November*	**novembre**
June	**juin**	*December*	**décembre**

Notice from the two tables above that the days and months are not capitalized in French, and they are all masculine.

Finally, a *season* in French is **"une saison."** The *seasons of the year* or to the right of **"les saisons de l'année"** are:

autumn, fall	**automne**[m]	*summer*	**été**[m]
spring	**printemps**[m]	*winter*	**hiver**[m]

6. DIRECTIONS I

A *direction* in French is **"une direction."** A *map* is **"une carte,"** and a *street* is **"une rue."**

The four geographical directions of a *compass* or **"une boussole"** are:

east	**est**[m]	*south*	**sud**[m]
north	**nord**[m]	*west*	**ouest**[m]

And the four main directions *right, left, up,* and *down* are:

right	**droite**	*up*	**haut**
left	**gauche**	*down*	**bas**

To describe the location of an object with respect to another, one can use:

above *on top (of)*	**au-dessus de**	*there*	**là**
here	**ici**	*to the left of*	**à gauche de**
inside (of)	**à l'intérieur (de)**	*to the right of*	**à droite de**
near	**près de**	*far (from)*	**loin (de)**
outside	**dehors**	*toward*	**vers**
straight ahead	**tout droit**	*under* *beneath*	**sous**

Derived from "**ici**" *(here)* and "**là**" *(there)*, the expressions "**voici**" and "**voilà**" are used to call the attention to something and are often translated as *"here is"* or *"here are"* in expressions such as: "**Voici le bus**" *(Here is the bus)*, "**Voici mes questions**" *(Here are my questions)*, "**Voilà pourquoi**" *(Here is why)*, "**Voilà**" *(Here it is)*, etc.

7. FAMILY I

A *family* in French is "**une famille**." The status of being *single* is "**célibataire**," *married* is "**marié(e)**" Some *members of the family*, or "**les membres de la famille**," are:

aunt	**tante**^f	*grandfather*	**grand-père**^m
boyfriend	**petit ami**^m **copain**^m	*grandmother*	**grand-mère**^f
couple	**couple**^m	*grandson*	**petit-fils**^m
cousin	**cousin(e)**	*husband*	**mari**^m
dad	**papa**^m	*mother*	**mère**^f
daughter	**fille**^f	*mom*	**maman**^f
daughter-in-law	**belle-fille**^f **bru**^f	*relatives*	**parents**^m
father	**père**^m	*son*	**fils**^m
fiancé	**fiancé**^m	*son-in-law*	**gendre**^m **beau-fils**^m
fiancée	**fiancée**^f	*spouse*	**conjoint(e)** **époux**^m/**épouse**^f
girlfriend	**petite amie**^f **copine**^f	*uncle*	**oncle**^m

8. ANATOMY I

Body in French is "**le corps**," and some *body parts*, or "**les parties du corps**," are:

arm	**bras**^m	*hand*	**main**^f
back	**dos**^m	*head*	**tête**^f
blood	**sang**^m	*heart*	**cœur**^m
brain	**cerveau**^m	*leg*	**jambe**^f
ear	**oreille**^f	*lip*	**lèvre**^f
eye	**œil**^m	*mouth*	**bouche**^f
face[1]	**visage**^m **figure**^f **face**^f	*nose*	**nez**^m
finger	**doigt**^m	*shoulder*	**épaule**^f
foot	**pied**^m	*stomach*	**estomac**^m
hair	**cheveux**^m	*toe*	**doigt**^m **de pied** **orteil**^m

9. PEOPLE I

The following is some vocabulary that we use to describe *people*, "**les gens**^m" or "**les personnes**^f" in French. Notice that, depending on the context, the word "**personne**" in singular form can mean a *person* or *nobody*.

baby	**bébé**^m	*minor*	**mineur(e)**
boss	**chef(fe)** **patron(ne)**	*neighbor*	**voisin(e)**
boy	**garçon**^m	*nobody*	**personne**
businessman	**homme**^m **d'affaires**	*people*	**gens**^m **personnes**^f
child	**enfant**^m	*person*	**personne**^f
criminal	**criminel(le)**	*player*	**joueur**^m **joueuse**^f
date appointment	**rendez-vous**^m	*president*	**président(e)**

---

[1] The word "**visage**" is more commonly used to refer to a person's face. The word "**face**" /fas/ is often used in medical terms or in some slang talk as an insult to someone.

everyone *everybody*	**tout le monde**	*queen*	**reine**[f]
friend	**ami(e)**	*roommate*	**colocataire**[m,f]
girl	**fille**[f]	*some people*	**certaines personnes**[f]
human	**humain**[m]	*someone*	**quelqu'un**
infant	**nourrisson**[m]	*student*	**étudiant(e)**
king	**roi**[m]	*thief*	**voleur**[m]**/voleuse**[f]
man	**homme**[m]	*woman*	**femme**[f]

10. ANIMALS I

The word *"animal"* in French is **"animal."** Below are some animal names in French:

bird	**oiseau**[m]	*hen*	**poule**[f]
bull	**taureau**[m]	*horse*	**cheval**[m]
cat	**chat**[m]	*mouse*	**souris**[f]
chicken	**poulet**[m]	*pet*	**animal**[m] **de compagnie**
cow	**vache**[f]	*pig*	**cochon**[m]
dog	**chien**[m]	*rabbit*	**lapin**[m]
donkey	**âne**[m]	*rat*	**rat**[m]
duck	**canard**[m]	*rooster*	**coq**[m]
fish	**poisson**[m]	*sheep*	**mouton**[m]
fly	**mouche**[f]	*turkey*	**dinde**[f]

LEVEL II: BEGINNER

I. Introductory Topics & Grammar

At this level, you will continue to familiarize yourself with some of the fundamental grammar rules and basic topics that will enhance your French-language knowledge.

1. PREPOSITIONS

Here are some of the most used prepositions in French with the most common meanings in different contexts.

Prep.	Meaning	Examples	
	to	Je vais **à** l'école le matin.	*I go **to** school in the morning.*
	at	Je finirai **à** midi.	*I will finish **at** noon.*
à	*by*	Fait **à** la main.	*Made **by** hand (handmade).*
	in	J'habite **à** Paris.	*I live **in** Paris.*
	on	Je rentrerai **à** pied.	*I'll come back home **on** foot.*
à côté de	*beside* *next to*	Il y a un chat **à côté de** la chaise.	*There is a cat **beside** the chair.*
à l'extérieur de	*outside*	Le garage est **à l'extérieur** du centre commercial.	*The garage is **outside** the shopping mall.*
à l'intérieur de	*inside*	Le ballon est **à l'intérieur de** la boîte.	*The ball is **inside** the box.*
à travers	*across* *through*	Il est possible se promener **à travers** les champs et les forêts.	*It is possible to walk **through** fields and forests.*
après	*after*	J'ai dormi **après** le déjeuner aujourd'hui.	*I slept **after** lunch today.*
autour de	*around*	J'ai installé des caméras **autour de** la maison.	*I installed cameras **around** the house.*
avant de	*before*	Je t'appellerai **avant de** partir.	*I will call you **before** leaving.*
avec	*with*	Il parle **avec** son ami.	*He speaks **with** his friend.*
contre	*against*	Je suis **contre** l'injustice.	*I am **against** injustice.*
dans	*in*	Le chat est **dans** la boîte.	*The cat is **in** the box.*
de	*of*	La couleur **de** cette voiture est bleue.	*The color **of** that car is blue.*
	from	J'ai voyagé **de** Londres à la Corée.	*I traveled **from** London to Korea.*
	about	Ils parlent **de** lui.	*They talk **about** him.*

dedans	*inside*	Les enfants sont **dedans**.	*The kids are **inside**.*
dehors	*outside*	J'ai trouvé cette balle **dehors**.	*I found this ball **outside**.*
depuis	*for (duration)*	J'y travaille **depuis** deux ans.	*I have worked there **for** two years.*
	since	J'y travaille **depuis** janvier.	*I have worked there **since** January.*
derrière	*behind*	L'arbre est **derrière** la maison.	*The tree is **behind** the house.*
devant	*in front of*	Je suis **devant** l'école.	*I am **in front of** the school.*
jusqu'à	*until*	J'ai travaillé **jusqu'à** minuit.	*I worked **until** midnight.*
	as far as	La lumière s'étend **jusqu'au** parc.	*The light reaches **as far as** the park.*
en	*in*	J'habite **en** France.	*I live **in** France.*
	by	Je vais voyager **en** voiture.	*I am going to travel **by** car.*
	to	J'irai **en** France.	*I will go **to** France.*
au-dessus de	*above over on top of*	La mouche est **au-dessus de** la table.	*The fly is **above** the table.*
en dessous de	*below underneath*	Ce liquide gèle **en dessous d'**une certaine température.	*This liquid freezes **below** a certain temperature.*
entre	*between*	L'oiseau est coincé **entre** les branches.	*The bird is stuck **between** the branches.*
le long de	*along*	Il y a des maisons **le long du** lac.	*There are houses **along** the lake.*
par	*by*	Je t'ai contacté **par** téléphone.	*I contacted you **by** phone.*
	per	Ça coûte 20 dollars **par** nuit.	*It costs 20 dollars **per** night.*
	through	Je passe **par** Paris.	*I'll go **through** Paris.*
	around	J'habite **par** ici.	*I live **around** here.*
parmi	*among*	Je suis le plus grand **parmi** mes amis.	*I am the tallest **among** my friends.*
pendant durant	*during*	Nous pouvons sortir **pendant** la journée.	*We can go out **during** the day.*
pour	*in order to*	On étudie **pour** apprendre.	*We study **in order to** learn.*
	for (destination)	Je partirai **pour** Barcelone demain.	*I will leave **for** Barcelona tomorrow.*
près de	*near*	J'habite **près de** la ville.	*I live **near** the city.*
selon	*according to*	**Selon** la loi, c'est interdit.	***According to** the law, it is prohibited.*

sans	*without*	Un poisson ne peut pas vivre **sans** eau.	*A fish can't live **without** water.*
sous	*under*	Le chat est **sous** la chaise.	*The cat is **under** the chair.*
sur	*on*	La clé est **sur** la table.	*The key is **on** the table.*
	about	Le débat **sur** cet incident est clos.	*The debate **about** that incident is over.*
vers	*toward*	Elle courut **vers** la sortie.	*She ran **toward** the exit.*

❖ The prepositions "**à**" and "**de**" contract when followed by the definite article "**le**" (in its non-contracted form) or "**les**." Other prepositions do not contract with the definite article.

	le	**la**	**l'**	**les**
à	au	à la	à l'	aux
de	du	de la	de l'	des

Here are some examples:

à	+ le	= au	J'irai avec toi **au** stade.	*I'll go with you **to the** stadium.*
à	+ les	= aux	Le professeur parle **aux** élèves.	*The teacher speaks **to the** students.*
de	+ le	= du	Toutes les photos sont supprimées **du** livre.	*All photos are removed **from the** book.*
de	+ les	= des	C'est l'un **des** meilleurs quartiers ici.	*It is one **of the** best areas here.*
de	+ la	= de la	La couleur **de la** voiture est bleue.	*The color **of the** car is blue.*

❖ The preposition "**à**" is used to mean *"in"* when referring to the proper name of a city (or a smaller area), e.g., "**Je vis <u>à</u> Rome**" *(I live <u>in</u> Rome)*. For larger areas, we use the preposition "**en**," e.g., "**Je vis en Californie**" *(I live <u>in</u> California)*, "**Je l'ai vu en Espagne**" *(I saw it <u>in</u> Spain)*, etc.

❖ The preposition "**à**" can also mean *"to"* or *"for"* when used to indicate purpose or reason. For example:

Quelque chose **à** boire	*Something **to** drink*
Une maison **à** vendre	*A house **for** sale*

❖ The preposition **"en"** generally means *"in"* in English. However, when referring to a destination that is larger than a city, the preposition **"en"** can also be translated as *"to,"* e.g., **"J'irai en Californie"** *(I will go <u>to</u> California)*, **"J'ai voyagé en Espagne"** *(I traveled <u>to</u> Spain)*, etc. When referring to a means of transportation, **"en"** is often translated as *"by,"* e.g., **"On voyage en train"** *(We travel by train)*.

❖ The preposition **"depuis"** is used as the equivalent of *"since"* and *"for"* in time expressions that typically use the present perfect or present perfect continuous tense in English. For example:

Je n'ai pas fumé **depuis** avril.	*I haven't smoked **since** April.*
Je n'ai pas fumé **depuis** deux ans.	*I haven't smoked **for** two years.*

❖ We use **"chez"** to refer to being at someone's house or workplace. In this context, **"chez"** is often translated as *"at"* or *"to."* For example:

Nous sommes **chez** Marco.	*We are **at** Marco's place.*
Es-tu **chez** Anne?	*Are you **at** Anne's place?*
Nous sommes **chez** Burger King.	*We are **at** Burger King.*
Je viendrai **chez** toi.	*I will come **to** your house.*
J'irai **chez** le dentiste demain.	*I will go **to** the dentist tomorrow.*

❖ To express the meaning of *"about"* (e.g., to talk *about* or watch a documentary *about* something), we often use **"sur."** For example:

J'ai regardé un documentaire **sur** cette guerre.	*I watched a documentary **about** that war.*
J'ai lu un livre **sur** la vie au Japon.	*I read a book **about** life in Japan.*

In some contexts, we could use **"de"** to mean *"about."* For example:

Ils parlent **de** lui.	*They talk **about** him.*
Je veux lire un livre **de** sciences.	*I want to read a book **about** science.*

2. Present Indicative Tense II

Some verbs deviate from the general conjugation rules in the present indicative tense outlined in **Level I, Lesson 6**. Some of these deviations are simple and easy to apply, while others may require some practice. Nevertheless, do not give up because conjugation in other tenses tends to be more straightforward with fewer irregularities. Use your Anki cards to practice more examples until you master this lesson. In addition, you can use the summary in the cheat sheets in **Appendix B** as a quick reference.

Let us examine the irregular verbs in the three verb groups "-**er**," "-**ir**," and "-**re**" in the present indicative tense.

#1: "-er" Verbs

The verb "**aller**" *(to go)* is essentially the *only* irregular "-**er**" verb that does not follow a particular pattern of conjugation. This is an important verb that should be practiced and memorized.

	je	tu	il/elle	nous	vous	ils/elles
aller *to go*	vais	vas	va	allons	allez	vont

Notice that the verb "**aller**" is used instead of the verb "**être**" *(to be)* in some contexts, e.g., "**Comment <u>allez</u>-vous?**" *(How <u>are</u> you?)*, "**Je <u>vais</u> bien**" *(I <u>am</u> well)*, etc.

Some "-**er**" verbs undergo minor spelling changes of the stem when conjugated in some forms. These are classified in the following five categories:

1. Verbs ending in "-**cer**"

Verbs ending in "-**cer**" add a *cedilla* to the "**c**" only when conjugated in the first-person plural form "**nous**." This is required to maintain the soft "**c**" sound when the "-**ons**" suffix is added. Other conjugations are unchanged. Here are some examples:

nous commençons	*we start*	**nous effaçons**	*we erase*
nous finançons	*we finance*	**nous influençons**	*we influence*

nous menaçons	*we threaten*	nous plaçons	*we place*
nous remplaçons	*we replace*	nous renonçons	*we renounce*

2. Verbs ending in "-**ger**"

Verbs ending in "-**ger**" add an "**e**" after the "**g**" only when conjugated in the first-person plural form "**nous**." This is required to maintain the soft "**g**" sound when the "-**ons**" suffix is added. Other conjugations are unchanged. Here are some examples:

nous bougeons	*we move*	nous changeons	*we change*
nous corrigeons	*we correct*	nous dégageons	*we release*
nous exigeons	*we demand*	nous mangeons	*we eat*
nous nageons	*we swim*	nous voyageons	*we travel*

3. Verbs ending in "-**yer**"

Verbs ending in "-**yer**" change the "**y**" to "**i**" in all forms except "**nous**" and "**vous**." For instance, the verb "**envoyer**" *(to send)* in the first-person singular is conjugated as "**j'envoie**" /jã-**vwa**/. Notice that the letter "**y**" is replaced with "**i**" and the "**y**" sound at the end no longer exists in pronunciation. Let us look at some examples:

	"**appuyer**" *(to lean on)*	"**dévoyer**" *(to mislead)*	"**ennuyer**" *(to bore or annoy)*	"**envoyer**" *(to send)*
je/j'	appuie	dévoie	ennuie	envoie
tu	appuies	dévoies	ennuies	envoies
il/elle/on	appuie	dévoie	ennuie	envoie
nous	appuyons	dévoyons	ennuyons	envoyons
vous	appuyez	dévoyez	ennuyez	envoyez
ils/elles	appuient	dévoient	ennuient	envoient

One exception is the verb "**payer**" *(to pay)* which can be conjugated both ways. For instance, the verb "**payer**" in the first-person singular can be conjugated as "**je paye**" /j(ə) pey/ or "**je paie**" /j(ə) pe/.

4. Verbs ending in "-**eler**"

Some verbs ending in "**-eler**" double the "**l**" at the end of their stem in all forms except "**nous**" and "**vous**." For instance, the verb "**appeler**" *(to call)* in the first-person singular is conjugated as "**j'appelle**" /ja-**pel**/. Here are some more examples:

	"épeler" *(to spell)*	"étinceler" *(to sparkle)*	"rappeler" *(to remind)*	"renouveler" *(to renew)*
je/j'	épelle	étincelle	rappelle	renouvelle
tu	épelles	étincelles	rappelles	renouvelles
il/elle/on	épelle	étincelle	rappelle	renouvelle
nous	épelons	étincelons	rappelons	renouvelons
vous	épelez	étincelez	rappelez	renouvelez
ils/elles	épellent	étincellent	rappellent	renouvellent

5. Verbs ending in "**-e-**" + *consonant* + "**-er**"

Some verbs ending in "**-e-**" followed by a *consonant* followed by "**-er**" add a *grave accent* to the "**e**" in the stem before the consonant in all forms except "**nous**" and "**vous**." This changes the "**e**" sound to an open "**e**" sound instead of a schwa sound. For instance, the verb "**lever**" /lə-**ve**/ *(to raise)* in the first-person singular is conjugated as "**je lève**" /j(ə) lev/. Here are some more examples:

	"acheter" *(to buy)*	"enlever" *(to remove)*	"mener" *(to lead)*	"peser" *(to weigh)*
je/j'	achète	enlève	mène	pèse
tu	achètes	enlèves	mènes	pèses
il/elle/on	achète	enlève	mène	pèse
nous	achetons	enlevons	menons	pesons
vous	achetez	enlevez	menez	pesez
ils/elles	achètent	enlèvent	mènent	pèsent

If the "**e**" in the stem before the consonant already has an acute accent in the infinitive, the acute accent is replaced with a grave accent in all forms except "**nous**" and "**vous**." Here are some examples:

	"célébrer" *(to celebrate)*	"espérer" *(to hope)*	"gérer" *(to manage)*	"préférer" *(to prefer)*
je/j'	célèbre	espère	gère	préfère
tu	célèbres	espères	gères	préfères

il/elle/on	célèbre	espère	gère	préfère
nous	célébrons	espérons	gérons	préférons
vous	célébrez	espérez	gérez	préférez
ils/elles	célèbrent	espèrent	gèrent	préfèrent

#2: "-ir" Verbs

We covered the conjugation of regular "-**ir**" verbs in **Level I, Lesson 6**. Here is an example of a regular "-**ir**" verb conjugated in the present indicative tense:

	je	tu	il/elle	nous	vous	ils/elles
finir *to finish*	fin**is**	fin**is**	fin**it**	fin**issons**	fin**issez**	fin**issent**

Unfortunately, not all "-**ir**" verbs are regular. There are many irregular verbs in this verb group. We will classify them into five main categories:

1. Verbs ending in "-**tir**," "-**mir**," and "-**vir**"

Many verbs in this category are conjugated with the same pattern. Notice the dropping of the last letter of the stem in the three singular forms.

	partir *(to leave)*	**dormir** *(to sleep)*	**servir** *(to serve)*
je	par**s**	dor**s**	ser**s**
tu	par**s**	dor**s**	ser**s**
il/elle/on	par**t**	dor**t**	ser**t**
nous	part**ons**	dorm**ons**	serv**ons**
vous	part**ez**	dorm**ez**	serv**ez**
ils/elles	part**ent**	dorm**ent**	serv**ent**

2. Verbs ending in "-**vrir**," "-**frir**," and "-**llir**"

Many verbs in this category are conjugated like regular "-**er**" verbs, for example:

	ouvrir *(to open)*	**offrir** *(to offer)*	**cueillir** *(to pick)*

je/j'	ouvre	offre	cueille
tu	ouvres	offres	cueilles
il/elle/on	ouvre	offre	cueille
nous	ouvrons	offrons	cueillons
vous	ouvrez	offrez	cueillez
ils/elles	ouvrent	offrent	cueillent

Other examples include: "**couvrir**" *(to cover)*, "**souffrir**" *(to suffer)*, "**découvrir**" *(to discover)*, "**assaillir**" *(to assault)*, and "**accueillir**" *(to welcome)*.

3. The verbs "**venir**," "**tenir**," and their derivations

Verbs in this category are conjugated as follows:

	venir	**tenir**	**devenir**	**obtenir**
	(to come)	*(to hold)*	*(to become)*	*(to obtain)*
je/j'	viens	tiens	deviens	obtiens
tu	viens	tiens	deviens	obtiens
il/elle/on	vient	tient	devient	obtient
nous	venons	tenons	devenons	obtenons
vous	venez	tenez	devenez	obtenez
ils/elles	viennent	tiennent	deviennent	obtiennent

Other examples include: "**advenir**" *(to happen)*, "**revenir**" *(to come back)*, "**convenir**" *(to suit)*, "**provenir**" *(to arise from)*, "**prévenir**" *(to prevent)*, "**survenir**" *(to occur)*, "**intervenir**" *(to intervene)*, "**détenir**" *(to hold or detain)*, "**retenir**" *(to retain or hold)*, "**abstenir**" *(to abstain)*, "**contenir**" *(to contain)*, "**soutenir**" *(to sustain or support)*, "**maintenir**" *(to maintain)*, "**appartenir**" *(to belong)*, and "**entretenir**" *(to entertain)*.

4. Verbs ending with "-oir"

Verbs ending in "**-oir**" do not follow a single conjugation pattern. Thus, one must practice and memorize as many verbs as possible in this category. Here are some common examples:

	je	**tu**	**il/elle**	**nous**	**vous**	**ils/elles**
avoir *to have*	ai	as	a	avons	avez	ont
savoir *to know*	sais	sais	sait	savons	savez	savent

devoir *must*	dois	dois	doit	devons	devez	doivent
pouvoir *can*	peux	peux	peut	pouvons	pouvez	peuvent
vouloir *to want*	veux	veux	veut	voulons	voulez	veulent
voir *to see*	vois	vois	voit	voyons	voyez	voient
falloir *to be necessary*	-	-	faut	-	-	-
pleuvoir *to rain*	-	-	pleut	-	-	-
asseoir *to sit*	assieds	assieds	assied	asseyons	asseyez	asseyent
décevoir *to disappoint*	déçois	déçois	déçoit	décevons	décevez	déçoivent
prévoir *to predict*	prévois	prévois	prévoit	prévoyons	prévoyez	prévoient
recevoir *to receive*	reçois	reçois	reçoit	recevons	recevez	reçoivent
valoir *to be worth*	-	-	vaut	-	-	-

5. Other irregular "-ir" verbs

There remain a few irregular "-ir" verbs that do not fall under any of the four previous categories, such as:

	je	tu	il/elle	nous	vous	ils/elles
acquérir *to acquire*	acquiers	acquiers	acquiert	acquérons	acquérez	acquièrent
conquérir *to conquer*	conquiers	conquiers	conquiert	conquérons	conquérez	conquièrent
bouillir *to boil*	bous	bous	bout	bouillons	bouillez	bouillent
courir *to run*	cours	cours	court	courons	courez	courent
parcourir *to run through*	parcours	parcours	parcourt	parcourons	parcourez	parcourent
secourir *to rescue*	secours	secours	secourt	secourons	secourez	secourent
mourir *to die*	meurs	meurs	meurt	mourons	mourez	meurent

#3: "-re" Verbs

The irregular "-re" verbs group includes some important verbs in French such as: "**être**" *(to be)*, "**faire**" *(to do or make)*, and "**boire**" *(to drink)*.

	être	**faire**	**boire**
	(to be)	*(to do or make)*	*(to drink)*
je	suis	fais	bois
tu	es	fais	bois
il/elle/on	est	fait	boit
nous	sommes	faisons	buvons
vous	êtes	faites	buvez
ils/elles	sont	font	boivent

Most verbs in this group fall under one of these eight categories that can help you recognize them:

1. The verb "**prendre**" and its derivations

The verb "**prendre**" and its derivations are conjugated with the same pattern. Notice the removal of the "**d**" in all three plural forms and the extra "**n**" in the third-person plural forms "**ils**" and "**elles**."

	prendre	**apprendre**	**comprendre**
	(to take)	*(to learn)*	*(to understand)*
je/j'	prends	apprends	comprends
tu	prends	apprends	comprends
il/elle/on	prend	apprend	comprend
nous	prenons	apprenons	comprenons
vous	prenez	apprenez	comprenez
ils/elles	prennent	apprennent	comprennent

Other examples include: "**entreprendre**" *(to undertake)*, "**surprendre**" *(to surprise)*, "**reprendre**" *(to retake)*, and "**méprendre**" *(to mistake)*.

2. The verbs "**mettre**," "**battre**," and their derivations

The verbs "**mettre**," "**battre**," and their derivations are conjugated with the same pattern. Notice the dropping of the second "**t**" in all three singular forms.

	mettre *(to put)*	**battre** *(to beat)*	**promettre** *(to promise)*	**débattre** *(to debate)*
je	met**s**	bat**s**	promet**s**	débat**s**
tu	met**s**	bat**s**	promet**s**	débat**s**
il/elle/on	met	bat	promet	débat
nous	mett**ons**	batt**ons**	promett**ons**	débatt**ons**
vous	mett**ez**	batt**ez**	promett**ez**	débatt**ez**
ils/elles	mett**ent**	batt**ent**	promett**ent**	débatt**ent**

Other examples include: "**admettre**" *(to admit)*, "**commettre**" *(to commit)*, "**compromettre**" *(to compromise)*, "**permettre**" *(to permit)*, "**soumettre**" *(to submit)*, "**transmettre**" *(to transmit)*, "**abattre**" *(to knock down)*, and "**combattre**" *(to combat)*.

3. The verb "**rompre**" and its derivations

The verb "**rompre**" and its derivations are conjugated with the same pattern. Notice that these verbs are conjugated just like regular "**-re**" verbs, except in the third-person singular form which takes the suffix "**t**."

	rompre *(to break)*	**corrompre** *(to corrupt)*	**interrompre** *(to interrupt)*
je/j'	romp**s**	corromp**s**	interromp**s**
tu	romp**s**	corromp**s**	interromp**s**
il/elle/on	romp**t**	corromp**t**	interromp**t**
nous	romp**ons**	corromp**ons**	interromp**ons**
vous	romp**ez**	corromp**ez**	interromp**ez**
ils/elles	romp**ent**	corromp**ent**	interromp**ent**

4. Verbs ending in "**-aindre**," "**-eindre**," and "**-oindre**"

Verbs in this category drop the "**d**" in their root in all forms, and add a "**g**" before the "**n**" in the three plural forms.

	craindre *(to fear)*	**peindre** *(to paint)*	**joindre** *(to join)*

je	crains	peins	joins
tu	crains	peins	joins
il/elle/on	craint	peint	joint
nous	craignons	peignons	joignons
vous	craignez	peignez	joignez
ils/elles	craignent	peignent	joignent

Other examples include: "**adjoindre**" *(to appoint)*, "**astreindre**" *(to compel or force)*, "**atteindre**" *(to attain or reach)*, "**ceindre**" *(to put on)*, "**contraindre**" *(to force)*, "**dépeindre**" *(to depict)*, "**disjoindre**" *(to disconnect)*, "**empreindre**" *(to imprint)*, "**éteindre**" *(to extinguish)*, "**feindre**" *(to feign)*, "**geindre**" *(to groan or whine)*, "**plaindre**" *(to pity)*, "**rejoindre**" *(to rejoin)*, "**restreindre**" *(to restrict)*, and "**teindre**" *(to dye)*.

5. Verbs ending in "-uire," "-dire," "-fire," and "-lire"

Verbs in this category are conjugated with the same pattern. Notice that these verbs add an "**s**" to the end of the stem in the three plural forms. One exception is the second-person plural of the verb "**dire**" (and its derivations), which is conjugated as "**vous di_tes_**."

	cuire	dire	confire	lire
	(to cook)	*(to beat)*	*(to preserve)*	*(to debate)*
je	cuis	dis	confis	lis
tu	cuis	dis	confis	lis
il/elle/on	cuit	dit	confit	lit
nous	cuisons	disons	confisons	lisons
vous	cuisez	di_tes_	confisez	lisez
ils/elles	cuisent	disent	confisent	lisent

Other examples include: "**conduire**" *(to drive)*, "**construire**" *(to build)*, "**contredire**" *(to contradict)*, "**déduire**" *(to deduce or deduct)*, "**détruire**" *(to destroy)*, "**élire**" *(to elect)*, "**induire**" *(to mislead)*, "**instruire**" *(to instruct)*, "**interdire**" *(to forbid)*, "**induire**" *(to mislead)*, "**introduire**" *(to insert or introduce)*, "**luire**" *(to shine)*, "**médire**" *(to malign)*, "**nuire**" *(to harm)*, "**prédire**" *(to predict)*, "**produire**" *(to produce)*, "**reconduire**" *(to renew)*, "**reconstuire**" *(to rebuild)*, "**réduire**" *(to reduce)*, "**séduire**" *(to seduce)*, "**suffire**" *(to suffer)*, and "**traduire**" *(to translate)*.

6. Verbs ending in "**-crire**"

Verbs in this category are conjugated with the same pattern. Notice that these verbs add a "**v**" to the end of the stem in the three plural forms.

	écrire *(to write)*	décrire *(to describe)*	souscrire *(to subscribe)*
je/j'	écris	décris	souscris
tu	écris	décris	souscris
il/elle/on	écrit	décrit	souscrit
nous	écrivons	décrivons	souscrivons
vous	écrivez	décrivez	souscrivez
ils/elles	écrivent	décrivent	souscrivent

Other examples include: "**inscrire**" *(to inscribe or write down)*, "**prescrire**" *(to prescribe)*, "**proscrire**" *(to prohibit or ban)*, "**récrire**" *(to rewrite)*, "**transcrire**" *(to transcribe)*, and "**circonscrire**" *(to contain or confine)*.

7. Verbs ending in "**-aître**"

Verbs in this category, except "**naître**," follow the same conjugation pattern. Notice the circumflex in the third-person singular form.

	apparaître *(to appear)*	connaître *(to know)*	paraître *(to seem)*
je/j'	apparais	connais	parais
tu	apparais	connais	parais
il/elle/on	apparaît	connaît	paraît
nous	apparaissons	connaissons	paraissons
vous	apparaissez	connaissez	paraissez
ils/elles	apparaissent	connaissent	paraissent

Other examples include: "**comparaître**" *(to appear in court)*, "**disparaître**" *(to disappear)*, "**méconnaître**" *(to be unaware of)*, "**reconnaître**" *(to recognize)*, "**reapparaître**" *(to reappear)*, and "**transparaître**" *(to show through)*.

8. Other irregular "**-re**" verbs

Finally, there remain a few verbs that do not belong to any of the previous categories like the verbs "**être**" *(to be)*, "**faire**" *(to do or make)*, and "**boire**" *(to drink)*, which we discussed at the beginning of this section. Here are a few other examples:

	je/j'	tu	il/elle	nous	vous	ils/elles
clore *to close*	clos	clos	clôt	-	-	closent
conclure *to conclude*	conclus	conclus	conclut	concluons	concluez	concluent
coudre *to sew*	couds	couds	coud	cousons	cousez	cousent
croire *to believe*	crois	crois	croit	croyons	croyez	croient
dissoudre *to dissolve*	dissous	dissous	dissout	dissolvons	dissolvez	dissolvent
distraire *to distract*	distrais	distrais	distrait	distrayons	distrayez	distraient
exclure *to exclude*	exclus	exclus	exclut	excluons	excluez	excluent
inclure *to include*	inclus	inclus	inclut	incluons	incluez	incluent
moudre *to grind*	mouds	mouds	moud	moulons	moulez	moulent
plaire *to please*	plais	plais	plait	plaisons	plaisez	plaisent
résoudre *to resolve*	résous	résous	résout	résolvons	résolvez	résolvent
rire *to laugh*	ris	ris	rit	rions	riez	rient
sourire *to smile*	souris	souris	sourit	sourions	souriez	sourient
suivre *to follow*	suis	suis	suit	suivons	suivez	suivent
vivre *to live*	vis	vis	vit	vivons	vivez	vivent

3. POSSESSIVE ADJECTIVES & PRONOUNS

Possessive adjectives (*my, your, his/her, our, their*) come before a noun, e.g., *"This is my house,"* while possessive pronouns (*mine, yours, his/hers, ours, theirs*) are used to replace a noun and its possessive adjective, e.g., *"This house is mine."*

In French, possessive adjectives and pronouns must agree in gender and number with the noun they describe.

The possessive adjectives are:

	Sing. Masc.	Sing. Fem.	Plural Masc.	Plural Fem.
my	mon	ma	mes	
your (informal singular)	ton	ta	tes	
his/her	son	sa	ses	
our	notre		nos	
your (plural or formal singular)	votre		vos	
their	leur		leurs	

On the other hand, the possessive pronouns in French are:

	Sing. Masc.	Sing. Fem.	Plural Masc.	Plural Fem.
mine	le mien	la mienne	les miens	les miennes
yours (informal singular)	le tien	la tienne	les tiens	les tiennes
his/hers	le sien	la sienne	les siens	les siennes
ours	le nôtre	la nôtre	les nôtres	
yours (plural or formal singular)	le vôtre	la vôtre	les vôtres	
theirs	le leur	la leur	les leurs	

❖ Note that the *masculine* form **"mon,"** **"ton,"** or **"son"** is used before a singular *feminine* noun that starts with a vowel or a mute **"h,"** e.g., **"mon armoire[b]"** *(my cabinet)*, **"son horloge[b]"** *(his clock)*, etc.

❖ Note that, unlike in English, the possessive adjective agrees in number and gender with the noun it describes and not the possessor, e.g., **"mes frères"** *(my brothers)*. Note that we use **"mes"** because the *noun* we describe is *plural*, although the possessor is singular. Similarly, in the example "**sa mère**" *(his/her mother)*, the possessive adjective "**sa**" agrees in gender and number with the noun it describes, "**mère**," and can mean *"his"* or *"her"* depending on the gender of the possessor. The context often clears up this ambiguity.

❖ Another way to express possession is using the proposition "**à**" followed by a noun or object pronoun, e.g., "**C'est à toi**" *(This is yours)*, "**Je ne sais pas c'est à qui**" *(I don't know whose it is)*, "**Ce n'est pas à Robert**" *(It's not Robert's)*, etc.

❖ One can also insert the adjective "**propre(s)**" *(own)* between the possessive pronoun and the noun for emphasis, e.g., "**son propre téléphone**" *(his/her own phone)*, "**ta propre maison**" *(your own house)*, "**ses propres mains**" *(his/her own hands)*, etc.

4. DEMONSTRATIVE PRONOUNS & ADJECTIVES

Demonstrative adjectives *(this, that, these, those)* come before a noun, e.g., *"I want this book,"* while possessive pronouns (same as demonstrative adjectives in English: *this, that, these, those*) are used to replace a noun and its possessive adjective, e.g., *"I want this."*

In French, demonstrative pronouns and adjectives must agree in gender and number with the noun being described.

Demonstrative Adjectives

Let us start with the demonstrative adjectives.

	Masc. Singular	Feminine Singular	Masc. Plural	Feminine Plural
this/that/these/those	ce/cet	cette	ces	

In French, the demonstrative adjectives "**ce**," "**cet**," and "**cette**" can mean both *"this"* and *"that."* The demonstrative adjective "**cet**" is used before a singular masculine noun that starts with a vowel or mute "**h**," e.g., "**cet arbre**" *(this/that tree)*, "**cet homme**" *(this/that man)*, etc., whereas "**ce**" is used before any other singular masculine noun, e.g., "**ce garcon**" *(this/that boy)*. The demonstrative adjective "**cette**" is used before a singular feminine noun.

Similarly, "**ces**" can mean both *"these"* and *"those."* There is no real distinction of nearness and farness in the simple forms of the demonstrative adjectives.

To make such a distinction, we can add "-**ci**" or "-**là**" after the noun, for example:

ce livre-ci	*this book*	ce livre-là	*that book*
cet homme-ci	*this man*	cet homme-là	*that man*
cette femme-ci	*this woman*	cette femme-là	*that woman*
ces chemises-ci	*these shirts*	ces chemises-là	*those shirts*

Demonstrative Pronouns

Let us now examine the demonstrative pronouns:

	Masc. Singular	Feminine Singular	Masc. Plural	Feminine Plural
this/that (one) these/those (ones)	celui	celle	ceux	celles

In general, "**celui**," "**celle**," "**ceux**," and "**celles**" do not appear on their own. They can appear with "-**ci**" or "-**là**" attached to the end of the demonstrative pronoun, or followed by "**que**," "**qui**," "**de**," or a prepositional phrase. In the latter case, the demonstrative pronoun is often translated as *"the one(s)."* Let us look at some examples:

*Do you want this book or **that one**?*	Voulez-vous ce livre ou **celui-là**?
*I have two cars; **this one** is my favorite.*	J'ai deux voitures; **celle-ci** est ma préférée.
*For **those** who are overweight, exercise is very important.*	Pour **ceux** qui sont en surpoids, l'exercice est très important.
*I'm looking for the car; not mine but Pierre's (**that** of Pierre).*	Je cherche la voiture; pas la mienne mais **celle** de Pierre.
*Which shirts? **The ones** that are there are not mine.*	Quelles chemises? **Celles** qui sont là ne sont pas les miennes.

When referring to a statement, an indefinite thing, or a previously mentioned idea, we use one of the following pronouns:

ce/c'	*this/that*	Used with the verb "**être**"	*informal*
ça	*this/that*	Used with verbs other than "**être**"	
ceci	*this*	Both "**ceci**" and "**cela**" can be used	*formal*
cela	*that*	with any verb including "**être**"	

The pronouns "**ce**" and "**ça**" are often used in familiar situations in daily spoken language. The pronoun "**ce**" (or "**c'**" before a vowel or a mute "**h**") is used before the verb "**être**" *(to be)*, whereas "**ça**" is used with other verbs.

On the other hand, the pronouns "**ceci**" *(this)* and "**cela**" *(that)* are more formal and are often encountered in written French.

Here are some examples:

That *is interesting.*	**C'est** intéressant.
This *is a good idea.*	**C'est** une bonne idée.
That *is good news.*	**Ce** sont de bonnes nouvelles.
Look at **that.**	Regarde **ça**.
I didn't say **that.**	Je n'ai pas dit **ça**.
This *is not acceptable.*	**Ceci** n'est pas acceptable.
That *has already been discussed.*	**Cela** a déjà été discuté.

5. OBJECT PERSONAL PRONOUNS

Object pronouns can be divided into three classes: *prepositional, direct,* and *indirect* object pronouns.

Prepositional Object Pronouns

Prepositional object pronouns come after a preposition, such as "**de**" *(of, from, or about)*, "**avec**" *(with)*, "**dans**" *(in)*, "**sans**" *(without)*, etc.

Personal Subject Pronoun	Prepositional Object Pronoun	Examples
je	moi	Ils parlent de **moi**. *They talk about* **me**.
tu	toi	Ce cadeau est pour **toi**. *This gift is for* **you**.
il	lui	Je sors avec **lui**. *I go out with* **him**.
elle	elle	Je sors avec **elle**. *I go out with* **her**.

nous	nous	Il n'est pas contre **nous**. *He is not against **us**.*
vous	vous	Ce cadeau est pour **vous**. *This gift is for **you**.*
ils/elles	eux	Je ne pars pas sans **eux**. *I won't go without **them**.*

❖ The reflexive prepositional pronouns are a special case of the prepositional object pronouns, such as *"myself," "yourself," "himself,"* etc., and are used when the subject and the object pronoun refer to the same person. More often than not, the reflexive prepositional object pronoun is followed by the adjective **"même(s),"** meaning *"same"* for emphasis, e.g., **"Ils parlent d'eux-mêmes"** *(They talk about themselves).*

Direct and Indirect Object Pronouns

The second and third classes of object pronouns are direct and indirect object pronouns. This tends to be one of the most challenging grammar lessons for English-speaking students. Nevertheless, the use of direct and indirect objects is so ubiquitous that we feel obliged to cover it at this beginner level. Feel free to return to this lesson at times of confusion if you do not fully grasp all of the details.

Before we delve into the details, let us first define the difference between the two classes, since the distinction in English is not always clear. The direct object is the noun directly acted upon, whereas the indirect object is usually the noun (or person) receiving the direct object. For example, in the expressions *"He gives it to us"* and *"I give it to you,"* the *"it"* is the direct object acted upon in both examples, whereas *"us"* is the indirect object in the first example and *"you"* in the second. In English, we use *"me," "you," "him," "her," "us,"* and *"them,"* regardless of whether we are referring to a direct or indirect object. In French, there are some differences.

❖ The direct and indirect object pronouns generally come before the verb, e.g., "**Il <u>nous</u> <u>le</u> donne**" (*He gives it to us*). Attachment to the end of the verb will be discussed as an exception.

❖ The indirect object comes *before* the direct object when they are both in the same sentence, except when the indirect object is in the third person, in which case the indirect object comes *after* the direct object.

❖ Unlike in English, we do not add the equivalent of *"to"* before the indirect object, e.g., *"I give it <u>to you</u>"* becomes "**Je <u>te</u> le donne**" where "**te**" means *"to you"* in this context.

Now, let us learn the direct and indirect object pronouns and their equivalents in English.

Direct Object Pronoun	Indirect Object Pronoun	English Equivalent
me (m')	me (m')	me
te (t')	te (t')	you (informal singular)
<u>le</u> (l')/ <u>la</u> (l')	<u>lui</u>	him/her
nous	nous	us
vous	vous	you (plural, formal singular)
<u>les</u>	<u>leur</u>	them

Notice that the direct and the indirect object pronouns are only different in the third-person singular and plural forms.

Let us look at some examples:

He knows <u>me</u>.	Il **me** connaît.	"**me**" is a direct object
He knows <u>us</u>.	Il **nous** connaît.	"**nous**" is a direct object
That book! I want <u>it</u>.	Ce livre! Je **le** veux.	Depending on the gender, "**le**" or "**la**" is used as the direct object *"it"*
That watch! I want <u>it</u>.	Cette montre! Je **la** veux.	
I know <u>him</u>.	Je **le** connais.	"**le**" is a direct object
I will give <u>him</u> something.	Je **lui** donnerai quelque chose.	"**lui**" is an indirect object
I know <u>her</u>.	Je **la** connais.	"**la**" is a direct object
I will give <u>her</u> something.	Je **lui** donnerai quelque chose.	"**lui**" is an indirect object

Those guys! I know them. *I will give them something.*	Ces garçons! Je **les** connais. Je **leur** donnerai quelque chose.	"**les**" is a direct object "**leur**" is an indirect object
Those girls! I know them. *I will give them something.*	Ces filles! Je **les** connais. Je **leur** donnerai quelque chose.	"**les**" is a direct object "**leur**" is an indirect object

Notice that, in the case of the affirmative imperative, the object pronoun is attached to the end of the verb, for example:

Ouvrez-le.	***Open*** *it*.
Demandez-lui de l'argent.	***Ask*** *him for money.*

If the imperative is in the negative, the object pronoun is not attached and is instead placed before the verb, for example:

Ne l'**ouvrez** pas.	*Don't* **open** *it*.
Ne lui **demande** pas d'argent.	*Don't* **ask** *him for money.*

Combining Direct and Indirect Object Pronouns

We will examine how to combine direct and indirect objects in the same sentence through the following two examples:

❖ Let us use the example: *"She sells me the house."* This translates to:

Elle me vend la maison.

In the above example, we recognize that **"la maison"** *(the house)* is the direct object being acted upon, i.e., being sold, whereas **"me"** *(me)* is the indirect object that receives the direct object, i.e., the house is being sold *to me*.

Let us first focus on the direct object in **"Elle vend la maison"** *(She sells the house)*. If we remove the direct object, **"la maison"** *(the house)*, to say *"She sells it,"* we must use **"le"** or **"la"** to refer to the direct object pronoun *"it."* Since **"la maison"** is feminine, we must use **"la"**:

Elle la vend.

Next, we add the indirect object "**me**" *before* the direct object "**la**" to say *"She sells it to me"*:

Elle me la vend.

❖ Let us use another example: *"I send him a gift."* This translates to:

Je lui envoie un cadeau.

Here, "**un cadeau**" *(a gift)* is the direct object, whereas "**lui**" *(him)* is the indirect object.

Let us first focus on the direct object in "**J'envoie un cadeau**" *(I send a gift)*. If we remove the direct object "**un cadeau**" *(a gift)* to say *"I send it,"* we must use "**le**" or "**la**" to refer to the direct object pronoun *"it."* Since "**un cadeau**" is masculine, we must use "**le**," abbreviated here as "**l'**":

Je l'envoie …

Now, we add the indirect object "**lui**" *after* the direct object "**le**" to say *"I send it to him"*:

Je le lui envoie.

Notice that when the indirect object is in the third person, i.e., "**lui**" *(to him/her)* or "**leur**" *(to them)*, the indirect object is placed *after* the direct object. Here are a few more examples:

*I send **them to her**.*	Je **les lui** envoie.
*I send **it to them**.*	Je **le leur** envoie.
*I send **her to them**.*	Je **la leur** envoie.

6. Relative Pronouns

Relative pronouns in French function differently from their English counterparts. Thus, it is difficult to have a direct translation. Consider the following examples of the relative pronouns "**qui**," "**que**," and "**dont**," which can refer to persons or things:

C'est le livre **qui** a remporté le prix.	*This is the book **that** won the award.*
C'est le livre **que** j'ai acheté.	*This is the book **that** I bought.*
C'est le livre **dont** je parlais.	*This is the book **that** I was talking <u>about</u>.*

In the above example, the relative pronouns "**qui**," "**que**," and "**dont**" are all translated as *"that."* The relative pronoun "**qui**" is used when referring to a *subject*, i.e., *"the book that won the award."* The relative pronoun "**que**" is used when referring to an *object*, i.e., *"the book that I bought."* Finally, the relative pronoun "**dont**" is used when referring to an *object* of a verb or verbal expression that includes the preposition "**de**," such as: "**parler de**" *(talk about)*, "**avoir besoin de**" *(to need)*, etc.

Similarly, the relative pronouns "**qui**," "**que**," and "**dont**" can refer to people and have different meanings:

C'est le garçon **qui** jouait ici.	*This is the boy **who** used to play here.*
C'est le médecin **que** j'ai consulté.	*This is the doctor **whom** I consulted.*
C'est le genre de joueur **dont** notre équipe a besoin.	*This is the kind of player **that** our team needs.*
C'est l'homme **dont** les deux fils sont médecins.	*This is the man **whose** two sons are doctors.*

Notice that "**qui**" is used when referring to a *subject*, i.e., *"the boy who used to play here;"* "**que**" is used when referring to an *object*, i.e., *"the doctor I consulted;"* and "**dont**" is used when referring to an *object* of a verb or verbal expression that includes the preposition "**de**," in this case: "**avoir besoin de**" *(to need)*, i.e., *"the player that our team needs."* The relative pronoun "**dont**" is also used to express possession if the verb is preceded by the subject and followed by the object. In this case, it is often translated as *"whose," "of which,"* or *"of whom."*

Another relative pronoun that can also mean *"that," "which,"* or *"whom"* is "**lequel**" and its gender and number variants: "**laquelle**," "**lequels**," and "**lesquelles**." When preceded by a preposition, these pronouns are often used to refer to things more specifically. When referring to people, "**qui**" preceded with a preposition is often used instead, for example:

Ce sont les joueurs <u>avec</u> **lesquels** je jouais.	*They are the players <u>with</u> **whom** I used to play.*
Je nettoierai la chaise <u>derrière</u> **laquelle** le chat joue.	*I will clean the chair <u>behind</u> **which** the cat plays.*
C'est le bâtiment <u>dans</u> **lequel** je vis.	*This is the building <u>in</u> **which** I live.*
C'est la personne **<u>à</u> qui** ils ont demandé.	*This is the person **whom** they asked.*

Notice that "**lequel**" (and its gender and number variants) is treated the same way as the definite article when contracted with the preceding preposition, e.g., "**C'est le projet <u>auquel</u> je pense**" *(This is the project I am thinking of).*

We have previously encountered the interrogative pronoun "**où**," meaning *"where." *As a relative pronoun, it is used meaning *"where"* or *"when,"* referring to a certain moment of time. Here are some examples:

C'est **où** je veux être maintenant.	*This is **where** I want to be now.*
Nous ne savons pas **où** aller.	*We don't know **where** to go.*
C'est le moment **où** j'ai pris la décision.	*This is the time **when** I made the decision.*
Il a probablement appelé au moment **où** j'étais occupé.	*He probably called at the time **when** I was busy.*

Another common pronoun that means *"when"* is "**lorsque**," e.g., "**Dis-moi lorsqe tu es de retour**" *(Tell me when you are back).* Remember that "**quand**" can be used as an interrogative or relative pronoun, whereas "**lorsque**" cannot be used as an interrogative pronoun to ask questions about time.

Here is a summary of some relative pronouns in French:

Relative pronoun	English meaning
que	*that, which, who*
qui	*that, which, who, whom*
dont	*that, whose, of which, of whom*
lequel (sing. m.) **laquelle** (sing. f.) **lesquels** (pl. m.) **lesquelles** (pl. f.)	*that, which, whom*
où	*where, when*

quand	*when*
lorsque	*when*

7. ORDINAL NUMBERS

Ordinal numbers describe the order of a noun. Ordinal numbers in French are formed using the suffix "**-ième**." The only exception is the ordinal number *"first,"* which has a masculine form "**premier**" and a feminine form "**première**."

un	1	premier/première	$1^{er}/1^{ère}$
deux	2	deuxième	2^e
trois	3	troisième	3^e
quatre	4	quatrième	4^e
cinq	5	cinquième	5^e
six	6	sixième	6^e
sept	7	septième	7^e
huit	8	huitième	8^e
neuf	9	neuvième	9^e
dix	10	dixième	10^e
vingt	20	vingtième	20^e
trente	30	trentième	30^e
cent	100	centième	100^e
mille	1,000	millième	1000^e

❖ The most common way to abbreviate ordinal numbers is using the superscript "**e**," except for "**premier**" and "**première**" which are abbreviated as "**1er**" and "**1ère**," respectively.

❖ Unlike in English, where dates are described using ordinal numbers, e.g., *"the 24th of October,"* in French, dates are expressed using cardinal numbers, e.g., "**le 24 octobre**." A notable exception is the first day of the month, in which case the ordinal number is used, e.g., "**le premier novembre**" *(the first of November)*.

❖ Numbers following the names of kings and queens, unlike in English, are cardinal, except for "**premier**" and "**première**," which are ordinal, and do not use the definite article before the number, e.g., "**Elizabeth Deux**" *(Elizabeth the Second)*, "**Edouard**

Trois" *(Edward the Third)*, **"Louis Quatorze"** *(Louis the Fourteenth)*, **"Benoît Premier"** *(Benedict the First)*, etc.

Fractional Numbers

❖ To describe the fractional number 1/2 *(half)*, we use the adjective **"demi,"** e.g., **"un demi-kilo"** *(half a kilo)*, **"une demi-heure"** *(half an hour)*, **"une demi-douzaine"** *(half a dozen)*, etc.

❖ We also use the feminine noun **"moitié"** to describe half the quantity of something, and it is often followed by **"de,"** e.g., **"la moitié du terrain"** *(half of the land)*.

❖ The main difference that you need to remember to distinguish between **"demi"** and **"moitié"** is that the former is often an adjective, whereas the latter is a noun, e.g., **"la moitié de la classe"** *(half of the class)*.

❖ The fractional number *third* is **"tiers"** in masculine and **"tierce"** in feminine, and the fractional number *fourth* is **"quart,"** e.g., **"un tiers des produits"** *(a third of the products)*, **"un quart des joueurs"** *(a fourth of the players)*, etc.

❖ Fractional numbers from *fifth* and above are the same as the ordinal numbers, e.g., **"un cinquième des ressources"** *(a fifth of the resources)*, etc. If the numerator is larger than one, the denominator is expressed in plural, e.g., 3/4 = **"trois quarts."**

❖ In numbers formed by an integer and a fraction, the **"un"** can be dropped only before 1/2 and 1/4, if preceded by an integer, e.g., 1 ½ (**un et demi**), 3 ¼ (**trois et quart**), 2 1/3 (**deux et un tiers**), 5 ⅛ (**cinq et un huitième**).

❖ The collective numbers **"une paire"** *(a pair)* and **"une douzaine"** *(a dozen)* may also be used to describe quantities. The adjectives **"double"** and **"triple"** are used for *"double"* and *"triple,"* respectively.

8. BASIC PHRASES

Learning greetings and short conversations is essential for taking the first steps to communicate in any language. Take some time to practice the following formal and informal basic phrases.

Salut	*Hi (informal)*
Bonjour.	*Good morning.*
Bon après-midi.	*Good afternoon.*
Bonsoir.	*Good evening.*
Bonne nuit.	*Good night.*
Comment allez-vous?	*How are you? (formal, singular)*
Comment vas-tu?	*How are you? (informal, singular)*
Quoi de neuf? Qu'est-ce qu'il y a?	*What's up?*
Je vais bien.	*I am fine. (formal)*
Ça va (bien).	*I am fine. (informal)*
Très bien.	*Very good.*
Pas très bien.	*Not so good.*
Comme ci comme ça.	*So-so.*
Au revoir.	*Goodbye.*
Bonne journée!	*Have a nice day.*
Merci.	*Thank you.*
De rien.	*You're welcome. It's nothing.*
S'il te plaît.	*Please. (informal)*
S'il vous plaît.	*Please. (informal)*
Pas grand chose.	*Nothing much.*
Désolé(e).	*Sorry.*
Excusez-moi.	*Excuse me. (formal)*
Excuse-moi.	*Excuse me. (informal)*
Enchanté(e).	*Nice to meet you.*
À plus tard. À toute à l'heure.	*See you later.*
À bientôt.	*See you soon.*
À demain.	*See you tomorrow.*
Bienvenu(e).	*Welcome.*
Comment t'appelles-tu?	*What is your name? (informal, singular)*
Comment vous appelez-vous?	*What is your name? (formal, singular)*
Je m'appelle…	*My name is …*
Je suis …	*I am …*

Quel âge as-tu?	*How old are you? (informal, singular)*
Quel âge avez-vous?	*How old are you? (formal, singular)*
J'ai 20 ans.	*I am 20 years old.*
D'où viens-tu?	*Where are you from? (informal, singular)*
D'où venez-vous?	*Where are you from? (formal, singular)*
De quelle partie?	*From which part?*
Je viens de …	*I am from … (I come from …)*
Je ne comprends pas.	*I don't understand.*
Parles-tu anglais?	*Do you speak English? (informal, singular)*
Parlez-vous anglais?	*Do you speak English? (formal, singular)*
Où habites-tu?	*Where do you live? (informal, singular)*
Où habitez-vous?	*Where do you live? (formal, singular)*
Combien ça coûte?	*How much does this cost?*
L'addition, s'il vous plaît.	*The bill, please.*
Peux-tu m'aider?	*Can you help me? (informal)*
Pouvez-vous m'aider?	*Can you help me? (formal)*
Peux-tu parler plus lentement?	*Can you speak more slowly? (informal)*
Pouvez-vous parler plus lentement?	*Can you speak more slowly? (formal)*
Comment puis-je[1] y arriver?	*How can I get there?*

II. Vocabulary Building

Here, we cover basic verbs and adjectives in the first two sections, then we go over nouns from different categories.

1. VERBS II

Below is a list of the next most common 60 verbs in French:

English	French	Examples
allow	**permettre** **laisser**	Ma maman ne me **permet** pas de manger des bonbons. *My mom doesn't **allow** me to eat candy.*
answer	**répondre**	Je ne pourrai pas **répondre** au téléphone. *I won't be able to **answer** the phone.*
ask (question)	**poser (une question)**[2]	Je veux **poser** une question importante. *I want to **ask** an important question.*

---

[1] When inverted to form a question, "**je peux**" *(I can)* becomes "**puis-je**" /pweej/ *(can I)*.

[2] We use "**poser une question**" *(to ask a question)* when we refer to asking questions. On the other hand, we use "**demander**" *(to ask for)* when we refer to requesting something or ordering from a restaurant.

ask (request)	**demander**[1]	Vous n'avez pas besoin d'attendre pour **demander** de l'aide. *You don't need to wait to ask for help.*
bother annoy	**déranger**	Les odeurs fortes me **dérangent**. *Strong scents bother me.*
build	**construire**	Je veux **construire** une clôture ici. *I want to build a fence here.*
buy	**acheter**	Carlo **achète** du pain tous les jours. *Carlo buys bread every day.*
cancel	**annuler**	Je devrais peut-être **annuler** mes plans. *Perhaps I should cancel my plans.*
choose	**choisir**	Je **choisis** souvent des saveurs de fruits. *I often choose fruit flavors.*
clean	**nettoyer**	Je dois **nettoyer** la salle de bains plus tard. *I must clean the bathroom later.*
cook	**cuisiner**	Mon frère **cuisine** tous les jours. *My brother cooks every day.*
cover	**couvrir**	Je devrais **couvrir** la pâte avec un chiffon. *I should cover the dough with a cloth.*
cry	**pleurer**	Je n'aime pas voir les gens **pleurer**. *I don't like to see people cry.*
die	**mourir**	Il veut rédiger un testament avant de **mourir**. *He wants to write a will before dying.*
dine	**dîner**	Nous irons **dîner** au restaurant français. *We'll go dine at the French restaurant.*
disappear	**disparaître**	Les moustiques **disparaissent** en hiver. *Mosquitoes disappear in winter.*
discover	**découvrir**	Je veux **découvrir** un café près de chez moi. *I want to discover a café close to home.*
draw	**dessiner**	Je veux **dessiner** ce paysage. *I want to draw this landscape.*
drive	**conduire**	Je veux apprendre à **conduire**. *I want to learn how to drive.*
express	**exprimer**	C'est bien d'**exprimer** ses émotions. *It's good to express emotions.*
find	**trouver**	Je dois **trouver** mes clés. *I must find my keys.*
forget	**oublier**	J'**oublie** toujours mon mot de passe. *I always forget my password.*
get obtain	**obtenir**	Où puis-je **obtenir** de la nourriture? *Where can I get food?*
go shopping	**faire du shopping**	Nous pouvons **faire du shopping** ce samedi. *We can go shopping this Saturday.*

grow	grandir pousser	Cet arbre **pousse** très rapidement. *This tree **grows** very fast.*
hear	entendre	J'**entends** une voix venant de loin. *I **hear** a voice coming from afar.*
help	aider	Mon fils **aide** toujours dans le jardin. *My son always **helps** in the garden.*
joke	plaisanter blaguer	Je **plaisante** beaucoup avec mes cousins. *I **joke** a lot with my cousins.*
kiss	embrasser	J'**embrasse** mon chat sur son nez tous les jours. *I **kiss** my cat on its nose every day.*
laugh	rire	C'est bon de **rire** de temps en temps. *It's good to **laugh** from time to time.*
lie	mentir	Mon fils **ment** sur son âge. *My son **lies** about his age.*
listen to hear	écouter	Vous devez **écouter** d'autres opinions. *You must **listen to** other opinions.*
lose	perdre	Je **perds** toujours les pièces les plus petites. *I always **lose** the smaller coins.*
mean	vouloir dire signifier	Que **voulez**-vous **dire**? *What do you **mean**?*
need	avoir besoin de	J'**ai besoin de** m'occuper de mes enfants. *I **need** to take care of my children.*
pay	payer	Je **paie** toutes mes factures au début du mois. *I **pay** all my bills at the start of the month.*
plan	planifier	Je **planifie** toujours ce que je vais manger. *I always **plan** what I'll eat.*
play (sports)	jouer	Mon cousin **joue** au football le samedi. *My cousin **plays** football on Saturdays.*
rain	pleuvoir	Il peut **pleuvoir** ce mercredi. *It may **rain** this Wednesday.*
relax	détendre relaxer	Il est bon de détendre vos jambes. *It's good to **relax** your legs.*
reply respond	répondre	Il ne **répond** jamais à mes messages. *He never **responds** to my messages.*
rest	reposer	J'aime me **reposer** près de la piscine. *I like to **rest** by the pool.*
rob steal	voler	Il y a des voleurs qui ne **volent** que des voitures. *There are thieves who only **steal/rob** cars.*
run	courir	Il est dangereux de **courir** vite dans la rue. *It is dangerous to **run** fast in the street.*
search for look for	chercher	Elle veut **chercher** les clés pour sortir. *She wants to **search for** the keys to go out.*

sell	**vendre**	Ce magasin **vend** uniquement des desserts. *This store only sells desserts.*
send	**envoyer**	Je devrais lui **envoyer** un message. *I should send him a message.*
share	**partager**	Tu dois **partager** avec ton frère. *You have to share with your brother.*
show	**montrer**	Je veux te **montrer** la cuisine. *I want to show you the kitchen.*
sing	**chanter**	Ce jeune homme **chante** magnifiquement. *That young man sings beautifully.*
smile	**sourire**	Je **souris** toujours pour les photos. *I always smile for photos.*
smoke	**fumer**	Il est interdit de **fumer** ici. *Smoking is not allowed here.*
snow	**neiger**	Il **neige** beaucoup en hiver. *It snows a lot in winter.*
swim	**nager**	Je vais **nager** dans la rivière. *I go swimming in the river.*
teach	**apprendre**	Je veux t'**apprendre** comment c'est fait. *I want to teach you how it's done.*
translate	**traduire**	Pouvez-vous **traduire** ce fichier? *Can you translate this file?*
try	**essayer** **tenter**	J'**essaie** toujours d'arriver tôt. *I always try to arrive early.*
wait (for)	**attendre**	Il doit **attendre** le bus. *He has to wait for the bus.*
wash	**laver**	Vous devez **laver** la vaisselle après le dîner. *You must wash the dishes after dinner.*
win	**gagner**	Je peux **gagner** la course. *I can win the race.*

In addition to the above new verbs, let us take advantage of English cognates to memorize the following verbs.

English	French	Examples
abandon	**abandonner**	Certaines personnes **abandonnent** leurs hobbies. *Some people abandon their hobbies.*
accuse	**accuser**	Il n'est pas acceptable d'**accuser** sans motifs. *It's not okay to accuse without grounds.*
appear	**apparaître**	Une célébrité peut **apparaître** aujourd'hui à l'émission. *A celebrity may appear today on the show.*
appreciate	**apprécier**	J'**apprécie** vraiment ce que mes parents font. *I really appreciate what my parents do.*

consider	**considérer**	Vous devez **considérer** les sentiments des autres. *You must **consider** how others feel.*
consult	**consulter**	J'ai besoin de **consulter** un professionnel. *I need to **consult** a professional.*
differentiate	**différencier**	Je suis incapable de **différencier** les chats. *I am unable to **differentiate** between the cats.*
distribute	**distribuer**	Le facteur **distribue** le courrier le matin. *The postman **distributes** the mail in the morning.*
divide	**diviser**	Cette rue **divise** les deux villes. *This street **divides** the two cities.*
estimate	**estimer**	J'**estime** que cela sera terminé dans 30 minutes. *I **estimate** it'll be done in 30 minutes.*
explore	**explorer**	J'adore **explorer** les villes que je ne connais pas. *I love **exploring** cities I don't know.*
ignore	**ignorer**	Ce n'est pas facile d'**ignorer** les bruits forts. *It's not easy to **ignore** loud noises.*
imitate	**imiter**	Mon petit frère m'**imite** toujours. *My little brother always **imitates** me.*
inform	**informer**	Tu dois m'**informer** si tu envisages de sortir. *You have to **inform** me if you plan on going out.*
limit	**limiter**	Je **limite** mes bonbons à un par semaine. *I **limit** my candies to one per week.*
manipulate	**manipuler**	Il n'est pas gentil de **manipuler** les gens. *It's not nice to **manipulate** people.*
mention	**mentionner**	Ce livre ne **mentionne** pas tous les détails. *This book doesn't **mention** all the details.*
minimize	**minimiser**	Nous ne devrions pas **minimiser** la situation. *We shouldn't **minimize** the situation.*
modify	**modifier**	Je dois **modifier** certaines données dans le document. *I must **modify** some data in the document.*
pass	**passer** [1]	Je pourrais **passer** chez toi plus tard. *I could **pass** by your house later.*
prefer	**préférer**	Je **préfère** les légumes au pain. *I **prefer** vegetables to bread.*
prolong **extend**	**prolonger**	Nous voulons **prolonger** notre séjour ici. *We want to **extend** our stay here.*
pronounce	**prononcer**	Il n'est pas facile de **prononcer** mon nom en anglais. *It's not easy to **pronounce** my name in English.*
prosper	**prospérer**	Les entreprises **prospèrent** en été. *Businesses **prosper** in the summer.*

---

[1] The verb "**passer**" can also mean *"to spend (time),"* e.g., "**J'aime passer du temps dans le parc**" *(I like spending time in the park).*

regulate	réguler	Le gouvernement veut **réguler** le marché. *The government wants to **regulate** the market.*
reside	résider	Elle **réside** près de la capitale. *She **resides** near the capital.*
select	sélectionner	Vous devez **sélectionner** la bonne réponse. *You must **select** the right answer.*
suffer	souffrir	Personne n'aime **souffrir** de maladies. *No one likes to **suffer** from illnesses.*

2. ADJECTIVES II

Below is a list of adjectives that we need at this level. Notice that an adjective must agree with the noun in number and gender.

English	French	Examples
additional	supplémentaire	J'ai besoin d'une enveloppe **supplémentaire**. *I need an **additional** envelope.*
any (whatever)	n'importe quel	J'aime la crème glacée de **n'importe quelle** saveur. *I like ice cream of **any** flavor.*
awake	éveillé	J'essaie de rester **éveillé** en classe. *I try to remain **awake** in class.*
basic	de base	Vous devriez connaître les règles **de base**. *You should know the **basic** rules.*
both	les deux	**Les deux** parents sont invités. ***Both** parents are invited.*
comfortable	confortable	Ce fauteuil est très **confortable**. *This armchair is very **comfortable**.*
each	chaque	**Chaque** personne est différente. ***Each** person is different.*
empty	vide	Le siège est **vide**. *The seat is **empty**.*
equal	égal	Les deux murs sont **égaux**. *Both walls are **equals**.*
fair just	juste	J'essaie toujours d'être **juste** avec mes enfants. *I always try to be **fair** with my children.*
faraway distant	lointain	Mes grands-parents vivent dans un pays **lointain**. *My grandparents live in a **faraway** country.*
favorite	préféré favori	Quel est ton film **préféré**? *What is your **favorite** movie?*
fresh	frais	L'eau avec du concombre a un goût **frais**. *Water with cucumber has a **fresh** taste.*

friendly	amical	Mon chat est très **amical**. *My cat is very **friendly**.*
full	plein	Je veux que le réservoir soit **plein**. *I want the tank to be **full**.*
healthy	sain	Manger des légumes tous les jours est **sain**. *Eating vegetables every day is **healthy**.*
light (weight)	léger	Je voyage avec une valise **légère**. *I travel with a **light** suitcase.*
lonely	solitaire	Mon chat est un animal **solitaire**. *My cat is a **lonely** animal.*
loud noisy	bruyant	Mon fils est très **bruyant**. *My son is very **loud**.*
lucky	chanceux	Vous êtes très **chanceux** si vous gagnez aujourd'hui. *You are very **lucky** if you win today.*
nearby close	voisin	L'université se trouve dans un quartier **voisin**. *The university is in a **nearby** neighborhood.*
nice cute (object)	joli sympa mignon	Je vais m'acheter une très **jolie** robe. *I'll buy myself a very **nice** dress.*
pleasant nice (person)	agréable	Mon oncle est une personne **agréable**. *My uncle is a **pleasant** person.*
polite	poli	Mon neveu est un enfant très **poli**. *My nephew is a very **polite** child.*
reasonable	raisonnable	Mon patron est très **raisonnable**. *My boss is very **reasonable**.*
salty	salé	J'aime le popcorn **salé**. *I like **salty** popcorn.*
shy	timide	Je suis désolé, il est très **timide**. *I'm sorry, he's very **shy**.*
silly	ridicule	C'est **ridicule** de s'inquiéter sans raison. *It's **silly** to worry without a reason.*
true	vrai	Un **vrai** ami ne te ment pas. *A **true** friend doesn't lie to you.*
unfair	injuste	Cet arbitre est très **injuste**. *That referee is very **unfair**.*
unlucky	malchanceux	Mon cousin est une personne **malchanceuse**. *My cousin is an **unlucky** person.*
useful	utile	Les ciseaux sont un outil **utile**. *Scissors are a **useful** tool.*
useless	inutile	Sans gaz, mon briquet est **inutile**. *Without gas, my lighter is **useless**.*

weird	étrange	Je sais que cela semble **étrange**.
strange	bizarre	*I know this looks **strange**.*
worried	inquiet	Je suis très **inquiet** pour toi!
	préoccupé	*I am very **worried** about you!*
wrong	faux	Je ne veux pas prendre la **fausse** route.
	tort	*I don't want to take the **wrong** way.*

In addition to the above new adjectives, we add a few more English cognates that are easy to memorize.

English	French	Examples
blond	blond	Les cheveux de mon voisin sont **blonds**.
		*My neighbor's hair is **blond**.*
brilliant	brillant	La fille de ma cousine est **brillante**.
		*My cousin's daughter is **brilliant**.*
complicated	compliqué	Faire ses propre pâtes est **compliqué**.
		*Making your own pasta is **complicated**.*
delicious	délicieux	Ce gâteau de mariage est **délicieux**.
		*This wedding cake is **delicious**.*
educational	éducatif	Regarder des vidéos **éducatives** est utile.
		*Watching **educational** videos is helpful.*
famous	fameux	Mon cousin est un écrivain **célèbre**.
	célèbre	*My cousin is a **famous** writer.*
feminine	féminin	Son style est assez **féminin**.
female		*Her style is pretty **feminine**.*
festive	festif	L'été est une période **festive**.
		*Summer is a **festive** time.*
generous	généreux	Ils veulent faire une **généreuse** donation à l'hôpital.
		*They want to make a **generous** donation to the hospital.*
mental	mental	La santé **mentale** est extrêmement importante.
		***Mental** health is extremely important.*
nervous	nerveux	Je suis **nerveux** à propos de l'examen.
		*I'm **nervous** about the exam.*
physical	physique	Je dois passer un examen **physique**.
		*I have to get a **physical** exam done.*
political	politique	Je ne recommande pas de parler de questions **politiques**.
		*I don't recommend talking about **political** matters.*
popular	populaire	Ma sœur est **populaire** à l'école.
		*My sister is **popular** at school.*
precious	précieux	Un diamant est une pierre **précieuse**.
		*A diamond is a **precious** stone.*

recent	récent	Les nouvelles sont très **récentes.** *The news is very* **recent.**
resident	résident	Finalement, j'obtiendrai le statut de **résident.** *Finally, I will obtain* **resident** *status.*
responsible	responsable	J'essaie d'être très **responsable** au travail. *I try to be very* **responsible** *at work.*
serious	sérieux	Mon grand-père est une personne très **sérieuse.** *My grandfather is a very* **serious** *person.*
significant	significatif	Le temps est très **significatif** pour moi. *Time is very* **significant** *to me.*
terrible	terrible	J'ai un **terrible** rhume. *I have a* **terrible** *cold.*
typical	typique	J'aime la cuisine **typique** de ma ville. *I like my town's* **typical** *food.*
violent	violent	Cet ouragan est très **violent.** *This hurricane is very* **violent.**

3. TRANSPORTATION I

Transportation in French is "**le transport.**" Below are some means of transportation and vocabulary related to transportation and traffic:

airplane	**avion**^{m}	*penalty*	**peine**^{f} **pénalité**^{f}
airport	**aéroport**^{m}	*pick-up truck*	**pick-up**^{m} **camionette**^{f}
bicycle	**vélo**^{m}	*police officer*	**officier**^{m} **de police**
boat	**bateau**^{m}	*ship*	**navire**^{m} **bateau**^{m}
brakes	**freins**^{m}	*sign*	**signe**^{m}
bus	**bus**^{m} **autobus**^{m}	*speed*	**vitesse**^{f}
car	**voiture**^{f}	*subway*	**métro**^{m}
driver	**conducteur**^{m}/ **conductrice**^{f}	*ticket (air, train)*	**billet**^{m} **ticket**^{m}
driver's license	**permis**^{m} **de conduire**	*ticket (fine)*	**amende**^{f}
engine	**moteur**^{m}	*tire*	**pneu**^{m}
envelope	**enveloppe**^{f}	*traffic*	**circulation**^{f}
flight	**vol**^{m}	*train*	**train**^{m}
gasoline	**essence**^{f}	*train station*	**gare**^{f}

	paquet^m		
package	colis^m	*truck*	camion^m
	emballage^m		

4. NATURE I

Some vocabulary related to *nature*, or "**la nature**," are:

air	air^m	*ocean*	océan^m
beach	plage^f	*park*	parc^m
camp	camp^m campement^m	*planet*	planète^f
canteen	cantine^f	*plant*	plante^f
cloud	nuage^m	*river*	rivière^f
coast	côte^f	*root*	racine^f
countryside	campagne^f	*sand*	sable^m
desert	désert^m	*sea*	mer^f
earth	terre^f	*sky*	ciel^m
fire	feu^m	*snow*	neige^f
flower	fleur^f	*space*	espace^m
grass	herbe^f	*star*	étoile^f
ground	sol^m terre^f	*sun*	soleil^m
ice	glace^f	*tree*	arbre^m
island	île^f	*universe*	univers^m
lake	lac^m	*weather*	temps^m
moon	lune^f	*wind*	vent^m
mountain	montagne^f	*world*	monde^m

5. PLACES

A *place* in French is "**un endroit**" or "**un lieu.**" This is a list of the most common places we encounter in our daily life:

apartment	appartement^m	*hospital*	hôpital^m
area	zone^f	*hotel*	hôtel^m
bakery	boulangerie^f	*location*	emplacement^m
bank	banque^f	*market*	marché^m
bar	bar^m	*office*	bureau^m

bookstore	librairie^f	parking	stationnement^m parking^m
bridge	pont^m	port harbor	port^m
building	bâtiment^m	restaurant	restaurant^m
center	centre^m	school	école^f
city	ville^f	shop	magasin^m boutique^f
club (sports)	club^m	suburb	banlieue^f
court (law)	cour^f tribunal^m	theater	théâtre^m
district	district^m quartier^m	university	université^f
factory	usine^f	village	village^m
farm	ferme^f	work	travail^m

6. FOOD I

An important subject in French is *food*, or "**la nourriture**." Here is some useful food vocabulary:

apple	pomme^f	lemon	citron^m
apricot	abricot^m	lettuce	laitue^f
banana	banane^f	mango	mangue^f
beef	bœuf^m	meat	viande^f
beer	bière^f	milk	lait^m
bread	pain^m	oil	huile^f
broccoli	brocoli^m	olive	olive^f
carrot	carotte^f	orange	orange^f
cheese	fromage^m	pork	porc^m
chicken	poulet^m	refreshment	rafraîchissement^m
coffee	café^m	rice	riz^m
egg	œuf^m	salad	salade^f
eggplant	aubergine^f	salt	sel^m
fruit	fruit^m	sugar	sucre^m
grape	raisin^m	tea	thé^m
grapefruit	pamplemousse^m	tomato	tomate^f
ice cream	glace^f	vegetable	légume^m
juice	jus^m	water	eau^f
lamb	agneau^m	wine	vin^m

7. CLOTHES I

The word for *clothes* in French is "**les vêtements**ᵐ." Here you can learn some vocabulary related to clothing:

belt	**ceinture**ᶠ	*pocket*	**poche**ᶠ
bra	**soutien-gorge**ᵐ	*purse*	**porte-monnaie**ᵐ **sac**ᵐ **à main**
coat	**manteau**ᵐ	*ring*	**anneau**ᵐ **bague**ᶠ
glasses	**lunettes**ᶠ	*shirt*	**chemise**ᶠ
glove	**gant**ᵐ	*sunglasses*	**lunettes**ᶠ **de soleil**
hat	**chapeau**ᵐ	*skirt*	**jupe**ᶠ
jacket	**veste**ᶠ	*t-shirt*	**t-shirt**ᵐ
makeup	**maquillage**ᵐ	*underwear*	**sous-vêtement**ᵐ
pants	**pantalon**ᵐ	*wallet*	**portefeuille**ᶠ

8. EDUCATION

The following are vocabulary related to *education* or "**l'éducation**ᶠ":

absence	**absence**ᶠ	*graduate*	**diplômé(e)**
academy	**académie**ᶠ	*history* *story*[1]	**histoire**ᶠ
arithmetic	**arithmétique**ᶠ	*homework*	**devoirs**ᵐ
astronomy	**astronomie**ᶠ	*list*	**liste**ᶠ
bachelor's degree	**baccalauréat**ᵐ **licence**ᶠ	*master's degree*	**maîtrise**ᶠ
backpack	**sac**ᵐ **à dos**	*meaning*	**signification**ᶠ
biology	**biologie**ᶠ	*method*	**méthode**ᶠ
board	**tableau**ᵐ	*microscope*	**microscope**ᵐ
break (pause)	**pause**ᶠ	*notebook*	**carnet**ᵐ **de notes**
career	**carrière**ᶠ	*physics*	**physique**ᶠ
chalkboard	**tableau**ᵐ	*requirement*	**exigence**ᶠ
chemistry	**chimie**ᶠ	*response* *answer*	**réponse**ᶠ
clarification	**clarification**ᶠ	*ruler*	**règle**ᶠ

---

[1] A factual account is often referred to as "**histoire**," whereas a fictional tale is referred to as "**conte**ᵐ."

class[1]	**classe**[f] **cours**[m]	*schedule*	**horaire**[m]
course	**cours**[m]	*scholarship*	**bourse**[f]
course material	**matériel**[m] **de cours**	*sheet (paper)*	**feuille**[f]
degree	**diplôme**[m]	*summary*	**résumé**[m]
doctorate	**doctorat**[m]	*system*	**système**[m]
eraser	**gomme**[f]	*technique*	**technique**[f]
faculty	**faculté**[f]	*theory*	**théorie**[f]
good grades	**bonnes notes**[f]	*way*	**façon**[f] **manière**[f]

9. SHOPPING

To go shopping in French is "**faire les courses.**" Here you learn some vocabulary related to shopping:

bill	**facture**[f]	*money*	**argent**[m]
brand	**marque**[f]	*opening time*	**heures**[f] **d'ouverture**
card	**carte**[f]	*order*	**commande**[f]
cash	**espèces**[f]	*payment*	**paiement**[m]
chain	**chaîne**[f]	*price*	**prix**[m]
complaint	**plainte**[f]	*purchase*	**achat**[m]
cost	**coût**[m]	*receipt*	**reçu**[m]
delivery	**livraison**[f]	*register*	**registre**[m]
discount	**réduction**[f] **rabais**[m] **remise**[f]	*row (line)*	**rangée**[f]
fee	**frais**[m]	*sale*	**vente**[f]
invoice	**facture**[f]	*shopping mall*	**centre commercial**[m]
label *tag*	**étiquette**[f]	*spree* *binge*	**frénésie**[f]
line *queue*	**file**[f] **queue**[f]	*surprise*	**surprise**[f]
market	**marché**[m]	*type*	**type**[m]
merchant	**marchand**[m]	*value*	**valeur**[f]

---

[1] The word "**cours**" *(course)* is used to refer to the time period we generally call a *"class"* in English, e.g., "**Je prends des cours**" *(I take classes)*. There is also the word "**classe**" in French which often refers to the classroom or the participants in a class, e.g., "**Personne ne s'est présenté en classe**" *(No one showed up in class)*.

10. MATERIALS

Vocabulary related to *materials*, or "**les matériaux**," can be useful to be familiar with. Here is a list of some common vocabulary:

cement	**ciment**[m]	*petroleum*	**pétrole**[m]
copper	**cuivre**[m]	*plastic*	**plastique**[m]
cotton	**coton**[m]	*powder*	**poudre**[f]
diamond	**diamant**[m]	*silk*	**soie**[f]
dust	**poussière**[f]	*silver*	**argent**[m]
fiber	**fibre**[f]	*steel*	**acier**[m]
glass	**verre**[m]	*substance*	**substance**[f]
gold	**or**[m]	*synthesis*	**synthèse**[f]
iron	**fer**[m]	*texture*	**texture**[f]
lead	**plomb**[m]	*thread*	**fil**[m]
leather	**cuir**[m]	*wood*	**bois**[m]
magnet	**aimant**[m]	*wool*	**laine**[f]

Notice that the word "**argent**" is used for *silver* and to refer to *money* in general.

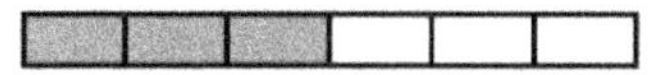

I. Introductory Topics & Grammar

Start by reading the introductory topics of this level. You will notice that some concepts are unique to the French language. You can also use Anki cards to practice with reviews and exercises.

1. COMPOUND PAST

The compound past tense, or the **passé composé** in French, is used to describe events that happened and were completed in the past or happened in the past and continue in the present. In French, this tense covers both the present perfect and the simple past tenses in English, that is, *"I spoke"* and *"I have spoken"* are both translated to the same tense in French.

Using the Conjugation Auxiliary "Avoir" vs. "Être"

The compound past is a compound tense, meaning it requires an auxiliary verb. In English, we use the verb *"to have"* in the present tense as an auxiliary to form the present perfect tense, e.g., *"I have done my homework."*

In French, some verbs use the auxiliary "**avoir**" *(to have)*, while others use the auxiliary "**être**" *(to be)* in the present tense, followed by the past participle.

The past participle of regular verbs using the auxiliary "**avoir**" *(to have)* is formed by adding the appropriate suffix for "**-er**," "**-ir**," and "**-re**" verbs.

"**-er**" verbs		"verb stem" + "**-é**"
"**-ir**" verbs	"**avoir**" in the present tense	"verb stem" + "**-i**"
"**-re**" verbs		"verb stem" + "**-u**"

The past participle of regular verbs using the auxiliary "**être**" *(to be)* is formed in a similar way. One additional requirement here is that the suffix of the past participle must agree with the subject in gender and number, that is, the past participle essentially requires the treatment of an adjective.

"-er" verbs	"être" in the present tense	"verb stem" + "-é"/ "-ée"/ "-és"/ "-ées"
"-ir" verbs		"verb stem" + "-i"/ "-ie"/ "-is"/ "-ies"
"-re" verbs		"verb stem" + "-u"/ "-ue"/ "-us"/ "-ues"

Let us look at some examples of verbs conjugated using the auxiliary "**avoir**":

		-er ending e.g., <u>parl</u>er	-ir ending e.g., <u>fin</u>ir	-re ending e.g., <u>vend</u>re
j'	ai			
tu	as			
il/elle/on	a	parl**é**	fini	vend**u**
nous	avons			
vous	avez			
ils/elles	ont			

Here are some more examples:

		Examples
j'	ai	J'**ai visité** l'Egypte l'année dernière. *I **visited** Egypt last year.*
tu	as	Tu **as terminé** ton travail. *You **have finished** your work.*
il/elle/on	a	Il **a parlé** avec sa mère. *He **spoke** with his mother.*
nous	avons	Nous **avons mangé** toute la nourriture. *We **have eaten** all the food.*
vous	avez	Je suis sûr que vous m'**avez entendu** hier soir. *I am sure you **heard** me last night.*
ils/elles	ont	Ils **ont travaillé** ici pendant deux ans. *They **worked** here for two years.*

Notice that in some of these examples, the compound past in French corresponds to the present perfect, whereas in others it corresponds to the simple past tense depending on the context.

Now, let us look at some examples of verbs conjugated using the auxiliary "**être**":

		-er ending **e.g., aller**	**-ir ending** **e.g., partir**	**-re ending** **e.g., descendre**
je	suis	all**é(e)**	part**i(e)**	descend**u(e)**
tu	es	all**é(e)**	part**i(e)**	descend**u(e)**
il/on	est	all**é**	part**i**	descend**u**
elle	est	all**ée**	part**ie**	descend**ue**
nous	sommes	all**é(e)s**	part**i(e)s**	descend**u(e)s**
vous	êtes	all**é(e)s**	part**i(e)s**	descend**u(e)s**
ils	sont	all**és**	part**is**	descend**us**
elles	sont	all**ées**	part**ies**	descend**ues**

Here are some more examples:

		Examples
je	suis	Je **suis allé** à la gym la semaine dernière. *I **went** to the gym last week.*
tu	es	Tu **es parti** tôt hier soir. *You **left** early last night.*
il/elle/on	est	Elle **est tombée** dans les escaliers. *She **fell down** the stairs.*
nous	sommes	Nous **sommes entrés** dans la salle. *We **have entered** the room.*
vous	êtes	Vous **êtes arrivés** tard hier soir. *You **arrived** late last night.*
ils/elles	sont	Ils **sont sortis** ensemble hier. *They **went out** together yesterday.*

Finally, you are perhaps wondering when to use the auxiliary "**avoir**" and the auxiliary "**être**" to form the past participle. The vast majority of French verbs, including all transitive[1] non-reflexive verbs, are conjugated using the auxiliary "**avoir**." Thus, it is easier to memorize the verbs that use "**être**." There are two main categories of verbs that use the auxiliary "**être**":

1. Some intransitive verbs related to *motion* (e.g., to go, to come, to return, to enter, to leave, to fall, to enter, etc.) and a few others related to *change or transformation* (e.g., to become, to be born, to die, to lose weight, etc.).

---

[1] A verb is transitive if it requires an object. For example, the *"to bring"* can only be transitive, because the meaning is not complete without an object, e.g., *"I bring."*

aller	*to go*	**échapper**	*to escape*
arriver	*to arrive*	**descendre**	*to go down or descend*
tomber	*to fall*	**tourner**	*to turn*
		retourner	
entrer	*to enter*	**revenir**	*to return*[1]
		rentrer	
partir	*to leave*	**sortir**	*to go out*
monter	*to climb or go up*	**venir**	*to come*
rester	*to stay*	**demeurer**	*to remain*
naître	*to be born*	**mourir**	*to die*
devenir	*to become*	**passer**	*to pass*
diminuer	*to diminish*	**maigrir**	*to lose weight*

Remember that all the verbs above that use "**être**" are either motion or transformation-related. However, not all motion and transformation-related verbs use "**être**." This should only serve as a guideline to help you memorize the verbs in this category.

Notice that the above verbs use "**être**" only when they are in intransitive form, that is when there is no direct object acted upon. If the verb is transitive, "**avoir**" must be used. For example:

Verb	Example	
retourner	Il <u>est</u> retourné au travail hier.	*He **returned** to work yesterday.*
to return	J'<u>ai</u> retourné l'enveloppe.	*I **returned** the envelope.*
passer	Je <u>suis</u> passé par le parc.	*I **passed** by the park.*
to pass or spend	J'y <u>ai</u> passé deux jours.	*I **spent** two days there.*
entrer	Il <u>est</u> entré dans la pièce.	*He **entered** the room.*
to enter	Il <u>a</u> entré les données dans le fichier.	*He **entered** the data into the file.*

---

[1] The three verbs "**retourner**," "**revenir**," and "**rentrer**" can all be used to mean *"to return"*:

- The verb "**retourner**" means *"to go back to where the speaker is not,"* e.g., "**J'habitais à Paris quand j'étais jeune. Je vais y retourner cet été**" *(I lived in Paris when I was young. I will return this summer)*. It can also mean *"to return (something),"* e.g., "**Je vais retourner le livre demain**" *(I will return the book tomorrow)*.
- The verb "**revenir**" means *"to return to where the speaker is, that is, to come back,"* e.g., "**Il est déjà parti mais il va bientôt revenir**" *(He has already left but will return soon)*.
- The verb "**rentrer**" means *"to return (home),"* where *"home"* can refer to a house, country, place of residence, etc., e.g., "**Je vais rentrer chez moi à midi**" *(I will return home at noon)*.

2. All reflexive verbs, which will be covered in detail in **Level IV, Lesson 3**, e.g., **"s'appeler"** *(to call oneself)*, **"se laver"** *(to wash oneself)*, etc.

Irregular Past Participles

Some verbs have irregular past participles and need to be memorized.

Verb	Past Participle	Meaning	Examples
acquérir	acquis	*to acquire*	Il a **acquis** la nouvelle maison. *He acquired the new house.*
apprendre	appris	*to learn*	Elle a **appris** le français si vite. *She learned French so quickly.*
avoir	eu	*to have*	J'ai **eu** mal à la tête. *I had a headache.*
boire	bu	*to drink*	Combien as-tu **bu**? *How much did you drink?*
comprendre	compris	*to understand*	J'ai **compris** les consignes. *I understood the instructions.*
conduire	conduit	*to drive*	J'ai **conduit** trois heures. *I drove three hours.*
craindre	craint	*to fear*	Ils ont **craint** l'ennemi. *They feared the enemy.*
devoir	dû	*must*	J'ai **dû** me lever tôt aujourd'hui. *I had to wake up early today.*
dire	dit	*to say*	Ils nous ont **dit** que c'était fermé. *They told us it was closed.*
écrire	écrit	*to write*	Elle a **écrit** une lettre. *She has written a letter.*
être	été	*to be*	Nous avons **été** occupés. *We have been busy.*
faire	fait	*to do*	J'ai **fait** tout le travail. *I have done all the work.*
falloir	fallu	*to have to*	Il a **fallu** ajuster la taille. *They had to adjust the size.*
lire	lu	*to read*	Avez-vous **lu** cet article? *Have you read this article?*
mettre	mis	*to put*	J'ai **mis** les affaires dans le van. *I put the stuff in the van.*
mourir	mort	*to die*	Il est **mort** l'année dernière. *He died last year.*

naître	né	*to be born*	Il est **né** et a été élevé ici. *He **was born** and raised here.*
offrir	offert	*to offer*	Il a **offert** son aide. *He **offered** to help.*
ouvrir	ouvert	*to lose*	J'ai **ouvert** la porte. *I have **opened** the door.*
peindre	peint	*to paint*	Il a **peint** le paysage. *He **painted** the landscape.*
plaire	plu	*to please*	J'espère que l'endroit t'a **plu**. *I hope you **liked** the place.*
pleuvoir	plu	*to rain*	Il a **plu** hier soir. *It **rained** last night.*
pouvoir	pu	*can*	Nous n'avons pas **pu** sortir hier. *We **couldn't** go out yesterday.*
prendre	pris	*to take*	Il a **pris** des photos de la voiture. *He **took** photos of the car.*
recevoir	reçu	*to receive*	Il a **reçu** ma lettre. *He **received** my letter.*
rire	ri	*to laugh*	J'ai **ri** quand ils me l'ont dit. *I **laughed** when they told me.*
savoir	su	*to know*	Il a **su** nous orienter. *He **knew** how to guide us.*
suivre	suivi	*to follow*	Elle a **suivi** les règles. *She has **followed** the rules.*
vivre	vécu	*to live*	Ils ont **vécu** ici pendant des années. *They have **lived** here for years.*
voir	vu	*to see*	Je ne l'ai pas **vu**. *I haven't **seen** him.*
vouloir	voulu	*to want*	Elle a **voulu** juste une tranche. *She **wanted** just one slice.*

Using the Past Participle as an Adjective

Many adjectives in French are the same as the past participle, especially when active meaning is conveyed, for example:

		Examples	
ouvert	*open*	La porte est **ouverte**.	*The door is **open**.*
fermé	*closed*	La fenêtre est **fermée**.	*The window is **closed**.*
corrompu	*corrupt*	Ce politicien est **corrompu**.	*This politician is **corrupt**.*
réveillé	*awake*	Je suis **réveillé**.	*I am **awake**.*

2. THE VERB "TO KNOW": "SAVOIR" VS. "CONNAÎTRE"

There are two verbs in French that mean *"to know"* in English. The two verbs are "**savoir**" and "**connaître**." Knowing when to use "**savoir**" and when to use "**connaître**" should not be difficult if you understand the subtle difference between the two concepts of *"knowing."*

In short, the verb "**savoir**" is used to describe knowledge of facts, concepts, skills, abilities, etc. On the other hand, the verb "**connaître**" is used to describe recognition or familiarity with a person, a place, or an object, including a movie, a site, a brand, etc.

When referring to a language, one could use either "**savoir**" or "**connaître**." The difference is that "**Je connais le français**" indicates that you know some French or that you are familiar with the language, whereas "**Je sais le français**" or "**Je sais parler français**" indicates that you know French well enough to speak it.

Below is a reminder of the present tense conjugation of both verbs.

	savoir	connaître
je	sais	connais
tu	sais	connais
il/elle/on	sait	connait
nous	savons	connaissons
vous	savez	connaissez
ils/elles	savent	connaissent

Here are some examples that use the verbs "**savoir**" and "**connaître**" and highlight the difference:

"savoir" and "connaître" Examples	Explanation
Sais-tu s'il y a quelqu'un à l'intérieur? *Do you **know** if there is someone inside?*	When referring to a fact (whether someone is inside or not), use "**savoir**."
Elle ne **sait** pas nager. *She doesn't **know** how to swim.*	When referring to a skill, use "**savoir**."

Je ne **sais** pas où il y a une école. *I don't **know** where there is a school.*	When referring to a fact (whether a school exists nearby), use "**savoir**."
Je ne **connais** pas très bien la ville. *I don't **know** the city very well.*	When referring to recognizing a place, use "**connaître**."
Ils ne **connaissent** pas mes parents. *They don't **know** my parents.*	When referring to recognizing a person, use "**connaître**."
Connaissez-vous ce film? *Do you **know** that movie?*	When referring to recognizing a movie, use "**connaître**."
Connaissez-vous l'anglais? (or) **Savez**-vous l'anglais? *Do you **know** English?*	When referring to a language, use "**connaître**" or "**savoir**."

"Connaître" meaning "To Enjoy" or "To Experience"

The verb "**connaître**" is used to mean *"to experience"* or *"to enjoy"* when referring to the figurative meaning of both concepts, for example:

L'économie **a connu** une forte croissance.	*The economy **has experienced** strong growth.*
Le pays **connaît** quatre saisons.	*The country **enjoys** four seasons.*

To know each other using "Connaître"

The verb "**connaître**" is used to refer to the reciprocal act of knowing each other, for example:

Nous **nous connaissons**[1] très bien.	*We **know each other** very well.*
Ils ne **se connaissent**[1] pas.	*They don't **know each other**.*

3. INDEFINITE ADJECTIVES & PRONOUNS

Indefinite adjectives describe a noun in a vague or non-specific way, e.g., "**autres** livres" (*other books*), "**chaque** personne" (*each person*), "**plusieurs** choses" (*several things*), "**toutes** les écoles" (*all schools*), etc. On the other hand, an indefinite pronoun replaces the noun in a vague and non-specific way, e.g., "**Je te dis quelque chose**" (*I tell you something*), "**Je parle à quelqu'un**" (*I speak to someone*), "**Tout est bien**" (*All is well*), etc. Many indefinite pronouns are identical to their

---

[1] More on the use of reflexive verbs will be covered in detail in **Level IV, Lesson 3**.

indefinite adjective counterpart, e.g., "**tout(e)**" *(all)*, "**autre**" *(other)*, "**beaucoup**" *(much* or *many)*, etc.

Unlike most adjectives in French, indefinite adjectives precede the noun they describe. Some also change form to agree with the noun in gender and number. Indefinite adjectives and pronouns are used abundantly in French. Thus, it is very useful to learn the most common ones.

Here is a list of the most common indefinite adjectives and pronouns:

	Meaning		**Examples**
assez	*enough*	indef. adj. & pron.	J'ai **assez** d'argent. *I have **enough** money.*
trop	*too much, too many*	indef. adj. & pron.	Il y a **trop** de monde ici. *There are **too many** people here.*
l'un l'autre **les uns les autres**	*each other*	indef. adj. & pron.	Ils doivent s'aider **les uns les autres.** *They must help **each other.***
l'un ou l'autre **l'une ou l'autre**	*one or the other*	indef. adj. & pron.	Il faut choisir **l'une ou l'autre** de ces maisons. *You must choose **one or the other** of these houses.*
les deux	*both*	indef. adj. & pron.	**Les deux** options sont disponibles. ***Both** options are available.*
les autres	*the others*	indef. adj. & pron.	**Les autres** ne sont pas disponibles. ***The others** are not available.*
le reste	*the rest*	indef. adj. & pron.	**Le reste** du monde souffre. ***The rest** of the world is suffering.*
même(s)	*same, self*	indef. adj. & pron.	C'est la **même** personne que nous avons vue hier soir. *It is the **same** person we saw last night.*
certain(e)(s)	*certain*	indef. adj. & pron.	Seules **certaines** personnes peuvent le faire. *Only **certain** people can do that.*
autre(s)	*other, another*	indef. adj. & pron.	Je voudrais un **autre** verre d'eau, s'il vous plaît. *I'd like **another** glass of water, please.*
tout(e)(s)	*all, every*	indef. adj. & pron.	**Toute** l'année, il pleut dans le pays. ***All** year round, it rains in the country.*
tous	*all, everybody*	indef. adj. & pron.	Nous venons **tous** d'Australie. ***All** of us are from Australia.*
peu	*little, few*	indef. adj. & pron.	Nous avons besoin de **peu** de temps pour arriver. *We need **little** time to arrive.*

beaucoup (de)	*much, many*	indef. adj. & pron.	Il existe **beaucoup** d'options pour les jeunes. *There are **many** options for young people.*
divers	*various*	indef. adj. & pron.	**Divers** champs sont ouverts à tous. ***Various** fields are open to everyone.*
plusieurs	*several*	indef. adj. & pron.	Vous pouvez lire **plusieurs** livres sur ce sujet. *You can read **several** books on this topic.*
n'importe quel **quelconque**	*any, whichever*	indef. adj. & pron.	Apportez-moi **n'importe quel** livre. *Bring me **any** book.*
quelque(s)	*some, few*	indef. adj. & pron.	J'ai **quelques** livres sur le sujet. *I have **some** books on the subject.*
chaque	*each, every*	indef. adj.	Brossez-vous les dents après **chaque** repas. *Brush your teeth after **each** meal.*
quelque chose	*something*	indef. pron.	Je veux dire **quelque chose** de très important. *I want to say **something** very important.*
quelqu'un(e)	*someone*	indef. pron.	J'ai parlé avec **quelqu'un** de très intéressant. *I talked with **someone** very interesting.*
rien	*nothing*	indef. pron.	Je ne ferai **rien** de la journée d'aujourd'hui. *I am going to do **nothing** all day today.*
personne	*nobody, not any*	indef. pron.	**Personne** n'est au bureau aujourd'hui. ***Nobody** is in the office today.*
quiconque **qui que ce soit**	*whoever*	indef. pron.	**Qui que ce soit**, ce n'est pas important. ***Whoever** it is, it is not important.*

Note that "**chaque**" *(each)* can only be used as an indefinite adjective because it is always followed by a noun, e.g., "**chaque livre**" *(each book)*, "**chaque numéro**" *(each number)*, "**chaque étudiant**" *(each student)*, etc. On the other hand, "**quelque chose**" *(something)*, "**quelqu'un**" *(somebody)*, "**rien**" *(nothing)*, and "**personne**" *(nobody)* can only be used as indefinite pronouns because they cannot be followed by a noun, e.g., "**Rien ne s'est passé**" *(Nothing happened)*.

4. Conjunctions

Conjunctions are important components of any language as they allow the speaker to join sentences and convey useful meanings.

The most common conjunctions in French are:

Conjunction	Meaning	Example
et	*and*	J'aime le printemps **et** l'été. I *like spring **and** summer.*
ou	*or*	Je boirai du thé **ou** du café. I *will drink tea **or** coffee.*
si	*if*	**Si** je suis fatigué, je ne sors pas. **If** *I am tired, I won't go out.*
mais	*but*	Je veux dormir, **mais** je ne peux pas. I *want to sleep, **but** I can't.*
alors	*so*	**Alors**, que devrions-nous faire? **So**, *what should we do?*
selon	*according to*	**Selon** les médecins, le café n'est pas mauvais. **According to** *the doctors, coffee is not bad.*
sauf excepté	*except*	Je vais à la gym tous les jours **sauf** le vendredi. I *go to the gym every day **except** Friday.*
puis ensuite	*then*	Il était là. **Puis**, il est parti. He *was there. **Then**, he left.*
cependant toutefois	*however*	Je suis fatigué. **Cependant**, je peux sortir avec toi. I *am tired. **However**, I can go out with you.*
pour que afin que de sorte que	*so that* *in order to*	Je vais résumer le livre **pour que** vous puissiez le comprendre. I *will summarize the book **so that** you can understand it.*
parce que	*because*	J'étudie l'espagnol **parce que** je veux vivre au Mexique. I *study Spanish **because** I want to live in Mexico.*
à cause de	*because of*	Nous ne pouvons pas sortir **à cause de** la neige. We *can't go out **because of the** snow.*
au lieu de	*instead of*	**Au lieu de** sortir ce soir, nous allons regarder un film. **Instead of** *going out tonight, we'll watch a movie.*
étant donné que	*given that*	Je vais aller au café **étant donné que** j'ai assez de temps libre. I'll *go to the coffee shop **given that** I have enough free time.*
donc par conséquent	*therefore*	Il était tard; **donc**, nous ne sommes pas sortis la nuit dernière. It *was late; **therefore**, we didn't go out last night.*
sinon autrement	*otherwise*	J'espère qu'il ne pleuvra pas; **sinon**, on ne sort pas. I *hope it doesn't rain; **otherwise**, we don't go out.*
bien que même si malgré que	*although*	Je comprends le problème, **même si** je ne peux pas l'expliquer. I *understand the problem, **although** I can't explain it.*

malgré	*in spite of* *despite*	**Malgré** sa petite taille, c'est un très bon joueur. *Despite being short, he is a very good player.*
c'est-à-dire	*that is*	Je parle anglais et espagnol, **c'est-à-dire** que je suis bilingue. *I speak English and Spanish, that is, I'm bilingual.*
autrement dit en d'autres termes	*in other words*	**Autrement dit**, nous devons travailler plus dur. *In other words, we must work harder.*
tout en tandis que pendant que	*while*	Achetons quelque chose **pendant que** nous sommes ici. *Let's buy something while we are here.*
tant que	*as long as*	**Tant que** vous êtes prêt, vous n'avez pas à vous inquiéter. *As long as you are prepared, you don't need to worry.*
soit … soit …	*either…* *or…*	**Soit** nous partons maintenant, **soit** plus tard. *We either leave now or later.*
ni … ni …	*neither …* *nor …*	Mon français n'est **ni** bon **ni** mauvais. *My French is neither good nor bad.*
en plus de outre	*besides*	**En plus de** la nourriture, je commanderai aussi des boissons. *Besides food, I will order drinks too.*
a part	*apart from*	**A part** le temps, je n'aime pas cet endroit. *Apart from the weather, I don't like this place.*
contrairement à	*unlike*	**Contrairement à** vous, je ne connais pas l'allemand. *Unlike you, I don't know German.*

5. SIMPLE FUTURE TENSE

One informal but common way to express the future tense in the indicative mood is by using the verb **"aller"** (*to go*) in the present simple tense followed by the infinitive. For example, **"Je vais voyager,"** literally means *"I go travel,"* but it is similar in purpose to the English expression *"I am going to travel."*

		-er ending parler *(to speak)*	**-ir ending** finir *(to finish)*	**-re ending** vendre *(to sell)*
je	vais			
tu	vas			
il/elle/on	va			
nous	allons	parler	finir	vendre
vous	allez			
ils/elles	vont			

The formal simple future tense is also used to express events in the future and is more common in written literature. To form the stem of the verb needed for regular verb conjugation, we use the *infinitive* as a stem and drop the final "**-e**" in the case of "**-re**" verbs. The endings are the same for the three types of verbs.

	-er ending parler *(to speak)*	-ir ending finir *(to finish)*	-re ending vendre *(to sell)*
je	parler**ai**	finir**ai**	vendr**ai**
tu	parler**as**	finir**as**	vendr**as**
il/elle/on	parler**a**	finir**a**	vendr**a**
nous	parler**ons**	finir**ons**	vendr**ons**
vous	parler**ez**	finir**ez**	vendr**ez**
ils/elles	parler**ont**	finir**ont**	vendr**ont**

Uses of the simple future tense in French are very similar to that in English. Nevertheless, there are sometimes little differences. For example, in sentences that describe two events occurring in the future linked with "**quand**" *(when)* or "**dès que**" *(once)*, both events are expressed in French using verbs in the simple future tense. While in English we say *"I'll call you when I arrive home,"* in French, we would say "**Je t'appellerai quand j'arriverai à la maison**." Notice that both verbs "**appeler**" *(to call)* and "**arriver**" *(to arrive)* are in the future tense.

Irregular Verbs

There are some verbs that are irregular in the simple future tense. Here, we list the most common ones:

	je	tu	il/elle	nous	vous	ils/elles
aller *to go*	irai	iras	ira	irons	irez	iront
avoir *to have*	aurai	auras	aura	aurons	aurez	auront
courir *to run*	courrai	courras	courra	courrons	courrez	courront
devenir *to become*	deviendrai	deviendras	deviendra	deviendrons	deviendrez	deviendront
devoir *must*	devrai	devras	devra	devrons	devrez	devront

	je	tu	il/elle	nous	vous	ils/elles
envoyer *to send*	enverrai	enverras	enverra	enverrons	enverrez	enverront
être *to be*	serai	seras	sera	serons	serez	seront
faire *to do*	ferai	feras	fera	ferons	ferez	feront
falloir *to have to*	-	-	faudra	-	-	-
mourir *to die*	mourrai	mourras	mourra	mourrons	mourrez	mourront
pleuvoir *to rain*	-	-	pleuvra	-	-	-
recevoir *to receive*	recevrai	recevras	recevra	recevrons	recevrez	recevront
revenir *to return*	reviendrai	reviendras	reviendra	reviendrons	reviendrez	reviendront
savoir *to know*	saurai	sauras	saura	saurons	saurez	sauront
tenir *to hold*	tiendrai	tiendras	tiendra	tiendrons	tiendrez	tiendront
valoir *to be worth*	-	-	vaudra	-	-	-
venir *to come*	viendrai	viendras	viendra	viendrons	viendrez	viendront
voir *to take*	verrai	verras	verra	verrons	verrez	verront
vouloir *to want*	voudrai	voudras	voudra	voudrons	voudrez	voudront

There are some verbs that undergo minor spelling changes. Here are some common examples:

	je	tu	il/elle	nous	vous	ils/elles
employer *to hire*	emploierai	emploieras	emploiera	emploierons	emploierez	emploieront
essuyer *to wipe*	essuierai	essuieras	essuiera	essuierons	essuierez	essuieront
nettoyer *to clean*	nettoierai	nettoieras	nettoiera	nettoierons	nettoierez	nettoieront
acheter *to buy*	achèterai	achèteras	achètera	achèterons	achèterez	achèteront
appeler *to call*	appellerai	appelleras	appellera	appellerons	appellerez	appelleront
jeter *to throw*	jetterai	jetteras	jettera	jetterons	jetterez	jetteront

Examples

Here are some examples that use the simple future tense:

J'**irai** en Italie l'année prochaine.	*I **will go** to Italy next year.*
Je n'**irai** pas à la gym aujourd'hui.	*I **won't go** to the gym today.*
Elle **achètera** une maison à Rome.	*She **will buy** a house in Rome.*
Tu **étudieras** dur seulement ce week-end.	*You **will study** hard only this weekend.*
Ils **vivront** dans une petite ville.	*They **will live** in a small city.*
Nous **dormirons** toute la journée demain.	*We **will sleep** all day tomorrow.*

6. Telling Time & Describing The Weather

Telling time and describing the weather are fundamental language skills for any language learner.

Expressing Time in Hours

In French, the verb "**être**" (*to be*) is used in the third-person form "**est**" to describe time.

Il est une heure.	*It's one o'clock.*
Il est trois heures.	*It's three o'clock.*
Il est onze heure.	*It's eleven o'clock.*

To ask what time it is, use the expression: "**Quelle heure est-il?**" meaning *"What time is it?"* in English, or more literally: *"What hour is it?"*

To ask *"At what time …?"*, we use "**À quelle heure …?**"

Expressing Minutes

To express time in hours and minutes, we simply add the minutes after the hour.

Il est une heure cinquante.	*It's one-fifty.*
Il est cinq heures vingt-quatre.	*It's five twenty-four.*

If you want to say: it is minutes to a certain hour, e.g., *"It's five to ten,"* use **"moins"** *(minus)*.

Il est deux heures **moins** dix.	*It's ten to two.*
Il est dix heures **moins** cinq.	*It's five to ten.*

The *"15 minutes"* and *"30 minutes"* can sometimes be replaced with **"quart"** *(quarter)* and **"demi"** *(half)*, respectively.

Il est une heure moins le **quart**.	*It's a quarter to one.*
Il est quatre heures et **demie**.	*It's four-thirty.*

Remember that the French officially use the 24-hour clock format. For example, *"1 p.m."* is **"13h"** in French.

Another minor note is that the letter **"h"** is often used in French instead of the colon, which is used to describe time in English, e.g., **"13h15"** *(1:15 p.m.)*.

Other Time Expressions

The expressions **"a.m."** and **"p.m."** are not commonly used in French, but you will may hear some people who tell the time in the twelve-hour clock format using expressions like: **"du matin"** *(in the morning)*, **"de l'après-midi"** *(in the afternoon)*, or **"du soir"** *(in the evening)*.

Here are some expressions that are used to express time with examples:

du matin	*in the morning*	*It's 9 a.m.* Il est neuf heures **du matin**.
de l'après-midi	*in the afternoon*	*It's 1 p.m.* Il est une heure **de l'après-midi**.
du soir	*in the evening*	*It's 7 p.m.* Il est sept heures **du soir**.
midi	*noon*	*It's noon.* Il est **midi**.
minuit	*midnight*	*It's midnight.* Il est **minuit**.

à l'aube	*at dawn*	*We'll meet* **at dawn.** Nous nous retrouverons **à l'aube.**
pile(s) **précise(s)**	*sharp*	*It's two o'clock* **sharp.** Il est deux heures **piles.**
environ	*about*	*It's* **about** *three o'clock.* Il est **environ** trois heures.

Weather Expressions

Describing the weather in French often involves the use of some idiomatic expressions that make little sense if translated into English literally. For example, the expression "**Il fait trop chaud**" translates literally to *"It makes much heat."* However, it just means that it is too hot. Similarly, the expression "**Il y a du soleil**," which means that the sun is shining, makes little sense when translated literally as *"There is the sun."*

Here, we list a few common ways of describing the weather using some idiomatic expressions as well as other simple expressions.

Weather Expressions using the verb "faire"

Quel temps fait-il?	*What's the weather like?*
Il fait beau.	*The weather is good.*
Il fait mauvais.	*The weather is bad.*
Il fait (trop) froid.	*It's (too) cold.*
Il fait chaud.	*It's hot.*

Weather Expressions using "il y a"

The expression "**il y a**" means *"there is"* or *"there are."* It is used in many weather expressions, such as:

Il y a des nuages.	*It's cloudy.*
Il y a du soleil.	*It's sunny.*
Il y a du vent.	*It's windy.*
Il y a de la neige.	*It's snowing.*
Il y a du brouillard.	*It's foggy.*
Il y a de la brume.	*It's misty.*
Il y a de l'humidité.	*It's humid.*
Il y a du tonnerre.	*There is thunder.*

Il y a un orage.	*There is a windstorm.*
Il y a de la foudre.	*There is lightning.*

Weather Expressions using the verb "être"

We can also use the verb "**être**" in the third-person singular form followed by an adjective to describe the weather.

C'est gelé.	*It's icy.*
C'est humide.	*It's humid.*
C'est nuageux.	*It's cloudy.*
C'est orageux.	*It's stormy.*
C'est agréable.	*It's pleasant.*
C'est venteux.	*It's windy.*
C'est pluvieux.	*It's rainy.*

Weather Expressions using a simple verb

One can also use a simple verb expression in the third-person singular form, such as "**Il pleut,**" where "**pleut**" is the third-person singular form of the present tense of the verb "**pleuvoir**" (*to rain*). Other examples include:

Il pleut.	*It's raining.*
Il neige.	*It's snowing.*
Il bruine.	*It's sprinkling.*
Il grêle.	*It's hailing.*
Il tonne.	*It's thundering.*

7. PRESENT PARTICIPLE & GERUND

We encountered the past participle in **Lesson 1** of this level when we studied the compound past. Another participle that is useful to learn is the *present participle*.

The conjugation of the present participle is straightforward. We start with the first-person plural form, that is, the "**nous**" form, and we replace the final "**-ons**" with "**-ant.**" The present participle has only one form. There is no gender or number associated with the present participle. Let us look at some examples of forming the present participle:

nous parlons	*we speak*	**parlant**	*speaking*
nous mangeons	*we eat*	**mangeant**	*eating*
nous choisissons	*we choose*	**choisissant**	*choosing*
nous buvons	*we drink*	**buvant**	*drinking*

Notice that any spelling change in the "**nous**" form is carried over to the present participle.

There are only three irregular verbs in the present participle: "**être**" *(to be)*, "**avoir**" *(to have)*, and "**savoir**" *(to know)*. The present participles of these verbs are: "**étant**," "**ayant**," and "**sachant**," respectively.

The present participle is used to describe the action of a noun or pronoun that is unrelated to the action described by the main verb. For example:

Nous avons vu l'homme **entrant** dans le bâtiment.	*We saw the man **entering** the building.*
Étant occupé, il a refusé de prendre rendez-vous.	***Being** busy, he declined to make an appointment.*
Voulant être entendu, il a décidé de se lever et de parler fort.	***Wanting** to be heard, he decided to stand up and speak loudly.*

Sometimes the past participle is used to replace a relative clause, for example:

Les personnes **portant** des sacs doivent attendre.	*People **carrying** (who carry) bags must wait.*
Les animaux domestiques **ayant** des papiers peuvent voyager.	*Pets **having** (that have) documentation can travel.*
Des techniciens **sachant** réparer les téléphones sont disponibles.	*Technicians **knowing** (who know) how to fix phones are available.*

When the present participle is preceded by the preposition "**en**," it is referred to as *gerund*. In this context, the preposition "**en**" can be translated as *"while," "upon,"* or *"by,"* for example:

Il s'est dormi **en regardant** la télé.	*He slept **while watching** TV.*
Il est devenu nerveux **en** me **voyant**.	*He got nervous **upon seeing** me.*

| **En étudiant** dur, il a réussi l'examen. | *By studying* hard, he passed the exam. |
| C'est **en suivant** les règles qu'il a réussi. | *It is* **by following** the rules that he succeeded. |

Sometimes "**tout**" *(all)* precedes the preposition "**en**" when forming the gerund. This cannot be translated literally, but often highlights a contradiction between two actions or events. The meaning becomes closer to *"even though,"* for example:

| **Tout en étant** malade, il a réussi à être le meilleur joueur sur le terrain. | *While being* sick, he managed to be the best player on the pitch. |
| **Tout en prétendant** être innocent, les preuves étaient contre lui. | *While claiming* to be innocent, the evidence was against him. |

The French language does not have a direct equivalent of the present and past continuous tense. Thus, the present participle is not used in this case. Alternative equivalents to the English continuous tenses will be discussed in **Level V, Lesson 7**.

8. ADVERBS

An adverb is a word that modifies a verb, an adjective, or another adverb. It usually answers a question such as how, how often, how long, when, where, etc.

A lot of French adverbs have the ending "**-ment**," e.g., "**rapidement**" *(quickly)*, "**fortement**" *(strongly)*, etc. This is, more or less, similar to the ending *"-ly"* in English. Nevertheless, there are many other adverbs and adverbial phrases that do not follow this simple rule. We will attempt to classify the most common adverbs into some categories for easier memorization.

Forming an Adverb

Many adverbs in French can be formed by simply adding "**-ment**" to the *feminine* singular adjective. Here are some examples:

Adverb in English	Masculine singular adjective	Feminine singular adjective	Adverb in French
slowly	lent	lente	lentement
quickly	rapide	rapide	rapidement
quietly	tranquille	tranquille	tranquillement
exactly	exact	exacte	exactement
relatively	relatif	relative	relativement
strongly	fort	forte	fortement
easily	facile	facile	facilement
normally	normal	normale	normalement
generally	général	générale	généralement
literally	littéral	littérale	littéralement
popularly	populaire	populaire	populairement
regularly	régulier	régulière	régulièrement
particularly	particulier	particulière	particulièrement

Some adverbs ending with "-**ment**" slightly deviate from the above rules. For example:

recent	récent	*recently*	récemment
violent	violent	*violently*	violemment

Not all adverbs in French are formed by adding the "-**ment**" ending, similar to the fact that not all English adverbs are formed by adding "-*ly*" to the corresponding adjective. Some adverbs do not follow any particular rules. For example, the adverb of "**bon**" *(good)* is "**bien**" *(well)*, and the adverb of "**mauvais**" *(bad)* is "**mal**" *(badly)*.

The Adverb "si"

Another common adverb in French is "**si**," which, depending on the context, can be translated as *"such"* or *"so."* For example:

C'est un **si** joli chat.	*He is **such** a pretty cat.*
Ce chat est **si** joli.	*This cat is **so** pretty.*

The Adverbs "Aussi" and "Non plus"

The adverb "**aussi**" is used to express agreement with an *affirmative* statement, whereas the adverb "**non plus**" is used to express agreement with a *negative* statement. For example:

A: Je parle français.	*A: I speak French.*
B: Moi **aussi**.	*B: Me **too**.*
A: Je ne parle pas français.	*A: I don't speak French.*
B: Moi **non plus**.	*B: Me **neither**.*

To show disagreement with affirmative and negative statements, we simply use "**non**" *(no)* and "**oui**" *(yes)*, respectively, for example:

A: Je parle français.	*A: I speak French.*
B: Moi **non**.	*B: I **don't**.*
A: Je ne parle pas français.	*A: I don't speak French.*
B: Moi **oui**.	*B: I **do**.*

The Adverbs "Encore" and "Déjà"

When followed by a verb in the present tense, "**encore**" generally means *"still"* in affirmative and negative expressions. However, "**encore**" can also mean *"yet"* in a negative expression when followed by a verb in the present perfect tense, for example:

J'habite **encore** en Italie.	*I **still** live in Italy.*
Je ne parle pas **encore** bien anglais.	*I **still** don't speak English well.*
Je ne suis pas **encore** rentré.	*I have not returned home **yet**.*

One can think of "**déjà**," meaning *"already,"* as the opposite response to "**pas encore**." Below are some examples in both the present tense and the present perfect tense:

a) Present Tense

Je ne parle pas **encore** bien anglais.	*I **still** don't speak English well.*
Je parle **déjà** bien l'anglais.	*I **already** speak English well.*

b) Present Perfect Tense

Je ne suis pas **encore** rentré.	*I have not returned home **yet**.*
Je suis **déjà** rentré chez moi.	*I have **already** returned home.*

In the present tense, the opposite of "**encore**" *(still)* is "**ne ... plus**" *(no longer)*. For example:

J'habite **encore** en Italie.	*I **still** live in Italy.*
Je **n'**habite **plus** en Italie.	*I **no longer** live in Italy.*

The Adverb "il y a"

The expression "**il y a**" is also used as an adverb of time meaning *"ago"* when describing something that happened and ended in the past. Here are some examples:

J'ai parlé à ma sœur **il y a** trois mois.	*I spoke to my sister three months **ago**.*
Je me suis réveillé **il y a** 15 minutes.	*I woke up 15 minutes **ago**.*

Adverbial Phrases with "Fois"

The feminine noun "**fois**" is used to describe the frequency of occurrence. The English equivalents are *"time,"* and its plural *"times,"* e.g., *"how many times did you win?"* Here is a list of some adverbial phrases that use "**fois**":

cette fois	*this time*	**de moins en moins**	*less and less*
la prochaine fois	*next time*	**la dernière fois**	*last time*
à chaque fois	*each time* *every time*	**une fois**	*one time* *once*
quelquefois	*at times* *sometimes*	**trois fois**	*three times*
parfois	*sometimes*	**plusieurs fois**	*many times*
beaucoup de fois	*many times*	**Combien de fois?**	*How many times?*

Other Adverbs

Given that an adverb can be created easily from a corresponding adjective, it is difficult to cover a vast number of adverbs in the limited space of this book.

Moreover, there are often multiple adverbs that convey a similar meaning. Here are some examples:

1. To say *"certainly"* or *"surely,"* you could use one of the following options: **"certainement,"** **"sûrement,"** **"bien sûr,"** or even **"sans doute"** *(undoubtedly)*.

2. To say *"really,"* *"truly,"* or *"actually,"* you could use: **"réellement,"** **"vraiment,"** or **"en réalité."** Remember that **"actuellement,"** in French, means *"currently,"* not *"actually."*

3. To say *"finally,"* you could use: **"finalement,"** **"à la fin,"** or **"enfin."**

In this section, we list some of the most common adverbs and adverbial phrases. You will learn more adverbs as you practice French by reading, listening, and understanding the general rules explained in this lesson.

Adverbs of Place

près **proche**	*near*	**loin**	*far*
devant	*in front* *ahead*	**derrière**	*behind*
dedans **à l'interieur**	*inside*	**dehors** **à l'exterieur**	*outside*
autour	*around*	**partout**	*everywhere*
nulle part	*nowhere*	**à bord**	*on board*

Adverbs of Time

bientôt	*soon*	**plus tard** **ensuite**	*later*
tôt	*early*	**tard**	*late*
à temps	*on time*	**après**	*after*
avant	*before*	**jamais**	*never*
toujours	*always*	**soudainement** **tout à coup**	*suddenly*
souvent	*often*	**puis**	*then*

généralement habituellement	*usually*	fréquemment	*frequently*
brièvement	*briefly*	à la fin	*in the end*
au début	*in the beginning*	tous les deux jours	*every other day*
tous les jours	*every day*	à long terme	*in the long term*
à court terme	*in the short term*	de suite	*right away* *immediately*
alors	*so* *then*	l'avant-dernière nuit	*the night before last*
avant-hier	*the day before yesterday*	quotidiennement journellement	*daily*
entre-temps en attendant	*meanwhile*	mensuellement	*monthly*
hebdomadairement	*weekly*	immédiatement aussitôt	*immediately*

Adverbs of Quantity

très	*very* *much*	seulement	*only*
		uniquement	*just*
trop	*too*	un peu	*a little*
aucun	*none*	moins	*less*
beaucoup	*so much*	assez	*enough*
presque	*almost*	pas du tout	*not at all*

Adverbs of Manner

comme	*as* *like*	comme ça cela	*like this*
ensemble	*together*	séparément	*separately*
petit à petit	*little by little*	pas à pas	*step by step*
juste	*just*	peut-être	*perhaps* *maybe*
à haute voix	*loudly*	en hate à la hâte	*in a hurry*
sérieusement	*seriously*	à peine	*barely*
de plus en outre	*moreover*	face à face	*face to face*
heureusement par bonheur par chance	*fortunately*	malheureusement	*unfortunately*

Adverbial Expressions

volontiers volontairement	*willingly*	à contrecœur	*unwillingly*
sciemment	*knowingly*	à la mode	*fashionably*
par cœur	*by heart*	à pied	*on foot*
en chemin en route	*on the way*	à l'étranger	*overseas abroad*

II. Vocabulary Building

Go over the vocabulary in this section. You could Anki cards to help you memorize the meaning of each verb in proper contexts.

1. VERBS III

Below is a list of some important verbs needed for this level:

English	French	Examples
access	accéder	En bas de ces escaliers, j'**accède** au sous-sol. *Down those stairs I **access** the basement.*
advance	avancer	Pour **avancer** à l'université, il faut étudier. *To **advance** in university, you have to study.*
break (object)	casser	Il faut **casser** trois œufs pour la recette. *You have to **break** three eggs for the recipe.*
breathe	respirer	Il faut **respirer** profondément avant de plonger. *You have to **breathe** deeply before diving in.*
bring	apporter amener	Pouvez-vous m'**apporter** ce verre? *Can you **bring** me that glass?*
carry	porter	Je **porterai** ces sacs jusqu'à la maison. *I will **carry** these bags to the house.*
convince	convaincre	Je ne suis pas facile à **convaincre**. *I'm not easy to **convince**.*
correct	corriger	Je **corrigerai** les examens demain. *I **will correct** the exams tomorrow.*
cross	traverser	Vous devez **traverser** le pont pour arriver. *You must **cross** the bridge to arrive.*
count	compter	Mon petit-fils sait **compter** jusqu'à dix. *My little son knows how to **count** to ten.*
describe	décrire	Je ne sais pas comment **décrire** cette ville. *I don't know how to **describe** that city.*
destroy	détruire	La guerre peut **détruire** une grande ville. *War can **destroy** a large city.*

direct	diriger	Il **dirige** très bien l'orchestre. *He **directs** the orchestra very well.*
discuss	discuter	Je ne **discuterai** pas de cela avec vous. *I **will** not **discuss** that with you.*
dream	rêver	Je **rêve** toujours d'aller en Australie. *I always **dream** of going to Australia.*
earn gain	gagner	Il **gagne** plus que ses frères. *He **earns** more than his brothers.*
fail	échouer	Ce n'est pas facile d'**échouer**. *It isn't easy to **fail**.*
fill	remplir	Je **remplis** toujours le bac à glaçons. *I always **fill** the ice tray.*
finish	finir terminer	Si je **finis** ceci, nous irons. *If I **finish** this, we'll go.*
fix (attach)	fixer	Donne-moi le tournevis pour **fixer** le cadre au mur. *Give me the screwdriver to **fix** the frame to the wall.*
fix (repair)	réparer	Je devrais **réparer** le robinet bientôt. *I should **fix** the faucet soon.*
fly	voler	Les moustiques **volent** dans les airs. *The mosquitoes **fly** in the air.*
follow	suivre	Vous pouvez me **suivre** sur les réseaux sociaux. *You can **follow** me on social media.*
guess	deviner	Je **devine** toujours mon cadeau d'anniversaire. *I always **guess** my birthday gift.*
happen	se passer arriver	Il a été franc à propos de ce qui pourrait **arriver**. *He was frank about what could **happen**.*
hate	détester	Je **déteste** quand les moustiques me piquent. *I **hate** it when mosquitoes bite me.*
have lunch	déjeuner	Je ne peux pas; je veux **déjeuner**. *I can't; I want to **have lunch**.*
hope	espérer	J'**espère** te voir bientôt. *I **hope** to see you soon.*
keep hold maintain	tenir	Je **tiens** toujours un registre de présence. *I always **keep** a record of attendance.*
keep save preserve	garder	Je **garde** toujours les restes. *I always **save** the leftovers.*
kill	tuer	Ce poison **tue** les puces. *That poison **kills** fleas.*
lack	manquer	Ce ragoût **manque** de saveur. *This stew **lacks** flavor.*

last	**durer**	Ces courses doivent **durer** un mois. *Those groceries must **last** for a month.*
let	**laisser**	Je ne veux pas **laisser** cela me ralentir. *I don't want to **let** this slow me down.*
mix **blend**	**mélanger**	Vous devez d'abord **mélanger** les ingrédients secs. *You must **mix** the dry ingredients first.*
must	**devoir**[1]	Vous **devez** rendre visite à votre grand-mère. *You **must** visit your grandmother.*
notify	**notifier** **prévenir**	Pouvez-vous me **prévenir** quand cela arrive? *Can you **notify** me when it arrives?*
perform **fulfill**	**réaliser** **effectuer**	Les scientifiques **réaliseront** une expérience. *The scientists **will perform** an experiment.*
possess	**posséder**	Il **possède** une compétence surprenante. *He **possesses** a surprising skill.*
pull	**tirer**	Vous devez **tirer** sur cette corde pour qu'elle tombe. *You have to **pull** on that rope for it to fall.*
push	**pousser**	Devrais-je te **pousser** en avant? *Should I **push** you forward?*
remind	**rappeler**	Pouvez-vous me **rappeler** la date, s'il vous plaît? *Can you **remind** me of the date, please?*
rent	**louer**	Je **loue** un appartement dans cet immeuble. *I **rent** an apartment in this building.*
resolve	**résoudre**	Je veux **résoudre** ce problème de mathématiques. *I want to **resolve** this math problem.*
ride[2] **(a horse)**	**monter**	C'est une belle journée ensoleillée pour **monter** à cheval. *It's a nice sunny day for **riding**.*
seem	**sembler**	Il **semble** que ce soit ainsi. *It **seems** it's that way.*
smell	**sentir**	Vous devez **sentir** cette cannelle. *You must **smell** this cinnamon.*
sound	**sonner**	La sonnette de la porte **sonne** trop fort. *The doorbell **sounds** too loud.*
split **break**	**diviser**	Cette rue **divise** la ville en deux. *This street **splits** the city in two.*
switch on **turn on**	**allumer**	Je dois **allumer** la lumière pour voir. *I have to **turn on** the light to see.*
taste	**goûter**	J'aime **goûter** à tous les aliments qui existent. *I like to **taste** all the food there is.*

---

[1] The verb "**devoir**" can also mean *"to owe,"* e.g., "**Je te dois 100 euros**" *(I owe you 100 euros).*

[2] The verb "**faire**" *(to do)* can also be used to mean *"to ride"* in some contexts, e.g., "**faire de l'équitation**" *(to go horseback riding)*, "**faire du vélo**" *(to ride a bike)*, "**faire un tour**" *(to go for a ride)*, etc.

thank	**remercier**	Je **remercie** mes amis de m'aider. *I **thank** my friends for helping me.*
train	**s'entraîner**	Je dois **m'entraîner** pour la course. *I have to **train** for the race.*
trust	**faire confiance**	Je **fais confiance** à ton jugement. *I **trust** your judgment.*
warn	**avertir prévenir**	Je te **préviens** que tu n'aimeras pas ça. *I **warn** you that you won't like it.*
wish	**souhaiter**	Les jeunes **souhaitent** être plus indépendants. *Young people **wish** to be more independent.*

In addition to the above new verbs, we add a few more English cognates that are easy to memorize.

English	French	Examples
abuse	**abuser**	Il n'est pas bon d'**abuser** de la confiance. *It's not good to **abuse** trust.*
accelerate	**accélérer**	J'essaie de ne pas **accélérer** trop lorsque je conduis. *I try to not **accelerate** too much when I drive.*
accompany	**accompagner**	Pouvez-vous m'**accompagner** jusqu'à la porte? *Can you **accompany** me to the door?*
arrange	**arranger**	J'**arrangerai** mes fichiers par ordre alphabétique. *I **will arrange** my files alphabetically.*
assist	**assister**[1]	Vous devez **assister** les gens quand vous le pouvez. *You must **assist** people when you can.*
cease	**cesser**	Cette marque **cessera** d'exister. *That brand **will cease** to exist.*
celebrate	**célébrer**	Je **célébrerai** mon anniversaire lors d'une croisière. *I **will celebrate** my birthday on a cruise.*
combat	**combattre**	Il est difficile de **combattre** les moustiques. *It's hard to **combat** the mosquitoes.*
condemn convict	**condamner**	Vous ne devriez pas **condamner** sans preuve. *You shouldn't **condemn** without proof.*
confine	**confiner**	L'armée **a confiné** les rebelles. *The army **has confined** the rebels.*
consent	**consentir**	Je lis les termes avant de **consentir**. *I read the terms before I **consent**.*

---

[1] The verb "**assister**" also means *"to attend,"* e.g., "**assister à un cours**" *(to attend a class)*, which is the more common use of the verb "**assister**." The verb "**aider**" is often used to describe the act of giving help or assistance. The verb "**attendre**," on the other hand, is often used to mean *"to wait for"* or *"to expect."*

contemplate	contempler	J'aime **contempler** l'art de rue. *I like to **contemplate** street art.*
continue	continuer	Je **continue** à regarder cette série. *I **continue** to watch that series.*
contrast	contraster	Cette couleur de porte **contraste** avec le mur. *That door color **contrasts** with the wall.*
contribute	contribuer	Je pense que je peux **contribuer** à ce projet. *I think I can **contribute** to this project.*
convert	convertir	Je **convertirai** l'image dans un autre format. *I **will convert** the image to another format.*
criticize	critiquer	Ma grand-mère **critique** toujours tout. *My grandmother always **criticizes** everything.*
demonstrate	démontrer	Je **démontrerai** comment c'est fait. *I **will demonstrate** how it's done.*
detect	détecter	Il peut **détecter** si vous augmentez votre vitesse. *It can **detect** if you increase your speed.*
devastate	dévaster	La maison est **dévastée**. *The house is **devastated**.*
employ	employer	Ma société **emploie** de nombreux travailleurs. *My company **employs** many workers.*
examine	examiner	Pouvez-vous **examiner** ce grain de beauté? *Can you **examine** this mole?*
indicate	indiquer	Pouvez-vous m'**indiquer** où se trouve la salle de bains? *Can you **indicate** to me where the bathroom is?*
influence affect	affecter	Être somnolent **affecte** mes réactions. *Being sleepy **affects** my reactions.*
intensify	intensifier	Le sel **intensifie** les saveurs. *Salt **intensifies** flavors.*
multiply	multiplier	Je n'aime pas **multiplier** les nombres. *I don't like to **multiply** numbers.*
offer	offrir	Le marché **offre** beaucoup de produits. *The market **offers** a lot of products.*
optimize	optimiser	Vous devez **optimiser** votre vitesse d'Internet. *You have to **optimize** your internet speed.*
recommend	recommander	Je **recommande** davantage cette marque. *I **recommend** this brand more.*
require	requérir	Ce travail **requiert** un certificat spécial. *This job **requires** a special certificate.*
serve	servir	Il est généreux de **servir** les autres lorsque c'est possible. *It is generous to **serve** others when possible.*
sign	signer	L'acteur aime **signer** des autographes. *The actor likes to **sign** autographs.*

supervise **oversee**	**superviser**	Mon chef **supervise** 30 personnes. *My boss **supervises** 30 people.*
test	**tester**	Vous devez **tester** le modèle avant la mise en œuvre. *You must **test** the model before implementation.*
torture	**torturer**	Il n'est pas humain de **torturer** les prisonniers. *It's not humane to **torture** prisoners.*
vandalize	**vandaliser**	Ils **ont vandalisé** le mur. *They **have vandalized** the wall.*
vibrate	**vibrer**	Mon téléphone portable **vibre** lorsque je reçois un message. *My cell phone **vibrates** when I receive a message.*

2. ADJECTIVES III

Below is a list of some common adjectives in French that we need at this level. Notice that an adjective must agree with the noun in number and gender.

English	French	Examples
alone	**seul**	J'aime me reposer **seul**. *I like to rest **alone**.*
ancient	**ancien**	Les pyramides d'Égypte sont **anciennes**. *Egypt's pyramids are **ancient**.*
attracted	**attiré**	Les papillons de nuit sont **attirés** par la lumière. *Moths are **attracted** to light.*
aware **conscious**	**conscient**	Je suis **conscient** de tous les défis. *I am **aware** of all the challenges.*
bitter	**amer**	J'aime mon café **amer**. *I like my coffee **bitter**.*
blind	**aveugle**	J'ai un serpent **aveugle**. *I have a **blind** snake.*
brave	**courageux**	Vous êtes très **courageux** de donner ce discours. *You're very **brave** giving that speech.*
bright **(light)**	**brillant** **lumineux**	Jupiter semble très **lumineuse** dans le ciel. *Jupiter looks very **bright** in the sky.*
cloudy	**nuageux**	La journée est un peu **nuageuse**. *The day is a bit **cloudy**.*
convenient	**pratique**	Il est **pratique** de ranger les vêtements ici. *It is **convenient** to store the clothes here.*
covered	**couvert**	Le sol est **couvert** de boue. *The floor is **covered** in mud.*
cowardly	**lâche**	Mon chien est très **lâche**. *My dog is very **cowardly**.*

dark	sombre	Cette forêt est très **sombre**. *This forest is very **dark**.*
deep profound	profond	C'est la partie **profonde** de la piscine. *This is the **deep** part of the pool.*
depressed	déprimé	J'écoute de la musique quand je me sens **déprimé**. *I listen to music when I feel **depressed**.*
depressing	déprimant	Les funérailles sont **déprimantes**. *Funerals are **depressing**.*
desirable	souhaitable	Vivre en ville est très **souhaitable**. *Living in the city is very **desirable**.*
drunk	ivre	Vous ne devez pas conduire si vous êtes **ivre**. *You must not drive if you are **drunk**.*
exhausted	épuisé	Couper du bois de chauffage me laisse **épuisé**. *Cutting firewood leaves me **exhausted**.*
fat	gros	Ce n'est pas poli de dire à quelqu'un qu'il a l'air **gros**. *It's not polite to tell someone they look **fat**.*
genius	génie	Einstein était un **génie** scientifique. *Einstein was a **genius** scientist.*
main principal	principal	Le point **principal** est de rester calme. *The **main** point is to remain calm.*
multiple	plusieurs	J'ai commandé **plusieurs** articles de cet endroit. *I've ordered from that place **multiple** items.*
naked bare	nue	Je veux connaître la vérité **nue**. *I want to know the **naked** truth.*
narrow	étroit	Fais attention à ces escaliers **étroits**. *Be careful with those **narrow** stairs.*
obvious	évident	Il est **évident** que la porte est ouverte. *It is **obvious** that the door is open.*
own	propre	Je vais acheter ma **propre** voiture. *I'm going to buy my **own** car.*
powerful	puissant	Cette machine est très **puissante**. *This machine is very **powerful**.*
proud	fier	Je suis **fier** de l'accomplissement de notre équipe. *I'm **proud** of our team's accomplishment.*
rainy	pluvieux	Ce sera **pluvieux** toute la fin de semaine. *It will be **rainy** all weekend.*
raw	cru	Ce poulet est **cru**. *That chicken is **raw**.*
relaxed	détendu	Le sommeil me laisse **détendu**. *Sleep leaves me **relaxed**.*
relaxing	relaxant	Se coucher tôt est **relaxant**. *Sleeping early is **relaxing**.*

English	French	Examples
retired	retraité	Mes grands-parents sont **retraités**. *My grandparents are **retired**.*
rude	impoli	Il ne faut pas être **impoli** envers les gens. *You shouldn't be **rude** to people.*
sensitive	sensible	J'ai une peau très **sensible**. *I have very **sensitive** skin.*
spicy	épicé	J'adore la cuisine **épicée**! *I love **spicy** food!*
successful	réussi	Il a subi une chirurgie **réussie**. *He underwent a **successful** surgery.*
thick	épais	Je ne veux pas une tranche **épaisse** de gâteau. *I don't want a **thick** slice of cake.*
thin	mince	Il a l'air très **mince** après avoir suivi un régime. *He looks very **thin** after dieting.*
tiring	épuisant	Rester debout toute la nuit est **épuisant**. *Staying up all night is **tiring**.*
united	unis	Ils sont **unis** contre l'ennemi. *They are **united** against the enemy.*
wide	large	Le canapé est très **large**. *The couch is very **wide**.*
winning	gagnant	Il a la recette **gagnante**. *He has the **winning** recipe.*
wise	sage	Mon professeur est très **sage**. *My professor is very **wise**.*

In addition to the above new adjectives, we add a few more English cognates that are easy to memorize.

English	French	Examples
approximate	approximatif	Pouvez-vous calculer le retard **approximatif**? *Can you calculate the **approximate** delay?*
arrogant	arrogant	Je n'aime pas les personnes **arrogantes**. *I don't like **arrogant** people.*
calm	calme	Je me sens **calme** quand je suis à la plage. *I feel **calm** when I am on the beach.*
defined	défini	Tes boucles sont très **définies**. *Your curls are very **defined**.*
double	double	Si je travaille le samedi, je suis payé en **double**. *If I work on Saturday, I get paid **double**.*
equivalent	équivalent	Une paire est **équivalente** à deux. *A pair is **equivalent** to two.*
financial	financier	Ma situation **financière** est privée. *My **financial** situation is private.*

historical	historique	Cette date commémore un événement **historique**. *That date commemorates a **historical** event.*
incorrect	incorrect	Il n'y a pas de manière **incorrecte** de le faire. *There is no **incorrect** way to do it.*
independent	indépendant	Les jeunes veulent être plus **indépendants**. *Young people wish to be more **independent**.*
intense	intense	Ce parfum est très **intense** pour moi. *That perfume is very **intense** to me.*
limited	limité	L'espace du patio est **limité**. *The patio's space is **limited**.*
logical	logique	Cette explication n'est pas **logique**. *This explanation is not **logical**.*
masculine male	masculin	Ces bottes ont l'air **masculines**. *Those boots look **masculine**.*
maximum	maximum	Je remplis la bouteille au **maximum**. *I fill the bottle to **maximum** capacity.*
medical	médical	J'ai un problème **médical**. *I have a **medical** issue.*
minimum	minimum	Il n'est pas recommandé de se contenter du **minimum**. *It's not recommended to just do the **minimum**.*
modest	modeste	Ce millionnaire est très **modeste**. *That millionaire is very **modest**.*
precious	précieux	Le vase de ma grand-mère est très **précieux**. *My grandma's vase is very **precious**.*
precise accurate	précis	Ils ont un horaire très **précis**. *They have a very **precise** schedule.*
ridiculous	ridicule	Ma réponse sera **ridicule**! *My answer will be **ridiculous**!*
separate	séparé	Ses parents sont **séparés**. *His parents are **separated**.*
sexual	sexuel	Le harcèlement **sexuel** est totalement inacceptable. ***Sexual** harassment is totally unacceptable.*
similar	similaire	Mes frères et sœurs et me sont très **similaires**. *My siblings and I are very **similar**.*
solid	solide	La surface ne semble pas **solide**. *The surface doesn't look **solid**.*
technical	technique	Je ne comprends pas les aspects **techniques** de la voiture. *I don't understand the **technical** aspects of the car.*

tender **gentle**	**tendre** [1]	La viande est très **tendre**. *The meat is very **tender**.*
traditional	**traditionnel**	J'aime la décoration plus **traditionnelle**. *I like the more **traditional** decor.*
unlimited	**illimité**	Ce qui peut être appris est **illimité**. *What can be learned is **unlimited**.*
valid	**valide**	Je crois qu'il a une raison **valide**. *I believe that he has a **valid** reason.*

3. RELIGION I

Below is some vocabulary related to *religion*, or "**la religion**," that you may need:

God	**Dieu**	*angel*	**ange**ᵐ
Koran	**Coran**ᵐ	*belief*	**croyance**ᶠ
Islam	**islam**ᵐ	*church*	**église**ᶠ
Muslim	**musulman(e)**	*faith*	**foi**ᶠ
Bible	**Bible**ᶠ	*devil*	**diable**ᵐ
Christianity	**christianisme**ᵐ	*demon*	**démon**ᵐ
Christian	**chrétien(ne)**	*heaven*	**paradis**ᵐ
Christmas	**Noël**ᵐ	*hell*	**enfer**ᵐ
Catholic	**catholique**ᵐ, ᶠ	*miracle*	**miracle**ᵐ
Catholicism	**catholicisme**ᵐ	*mosque*	**mosquée**ᶠ
Protestantism	**protestantisme**ᵐ	*pope*	**pape**ᵐ
Protestant	**protestant(e)**	*prayer*	**prière**ᶠ
Judaism	**judaïsme**ᵐ	*prophet*	**prophète**ᵐ
Jewish	**juif**ᵐ/**juive**ᶠ	*sin*	**péché**ᵐ
Buddhism	**bouddhisme**ᵐ	*soul*	**âme**ᶠ
Buddhist	**bouddhiste**ᵐ,ᶠ	*atheism*	**athéisme**ᵐ
Hinduism	**hindouisme**ᵐ	*atheist*	**athée**ᵐ, ᶠ
Hindu	**hindou(e)**	*Satan*	**Satan**ᵐ

4. MEDIA I

The *media*, a singular word in English, is a plural word in French, that is, "**les médias**ᵐ." Here is some related vocabulary:

advertising	**publicité**ᶠ	*press*	**presse**ᶠ
antenna	**antenne**ᶠ	*public TV*	**télévision publique**ᶠ

---

[1] The adjective "**tendre**" *(tender)* can also refer to human behavior, e.g., "**Ils sont tendres avec leurs enfants**" (*They are tender with their children*).

cable TV	**télédistribution**[f]	*radio station*	**station**[f] **de radio**
cinema	**cinéma**[m]	*rumor*	**rumeur**[f]
documentary	**documentaire**[m]	*scandal*	**scandale**[m]
fact check	**vérification**[f] **des faits**	*soap opera*	**feuilleton**[m]
magazine	**magazine**[m]	*television*	**télévision**[f] **télé**[f]
movie	**film**[m]	*TV channel*	**chaîne**[f] **de télévision**
news	**nouvelles**[f]	*TV series*	**série télévisée**[f]
news report	**reportage**[m]	*TV show*	**émission**[f] **de télévision**
newspaper	**journal**[m]	*voice*	**voix**[f]

5. HOUSE I

Here we learn a set of vocabulary related to the *house*, or **"la maison,"** in French:

address	**adresse**[f]	*glass (of water)*	**verre**[m] **(d'eau)**
alarm clock	**réveil**[m]	*glue*	**colle**[f]
armchair	**fauteuil**[m]	*ground floor*	**rez-de-chaussée**[m]
bag	**sac**[m]	*headboard*	**tête**[f] **de lit**
balcony	**balcon**[m]	*kettle*	**bouilloire**[f]
basement	**sous-sol**[m]	*key*	**clé**[f]
basin	**lavabo**[m]	*kitchen*	**cuisine**[f]
basket	**panier**[m] **corbeille**[f]	*knife*	**couteau**[m]
bathroom	**salle**[f] **de bain**	*ladle*	**louche**[f]
bathtub	**baignoire**[f]	*lamp*	**lampe**[f]
bed	**lit**[m]	*living room*	**salon**[m]
bedroom	**chambre**[f] **à coucher**	*mail*	**courrier**[m]
blanket	**couverture**[f]	*mirror*	**miroir**[m]
book	**livre**[m]	*outlet (electricity)*	**prise**[f]
bottle	**bouteille**[f]	*oven*	**four**[m]
bowl	**bol**[m]	*painting*	**peinture**[f]
box	**boîte**[f]	*photo*	**photo**[f]
carpet	**tapis**[m]	*pillow*	**oreiller**[m]
ceiling	**plafond**[m]	*refrigerator*	**réfrigérateur**[m] **frigo**[m]

cellar	**cave**f	*roof*	**toit**m
chair	**chaise**f	*room*	**chambre**f **salle**f **pièce**f
chimney	**cheminée**f	*saucepan*	**casserole**f
cigar	**cigare**m	*scale (kitchen)*	**balance**f
cigarette	**cigarette**f	*sink*	**évier**m
clock	**horloge**f	*sofa*	**canapé**m **sofa**m
cup	**tasse**f **coupe**f	*spoon*	**cuillère**f
desk	**bureau**m	*stairs*	**escaliers**m
dishes *plates*	**assiettes**f **vaisselle**f **plats**m	*stove*	**poêle**m **cuisinière**f
door	**porte**f	*study (room)*	**bureau**m
extractor	**extracteur**m	*table*	**table**f
fan	**ventilateur**m	*telephone*	**téléphone**m
faucet	**robinet**m	*thing*	**chose**f
floor	**sol**m	*towel*	**serviette**f
fork	**fourchette**f	*trash* *garbage*	**poubelle**f **ordures**f **déchets**m
freezer	**congélateur**m	*wall*	**mur**m
frying pan	**poêle**f **à frire**	*wardrobe*	**garde-robe**f **armoire**f
garage	**garage**m	*window*	**fenêtre**f

6. SPORTS I

Sport, or "**le sport**," contains a lot of vocabulary that we encounter in our daily life. Here we have some commonly used ones:

ball	**balle**f **ballon**m	*national team*	**équipe nationale**f
baseball	**baseball**m	*offside*	**hors-jeu**m
basketball	**basketball**m	*period*	**période**f
boxing	**boxe**f	*punch*	**coup**m **de poing**
championship	**championnat**m	*race*	**course**f
chess	**échecs**m	*referee*	**arbitre**m
court *field*	**terrain**m	*round*	**partie**f **tour**m

draw (tie)	**égalité**[f]	*scorer*	**buteur**[m]
entry / admission	**entrée**[f] **admission**[f]	*shot (soccer)*	**tir**[m]
exercise	**exercice**[m]	*stadium*	**stade**[m]
game	**jeu**[m]	*swimming*	**natation**[f]
goal	**but**[m]	*team*	**équipe**[f]
in top shape	**en pleine forme**	*tennis*	**tennis**[m]
injury	**blessure**[f]	*trainer coach*	**entraîneur**[m] / **entraîneuse**[f]
locker room	**vestiaire**[m]	*training*	**entraînement**[m]
match	**match**[m]	*wound*	**plaie**[f] **blessure**[f]

7. COLORS II

Some more colors and color-related words to add to your French vocabulary are:

burgundy	**bordeaux**[m,f]	*shade*	**ombre**[f]
magenta	**magenta**[m,f]	*tone*	**ton**[m]
pink	**rose**[m,f]	*violet*	**violet(te)**

8. TECHNOLOGY

Let us go over some vocabulary related to *technology* or "**la technologie**":

alert	**alerte**[f]	*input (device)*	**entrée**[f]
appliance	**appareil**[m]	*keyboard*	**clavier**[m]
atom	**atome**[m]	*laboratory*	**laboratoire**[m]
attachment	**pièce jointe**[f]	*laptop*	**ordinateur portable**[m]
backup file	**fichier**[m] **de sauvegarde**	*network*	**réseau**[m]
battery	**batterie**[f] **pile**[f]	*password*	**mot**[m] **de passe**
binary	**binaire**[m,f]	*patent*	**brevet**[m]
button	**bouton**[m]	*permission*	**autorisation**[f] **permission**[f]
cable	**câble**[m]	*printer*	**imprimante**[f]
calculator	**calculatrice**[f]	*program*	**programme**[m]
camera	**caméra**[f]	*reminder*	**rappel**[m]
CD player	**lecteur CD**[m]	*remote control*	**télécommande**[f]

cell phone	**téléphone cellulaire**[m] **téléphone portable**[m]	*satellite*	**satellite**[m]
charger	**chargeur**[m]	*search*	**recherche**[f]
circuit	**circuit**[m]	*screen*	**écran**[m]
code	**code**[m]	*short circuit*	**court-circuit**[m]
computer	**ordinateur**[m]	*speaker*	**haut-parleur**[m]
database	**base**[f] **de données**	*symbol*	**symbole**[m]
domain	**domaine**[m]	*telescope*	**télescope**[m]
downloading	**téléchargement**[m]	*testing*	**essai**[m] **test**[m]
email	**e-mail**[m]	*transmitter*	**émetteur**[m]
energy	**énergie**[f]	*uploading*	**téléchargement**[m]
file	**fichier**[m] **dossier**[m]	*volume*	**volume**[m]
fuse	**fusible**[m]	*weblink*	**lien web**[m]
headphones	**écouteurs**[m]	*wire*	**fil**[m]
home appliances	**électroménager**[m]	*wireless*	**sans fil**

9. TRAVEL

Travel, or "**le voyage,**" is another important topic with commonly used vocabulary, such as:

adventure	**aventure**[f]	*outskirts*	**périphérie**[f] **banlieue**[f]
accommodation	**logement**[m] **hébergement**[m]	*passenger*	**passager**[m]
arrival	**arrivée**[f]	*passport*	**passeport**[m]
carry-on luggage	**bagage**[m] **à main**	*public transportation*	**transport public**[m]
customs	**douane**[f]	*remote zone*	**zone reculée**[f]
delay	**retard**[m]	*security safety*	**sécurité**[f]
departure	**départ**[m]	*souvenir*	**souvenir**[m]
duty free	**hors taxes**	*suitcase*	**valise**[f]
guide	**guide**[m]	*tour*	**tour**[m] **excursion**[f]
holidays vacation	**vacances**[f]	*tourist*	**touriste**[m,f]
itinerary	**itinéraire**[m]	*traveler*	**voyageur**[m]
luggage	**bagage**[m]	*trip journey*	**voyage**[m]

10. LANGUAGE

There is a subtle difference between "**la langue**" and "**le langage**," both meaning language. Whereas "**langue**" is used to describe the real spoken language, e.g., "**la langue française**" *(the French language)*, "**langage**" is used to describe the way and the ability of humans and other beings to communicate, e.g., "**le langage parlé**" *(oral language)*. To describe computer languages, we also use "**langage**," e.g., "**le langage Java**" *(the Java language)*. Here is some vocabulary related to language:

acronym	**acronyme**[m]	*native*	**indigène**[m,f]
adjective	**adjectif**[m]	*noun*	**nom**[m]
alphabet	**alphabet**[m]	*paragraph*	**paragraphe**[m]
Arabic	**arabe**[m]	*passage*	**passage**[m]
auxiliary	**auxiliaire**[m]	*passive*	**passif**[m]
clause	**clause**[f]	*phrase*	**phrase**[f]
conjunction	**conjonction**[f]	*Portuguese*	**portugais**[m]
conjugation	**conjugaison**[f]	*preposition*	**préposition**[f]
dialect	**dialecte**[m]	*pronoun*	**pronom**[m]
dictionary	**dictionnaire**[m]	*proverb*	**proverbe**[m]
discourse	**discours**[m]	*semantics*	**sémantique**[f]
emphasis	**accent**[m]	*sentence*	**phrase**[f]
figurative	**figuratif**[m]	*slang*	**argot**[m]
fluency	**maîtrise**[f] **aisance**[f]	*subjunctive*	**subjonctif**[m]
fluent	**courant(e)**	*suffix*	**suffixe**[m]
grammar	**grammaire**[f]	*superlative*	**superlatif**[m]
Hindi	**hindi**[m]	*syllable*	**syllabe**[f]
idiom	**idiome**[m]	*tale*	**conte**[m]
indicative	**indicatif**[m]	*translation*	**traduction**[f]
infinitive	**infinitif**[m]	*Urdu*	**ourdou**[m]
interjection	**interjection**[f]	*verb*	**verbe**[m]
letter	**lettre**[f]	*verb tense*	**temps**[m] **des verbes**
level	**niveau**[m]	*vocabulary*	**vocabulaire**[m]
Mandarin	**mandarin**[m]	*vowel*	**voyelle**[f]
mood	**humeur**[f]	*word*	**mot**[m]

L E V E L   I V :   I N T E R M E D I A T E

I. Introductory Topics & Grammar

At this intermediate level, we encounter new topics. Some will be familiar thanks to our knowledge of English, and some new topics are unique to the French language. Use the Anki cards to reinforce these topics in your memory with reviews and exercises.

1. DEGREES OF COMPARISON

In this lesson, we will examine different ways of comparing nouns, indicating their equality, inequality, or the extreme degree of an adjective. We will study the comparison of equality, the comparison of inequality, and superlatives.

Comparatives of Equality

The most common expressions in this category are:

1. **aussi** + (adjective/adverb) + **que** …   *as (adj./adv.) as …*

Cette voiture est **aussi** chère **qu'**une maison.	*This car is **as** expensive **as** a house.*
Elle est **aussi** grande **que** sa sœur.	*She is **as** tall **as** her sister.*
Il parle **aussi** clairement **qu'**un professeur.	*He speaks **as** clearly **as** a teacher.*

2. **autant de** + (noun) + **que** …   *as much/many (noun) as …*

Il a **autant d'**argent **qu'**un millionnaire.	*He has **as much** money **as** a millionaire.*
Il y a **autant de** monde ici **qu'**à Londres.	*There are **as many** people here **as** in London.*

Comparatives of Inequality

The following formula is used to express inequality when comparing two adjectives, adverbs, or nouns:

plus/moins (de)… que …   *more/less … than …*

For example:

Elle est **plus** grande **que** sa sœur.	*She is taller than her sister.*
Il parle **plus** clairement **qu'**un professeur.	*He speaks more clearly than a teacher.*
Il a **plus d'**argent **que** le président.	*He has more money than the president.*
Nous sommes **moins** riches **que** nos parents.	*We are less rich than our parents.*
Il parle **moins** clairement **qu'**un professeur.	*He speaks less clearly than a teacher.*
Il a **moins de** patience **que** mon frère.	*He has less patience than my brother.*

Notice that "**de**" is added only when comparing nouns, but not when comparing adjectives or adverbs.

It is also possible to use the above structure to compare an adjective to another adjective of the same noun. For example:

Son discours est **plus** émotif **que** précis.	*His speech is **more** emotional **than** it is accurate.*
Ils sont **plus** professionnels **qu'**expérimentés.	*They are **more** professional **than** they are experienced.*

Only few adjectives and adverbs have irregular forms, or both regular and irregular forms. Here are the most common irregular adjectives (in the singular masculine form) and adverbs:

bon	*good*	**meilleur**	*better*
mauvais	*bad*	**pire** (or) **plus mauvais**	*worse*
petit	*little*	**moins**	*less*
bien	*well*	**mieux**	*better*
mal	*badly*	**pire** (or) **plus mal**	*worse*
peu	*little*	**moins**	*less*

Superlatives

There are two ways to express the large or extreme degrees of an adjective.

1. Relative Superlatives

| **le/la/les** + **plus/moins** + (adjective) | *the* + *most/least* + *(adjective)* |

Here are some examples:

Elle est **la plus** intelligente de sa classe.	*She is **the most** intelligent in her class.*
Nous sommes **les moins** touchés par la crise.	*We are **the least** affected by the crisis.*
C'est le sujet **le plus** important du pays.	*This is **the most** important topic in the country.*
Il est le politicien **le moins** corrompu du parlement.	*He is **the least** corrupt politician in the parliament.*
Ce sont les femmes **les plus** courageuses que j'ai jamais vues.	*They are **the most** courageous women I have ever seen.*

The following adjectives (listed here in their singular masculine form) and adverbs have irregular forms as relative superlatives:

bon	*good*	**le meilleur**	*best*
mauvais	*bad*	**le pire** (or) **le plus mauvais**	*worst*
petit	*little*	**le moindre**	*least*
bien	*well*	**le mieux**	*best*
mal	*badly*	**le pire** (or) **le plus mal**	*worst*
peu	*little*	**le moins**	*least*

2. Absolute Superlatives

One can express an absolute superlative by simply preceding the adjective with an adverb such as "**très**" (*very*) or "**extrêmement**" (*extremely*). For example:

| Ce stade est **très** froid. | *This stadium is **very** cold.* |
| Le café est **extrêmement** chaud. | *The coffee is **extremely** hot.* |

2. PARTITIVES

To refer to an unidentified quantity of something in English, we often use words or phrases like *"some," "a few,"* and *"a little bit of."* These are called *partitives* because they refer to a part of something, whether it is countable, e.g., *"some trees,"* or uncountable, e.g., *"some water."*

In French, the most common way to form a partitive is using the preposition "**de**" followed by a definite article, also known as a *partitive article*. This would literally translate to *"of the."* However, it serves more as an equivalent to the partitive *"some"* in English.

Countable Nouns

Because countable nouns have a plural form, we use the partitive article "**des**," which comes from the contraction of the preposition "**de**" and the plural definite article "**les**."

Let us look at some examples with countable nouns:

un garçon	*a boy*	des garçons	*some boys*
un arbre	*a tree*	des arbres	*some trees*
une maison	*a house*	des maisons	*some houses*
une erreur	*a mistake*	des erreurs	*some mistakes*

Remember that using partitive articles is not the only way to describe an undefined quantity of countable nouns. For example, the partitive word "**quelques**," meaning *"some,"* can be used. The more specific partitive "**certain(e)s**" *(certain)* can also be used depending on the context.

Let us look at some examples:

| un livre | *a book* | quelques livres | certains livres | *some books* |
| une fille | *a girl* | quelques filles | certaines filles | *some houses* |

Uncountable Nouns

By countable nouns, we refer to nouns that are not often used in plural form, even if a plural form can be used in some contexts. For example, in English, we could say *"three fruits"* referring to three pieces of fruit. However, the word *"fruit"* is often used as an uncountable noun. Here, we discuss how to refer to an undefined quantity of such nouns when used in their uncountable form.

To refer to an uncountable noun using a partitive article, we treat it as a singular noun. Thus, we use the preposition **"de"** followed by the singular definite article **"le," "la,"** or **"l'."** This results in the three following partitive articles:

	l'	=	de l'	Before a **masculine** or a **feminine** noun that begins with a vowel or a mute **"h"**
de +	le	=	du	Before a **masculine** noun that does not begin with a vowel or a mute **"h"**
	la	=	de la	Before a **feminine** noun that does not begin with a vowel or a mute **"h"**

Let us look at some examples with uncountable nouns:

l'eau	*the water*	**de l'eau**	*some water*
le sucre	*the sugar*	**du sucre**	*some sugar*
la viande	*the meat*	**de la viande**	*some meat*
le pain	*the bread*	**du pain**	*some bread*
la pluie	*the rain*	**de la pluie**	*some rain*
le lait	*the milk*	**du lait**	*some milk*

As an alternative to partitive articles, one can, depending on the context, use the partitive word **"un peu de"** *(a bit of)* to refer to an undefined quantity of an uncountable noun.

Here are some examples:

l'eau	*the water*	**un peu d'eau**	*a bit of water*
le sucre	*the sugar*	**un peu de sucre**	*a bit of sugar*
la viande	*the meat*	**un peu de viande**	*a bit of meat*

Further Notes on Partitive Articles

❖ Remember that if an adjective precedes the noun, the definite article, and thus the partitive article, must change according to the beginning of the adjective, e.g., **"d'orge"** *(some barley)* vs. **"de la nouvelle orge"** *(some new barley)*.

❖ Some verbs in French require the preposition **"de,"** e.g., **"avoir besoin de"** *(to need)*. In this case, an alternative partitive such as "**quelques**" or "**un peu de**" can be used instead, e.g., "**J'ai besoin de <u>quelques</u> livres à lire sur le sujet**" *(I need <u>some</u> books to read on the subject).*

❖ In negative sentences, the partitive is omitted and replaced with "**de**," whether the noun is countable or uncountable, e.g., "**Je n'ai pas <u>d'</u>oncles**" *(I don't have uncles),* "**Je ne veux pas <u>de</u> sucre**" *(I don't want sugar),* "**Il n'y a pas <u>de</u> pain**" *(There isn't bread),* etc. The only exception is when the verb "**être**" *(to be)* is used. In this case, the partitive article is used, e.g., "**Ce n'est pas <u>de l'</u>eau**" *(This is not water),* "**Ce n'est pas <u>de la</u> viande**" *(This is not meat).*

❖ In negative sentences with countable nouns, the negative meaning of *"any,"* as in *"There aren't any books,"* can be rendered by the use of "**aucun(e)**." The word "**aucun(e)**" is treated like an indefinite article. It conveys the meaning of *"not one"* or *"not any,"* and it is always followed by a singular noun even if the meaning is plural. Here are some examples:

Il n'y a **aucun** arbre dans le désert.	*There aren't **any** trees in the desert.*
Il n'y a **aucune** maison dans cette zone.	*There aren't **any** houses in this area.*

Remember, however, that "**aucun(e)**" cannot be used with uncountable nouns.

3. REFLEXIVE PRONOUNS & VERBS

A verb is considered reflexive if the subject and the object of the verb are the same. This means that the subject is doing the action to itself, not to something or someone else. For instance, *"I wash myself"* is reflexive, while *"I wash my car"* is not reflexive.

Some verbs in French are commonly used in the reflexive form. Let us take a look at one example that you may be familiar with. The verb "**appeler**" means *"to call,"* e.g., "**Ma mère m'appelle tous les vendredis**" *(My mom calls me every Friday).* However, the reflexive form of the verb "**s'appeler**," which literally means *"to call oneself,"* is used to express one's name. For instance, "**Je m'appelle Pierre**" means

"My name is Pierre," which is literally *"I call myself Pierre."* A reflexive verb is formed by preceding the verb in the infinitive with **"se"** or **"s'"** before a vowel or mute **"h,"** often translated as *"oneself."*

There are many verbs in French that have reflexive forms. We will discuss some examples; however, let us first learn how to conjugate reflexive verbs. Consider the verb **"se laver"** *(to wash oneself)* as an example.

	Object Personal Pron.	**e.g., se laver**
je	me	lave
tu	te	laves
il/elle/on	se	lave
nous	nous	lavons
vous	vous	lavez
ils/elles	se	lavent

As shown in the table, we add the object personal pronoun before the verb. Note that the subject and object personal pronouns are of the same gender and number because the subject and the object are essentially the same.

Remember that when the verb is used in reflexive form, the infinitive is preceded with **"se,"** e.g., **"se laver."** Here are more examples of reflexive verbs.

se lever	*to get up*	**s'ennuyer**	*to get bored*
se fâcher	*to get mad*	**s'arrêter**	*to stop oneself*
s'amuser	*to have fun*	**se doucher**	*to take a shower*
se preparer / **s'apprêter**	*to get ready*	**se brosser**	*to brush (one's hair or teeth)*
se coucher	*to go to bed*	**se coiffer**	*to fix one's hair*
se reposer	*to rest*	**se rassembler**	*to gather*
se relaxer	*to relax*	**se perdre**	*to get lost*
se faire mal	*to hurt oneself*	**s'inquiéter (de)**	*to worry (about)*
se promener	*to walk*	**se raser**	*to shave*
se souvenir	*to remember*	**se réjouir**	*to rejoice*
se dépêcher	*to hurry*	**se remettre (de)**	*to recover*
s'asseoir	*to sit down*	**se sentir**	*to feel*
se fouler	*to twist or sprain*	**se déshabiller**	*to undress oneself*

se fatiguer	*to get tired*	**se réveiller**	*to wake up*
se saouler	*to get drunk*	**s'habiller**	*to get dressed*
se peigner	*to comb one's hair*	**se nuire**	*to harm oneself*
se noyer	*to drown*	**se moucher**	*to blow one's nose*
se marier	*to get married*	**se maquiller**	*to put on makeup*
s'intéresser à	*to be interested in*	**s'habituer à**	*to get used to*
s'imaginer	*to imagine*	**s'inscrire à**	*to enroll or register*
se fier à	*to trust*	**se faire**	*to make oneself (a coffee, meal, etc.)*
s'enrhumer	*to catch a cold*	**s'énerver**	*to get annoyed*
s'endormir	*to fall asleep*	**se couper**	*to cut oneself*
s'éloigner	*to move away*	**s'effrayer**	*to be frightened*

Let us look at some examples:

Je **m'ennuie** vite à la maison.	*I **get bored** fast at home.*
Elle **se lève** toujours tôt.	*She always **gets up** early.*
Nous **nous amusons** beaucoup ensemble.	*We **have** a lot of **fun** together.*
Je **me rase** deux fois par semaine.	*I **shave** twice a week.*

One can add the reflexive pronoun to verbs that are not usually reflexive to make them reflexive, for example:

se parler	*to speak to each other*	**se voir**	*to see each other*
se comprendre	*to understand each other*	**s'acheter**	*to buy oneself something*

Some verbs are used *only* in reflexive form, such as **"se suicider"** *(to commit suicide)*.

Some verbs change their meaning when they are used in reflexive form, for example:

ennuyer	*to bore*	**s'ennuyer**	*to get bored*
coucher	*to lay down*	**se coucher**	*to lie down or go to bed*
marier	*to join in marriage*	**se marier**	*to get married*
endormir	*to put to sleep*	**s'endormir**	*to fall asleep*

Finally, keep in mind that all reflexive verbs use the auxiliary **"être"** when conjugated in the compound past, regardless of the auxiliary used by the non-reflexive form of the verb. For example:

Je **me <u>suis</u> ennuyé** hier soir.	*I **got bored** last night.*
Elle **s'<u>est</u> réveillée** tôt aujourd'hui.	*She **woke up** early today.*

Nous **nous** <u>**sommes**</u> beaucoup **amusés** hier.	*We **had** a lot of **fun** yesterday.*
Je **me** <u>**suis**</u> **rasé** la semaine dernière.	*I **shaved** last week.*
Elles **se** <u>**sont**</u> **veus** par hasard.	*They **saw each other** by accident.*

Remember that when "**être**," is used as an auxiliary, the past participle takes the treatment of an adjective and must agree in gender and number with the subject.

4. EXPRESSIONS USING "AVOIR" & "FAIRE"

Some expressions in French do not make sense if literally translated into English. In this section, we will learn some expressions using "**avoir**" *(to have)* and "**faire**" *(to do or to make)* that are common in French.

1. Expressions using "**Avoir**"

In addition to the obvious use of "**avoir**" to indicate possession, e.g., "**J'ai deux chats**" (*I have two cats*), there are some less obvious uses of the verb "**avoir**" in French.

In English, we use the verb *"to be"* to describe age, as in *"how old <u>are</u> you?"* and *"I <u>am</u> 30 years old."* In French, the verb "**avoir**" is used instead; that is, we literally say, *"I have 30 years old"* rather than, *"I am 30 years old."* Here are a few more examples:

Quel âge **as**-tu?	*How old **are** you?*
J'ai 40 ans.	*I **am** 40 years old.*
Il **a** 20 ans.	*He **is** 20 years old.*

Some expressions in French describe a feeling or desire using the verb "**avoir**," while their equivalents in English use the verb *"to be,"* e.g., "**J'ai peur**" *(I <u>am</u> afraid).* The word "**peur**" means *"fear."* Thus, we literally say, *"I have fear."* Some other examples include:

avoir faim	*to be hungry*	**avoir soif**	*to be thirsty*
avoir froid	*to be cold*	**avoir chaud**	*to be hot*
avoir sommeil	*to be sleepy*	**avoir peur**	*to be afraid*

Finally, there are many other idioms and expressions that use the verb "**avoir**," such as:

avoir raison	*to be right*	**avoir tort**	*to be wrong*
avoir du succès	*to be successful*	**avoir lieu**	*to take place*
avoir mal à	*to have pain in*	**avoir de la chance**	*to be lucky*
avoir la parole	*to have the floor*	**avoir besoin de**	*to need*
avoir envie de	*to feel like*	**avoir un fou rire**	*to giggle*
avoir horreur de	*to hate something*	**avoir l'air**	*to look like*
avoir du charme	*to be charming*	**avoir honte de**	*to be ashamed of*
avoir le coup de foudre	*to fall in love at first sight*	**avoir l'habitude de**	*to be used to*

2. Expressions using "**Faire**"

There are many expressions that use the verb "**faire**" *(to do or to make)* in French, when similar expressions in English would not. We have encountered the verb "**faire**" used with weather expressions in **Level III, Lesson 6**, e.g., "**Il fait froid**" *(It is cold)*.

Let us examine some other expressions that use the verb "**faire**." In general, we use the verb "**faire**" when referring to sports and hobbies. Here are some examples:

faire du sport	*to play sports*	**faire de la gym**	*to go to the gym*
faire du surf	*to do surfing*	**faire une promenade**	*to take a walk*
faire du vélo	*to go cycling*	**faire du snowboard**	*to snowboard*

The verb "**faire**" is also used with many house chores and day-to-day tasks. Examples include:

faire des devoirs	*to do homework*	**faire la lessive**	*to do laundry*
faire le lit	*to make the bed*	**faire le plein**	*to fill up on gas*
faire les courses	*to buy groceries*	**faire les magasins**	*to go shopping*
faire le ménage	*to do the chores*	**faire le ménage**	*to do the cleaning*

There are many other idioms and expressions that use the verb "**faire**" that do not fall under any of the aforementioned categories, such as:

faire la queue	*to wait in line*	**Ça ne fait rien.**	*It doesn't matter.*
faire mal	*to hurt or to be painful*	**faire une pause**	*to take a break*

faire une sieste	*to take a nap*	**faire soi-même**	*DIY*
faire attention	*to pay attention*	**faire des économies**	*to save money*
faire la grasse matinée	*to sleep in*	**faire la sourde oreille**	*to turn a deaf ear*
faire la fête	*to party*	**faire la tête**	*to be in a bad mood*
faire la manche	*to beg*	**faire des cauchemars**	*to have nightmares*

Finally, the verb "**faire**" can be used in many causative expressions meaning *"to have someone do something."* For example:

Il me **fait voir** la différence.	*He **makes** me **see** the difference.*
Je lui **fais écrire** pour moi.	*I **have** him **write** for me.*

5. Present Subjunctive Tense I

All the tenses we have encountered so far were in the indicative mood. The indicative mood is what we use to express facts. This is the mood we encounter often. There are five moods in total in French: infinitive, indicative, subjunctive, imperative, and conditional. The subjunctive mood is used to express opinion, possibility, and feelings, such as fear, doubt, hope, desire, etc. Generally speaking, the indicative describes facts, whereas the subjunctive describes non-facts.

To conjugate verbs in the present subjunctive, we begin from the *third-person plural in the present indicative*, that is, the "**ils/ells**" form, e.g., "**parlent**," "**finissent**," "**vendent**," etc., and we extract the stem from these verbs "**parl-**," "**finiss-**," "**vend-**," etc., by dropping the last "**-ent**." Then, we add the endings shown in the following table:

	parler *(to speak)*	**finir** *(to finish)*	**vendre** *(to sell)*
	ils <u>parl</u>ent	ils <u>finiss</u>ent	ils <u>vend</u>ent
je	parl**e**	finiss**e**	vend**e**
tu	parl**es**	finiss**es**	vend**es**
il/elle/on	parl**e**	finiss**e**	vend**e**
nous	parl**ions**	finiss**ions**	vend**ions**
vous	parl**iez**	finiss**iez**	vend**iez**
ils/elles	parl**ent**	finiss**ent**	vend**ent**

It is important that you remember to use the stem from the **"ils/elles"** form in the present indicative, not the stem from the infinitive. This is especially important with verbs that are irregular in the **"ils/elles"** form in the present indicative.

There are some irregular verbs that do not follow the aforementioned conjugation patterns. These include the following:

1. The verbs **"être"** *(to be)* and **"avoir"** *(to have)* are irregular and must be memorized.

	être	**avoir**
je	sois	aie
tu	sois	aies
il/elle/on	soit	ait
nous	soyons	ayons
vous	soyez	ayez
ils/elles	soient	aient

2. In some verbs, the **"nous"** and **"vous"** forms are conjugated differently. The stem is formed from the *first-person plural in the present indicative*, that is, the **"nous"** form, by dropping the suffix **"-ons."** Here are some examples:

	je	tu	il/elle	nous	vous	ils/elles
appeler *to call*	appelle	appelles	appelle	appelions	appeliez	appellent
acheter *to buy*	achète	achètes	achète	achetions	achetiez	achètent
boir *to drink*	boive	boives	boive	buvions	buviez	boivent
croire *to believe*	croie	croies	croie	croyions	croyiez	croient
jeter *to throw*	jette	jettes	jette	jetions	jetiez	jettent
mourir *to die*	meure	meures	meure	mourions	mouriez	meurent
préférer *to prefer*	préfère	préfères	préfère	préférions	préfériez	préfèrent
prendre *to take*	prenne	prennes	prenne	prenions	preniez	prennent

	je	tu	il/elle	nous	vous	ils/elles
recevoir *to receive*	reçoive	reçoives	reçoive	recevions	receviez	reçoivent
tenir *to hold*	tienne	tiennes	tienne	tenions	teniez	tiennent
venir *to come*	vienne	viennes	vienne	venions	veniez	viennent
voir *to see*	voie	voies	voie	voyions	voyiez	voient

3. Some verbs have irregular stems but regular endings. The most common ones are:

	je	tu	il/elle	nous	vous	ils/elles
aller *to go*	aille	ailles	aille	allions	alliez	aillent
faire *to do*	fasse	fasses	fasse	fassions	fassiez	fassent
pouvoir *to rain*	puisse	puisses	puisse	puissions	puissiez	puissent
savoir *to know*	sache	saches	sache	sachions	sachiez	sachent
valoir *to be worth*	vaille	vailles	vaille	valions	valiez	vaillent
vouloir *to want*	veuille	veuilles	veuille	voulions	vouliez	veuillent

In addition, the verb "**falloir**" *(to be necessary)* is impersonal and has only a third-person singular form, which is irregular in the subjunctive, i.e., "**il faille**" *(it is necessary)*.

The subjunctive is usually used in subordinate clauses that use the conjunction "**que**" *(that)*, where the main clause expresses opinions and feelings such as fear, doubt, hope, desire, etc.

	Examples
Impersonal opinion	**Il est important que** vous mangiez bien. *It is important that you eat well.*
Emotion	**Je suis content qu'**ils aillent bien. *I'm glad they are well.*
Doubt	**Je doute qu'**il y ait du soleil aujourd'hui. *I doubt that it is sunny today.*
Desire	**Je veux qu'**il étudie bien. *I want him to study well.*

Expressing Opinions

Knowing when to use the indicative mood and when to use the subjunctive mood when expressing an opinion in French can be a little tricky. Nevertheless, these are the main guidelines:

1. Impersonal Opinions

For impersonal opinions, such as *"it is important that …,"* *"it is good that …,"* and *"it is bad that …,"* we generally use the subjunctive mood, for example:

Il est important que vous <u>rendiez</u> visite à votre famille.	***It is important that*** *you <u>visit</u> your family.*
C'est bien que vous <u>soyez</u> ici aujourd'hui.	***It is good that*** *you <u>are</u> here today.*
Il faut que vous <u>suiviez</u> les règles.	***It is necessary that*** *you <u>follow</u> the rules.*

However, if the impersonal opinion expresses some sense of certainty, such as *"it is true that …"* or *"it is clear that …,"* the indicative mood is used, for example:

C'est vrai que je <u>veux</u> sortir aujourd'hui.	***It is true that*** *I <u>want</u> to go out today.*
Il est clair qu'ils <u>peuvent</u> gagner ce match.	***It is clear that*** *they <u>can</u> win this match.*

If any of the above expressions are used to express doubt, the subjunctive mood must be used, for example:

Il n'est pas certain qu'ils <u>puissent</u> gagner ce match.	***It is not certain that*** *they <u>can</u> win this match.*

2. Personal Opinions

If the main clause expresses an opinion in the negative, the subordinate clause is in the subjunctive mood, for example:

Je ne pense pas que cette maison <u>soit</u> trop grande.	***I don't think that*** *this house <u>is</u> too big.*

| **Je ne crois pas qu'il y ait** des gens qui vivent là-bas. | *I don't believe that there are people living there.* |

If the main clause is in the affirmative, the subordinate clause must be in the indicative, not in the subjunctive mood, for example:

| **Je pense que** cette maison est trop grande. | *I think that this house is too big.* |
| **Je crois qu'il y a** des gens qui vivent là-bas. | *I believe that there are people living there.* |

Note also that it is the main clause that determines the use of the indicative or the subjunctive. For instance, in the sentence "**Je pense que cette maison n'est pas grande**" *(I believe that the house is not big)*, we use the indicative because the main clause "**Je pense que**" is in the affirmative.

Expressing Possibilities

Most expressions that express the possibility or probability of something being one way or the other use the subjunctive mood. For example:

| **Il est possible que** ce soit nuageux à l'extérieur. | *It is possible that it is cloudy outside.* |
| **Il se pourrait que** Mark soit coincé dans les embouteillages. | *It could be that Mark is stuck in traffic.* |

A notable exception that uses the indicative is "**peut-être**," meaning *"perhaps"* or *"maybe,"* for example:

| **Peut-être** que c'est nuageux dehors. | *Maybe it is cloudy outside.* |

Expressing Desires, Wishes, Feelings, and Requests

In general, desires, wishes, feelings, and requests are expressed in the subjunctive mood. The main clause can be in the present or the past, for example:

| **Je veux que** tu sois poli. | *I want you to be polite.* |

Je demande que nous <u>ayons</u> plus de temps.	*I request that we <u>have</u> more time.*
Je suis content que tu <u>fasses</u> ton travail à temps.	*I'm glad you <u>do</u> your job on time.*
Je voulais que tu <u>viennes</u> chez moi.	*I wanted you to <u>come</u> to my house.*

When the verb in the main clause is used to express desire, the subjunctive mood is only used if the subject and the performer of the action are not the same. For example:

Je veux que tu <u>fasses</u> cette tâche.	*I want you to <u>do</u> this task.*

If the subject and the performer of the action are the same, we use the infinitive following the verb. For example:

Je veux <u>faire</u> cette tâche.	*I want to <u>do</u> this task.*

6. IMPERSONAL VERBS & EXPRESSIONS

Some verbs are used only in third-person singular, i.e., "**il**" form. For example, some weather expressions such as "**il pleut**" *(it is raining)* and "**il neige**" *(it is snowing)* are always in the third-person singular form. Such verbs are called impersonal verbs.

In addition to impersonal verbs, there are impersonal expressions. These are often expressed in English using statements that start with *"it is."* In French, "**il est**" or "**c'est**" is often used, e.g., "**C'est vrai que la situation est mauvaise**" *(It is true that the situation is bad)*. Remember that some impersonal expressions require the use of the subjunctive.

One common impersonal expression in French is "**il s'agit de**," which is often translated as *"it is about"* or *"it is a matter of."* Here are some examples:

Il s'agit de priorités.	*It is about priorities.*
Il ne **s'agit** pas seulement **de** financement.	*It is not only about funding.*
Ce livre, **il s'agit d'**une histoire réelle.	*This book is about a real story.*
De quoi **s'agit-il?**	*What is it about?*

Some verbs can only be in the third-person singular, that is, in impersonal form, such as **"falloir"** *(to be necessary)* and **"valoir"** *(to be worth)*. On the other hand, there are verbs that have a personal meaning, but can also be used in impersonal form, in which case the meaning is different. For example, when the verb **"arriver"** *(to arrive)* is used in impersonal form, it means *"to happen,"* e.g., **"Je ne sais pas ce qui va arriver"** *(I don't know what will happen)*.

Here is a list of some common impersonal verbs that may or may not have a personal meaning:

arriver	Il **arrive** rarement que l'expédition soit retardée.
to happen	*It rarely **happens** that the shipment is delayed.*
falloir	Il **faut** d'abord que vous prépariez les documents.
to be necessary	*It **is necessary** that you first prepare the documents.*
importer	Peu **importe** qui ils sont.
to be important	*It doesn't **matter** who they are.*
manquer	Il **manque** deux reçus aux documents.
to be missing	*Two receipts **are missing** from the documents.*
rester	Il **reste** cinq minutes jusqu'à la fin.
to remain	*There **remains** five minutes until the end.*
se trouver	Il **se trouve** que cette fois le résultat est le même.
to happen to be	*It **happens** that this time the result is the same.*
se passer	Qu'est-ce qui **s'est passé**?
to happen	*What **happened**?*
se pouvoir	Il **se peut** que certains détails nous échappent.
to be possible	*It **is possible** that we miss out on some details.*
sembler	Ça **semble** à première vue difficile à prévoir.
to seem	*It **seems** hard to predict at first.*
suffire	Ça **suffit** pour moi.
to be enough	*That **is enough** for me.*
valoir le coup	C'est un peu cher mais ça **vaut le coup**.
to be worth it	*It is a bit pricey but it **is worth it**.*
valoir le mieux	Il **vaut mieux** préserver votre vie privée.
to be better	*It **is better** to preserve your privacy.*
venir	Il **vient** un moment où il faut prendre une décision.
to come	*There **comes** a time when you have to make a decision.*

7. FUTURE PERFECT TENSE

The future perfect tense, similar to its use in English, describes events that will happen and be completed in the future by a certain time or after another event is completed in the future.

We use the auxiliary "**avoir**" or "**être**" in the future tense followed by a past participle. The auxiliary "**avoir**" or "**être**" in future tense serves a similar function to the auxiliary *"will have"* in English, e.g., *"I will have done my homework by the time they come."*

The verb "**avoir**" in the future form is conjugated as follows:

		-er ending parlare	-ir ending finir	-re ending vendre
j'	aurai			
tu	auras			
il/elle/on	aura			
nous	aurons	parlé	fini	vendu
vous	aurez			
ils/elles	auront			

On the other hand, the verb "**être**" in the future form is conjugated as follows:

		-er ending e.g., aller	-ir ending e.g., partir	-re ending e.g., descendre
je	serai	allé(e)	parti(e)	descendu(e)
tu	seras	allé(e)	parti(e)	descendu(e)
il/on	sera	allé	parti	descendu
elle	sera	allée	partie	descendue
nous	serons	allé(e)s	parti(e)s	descendu(e)s
vous	serez	allé(e)s	parti(e)s	descendu(e)s
ils	seront	allés	partis	descendus
elles	seront	allées	parties	descendues

Recall from **Level III, Lesson 1** that some verbs have irregular past participle forms.

Let us look at some examples of the future perfect tense:

J'**aurai visité** l'Egypte en janvier.	*I **will have visited** Egypt in January.*
Tu **auras bu** le café.	*You **will have drunk** the coffee.*

Elle **aura parlé** à sa mère.	*She **will have spoken** to her mother.*
Nous **aurons mangé**.	*We **will have eaten**.*
Vous **serez arrivés**.	*You **will have arrived**.*

8. Interjections

Interjections are mere exclamation words or expressions that usually represent feelings like surprise or anger. Interjections are often followed by an exclamation mark.

		Examples
Quel …!	*What…!*	**Quel** beau chat! ***What** a beautiful cat!*
Comment …!	*How…!*	**Comment** il chante! ***How** he sings!*
Combien…!	*How much…!*	**Combien** je l'aime! ***How** much I love her!*
Aïe!	*Ouch!*	**Aïe**, ça fait mal. ***Ouch**, it hurts.*
Attention!	*Careful!*	**Attention**! C'est sombre. ***Careful**! It's dark.*
Assez!	*Enough!*	**Assez**! Je suis fatigué. ***Enough**! I'm tired.*
Bien!	*Alright!*	**Bien**! Attendons et on verra. ***Alright**! Let's wait and see.*
Bon appétit!	*Enjoy your meal!*	Voici. **Bon appétit!** *Here you go. **Enjoy your meal!***
Bonne chance!	*Good luck!*	À bientôt. **Bonne chance!** *See you soon. **Good luck!***
Bien sûr!	*Of course!*	-Avez-vous faim? -**Bien sûr!** *-Are you hungry? -**Of course.***
Hein!	*Huh?* *What?*	Pas mal, **hein?** *Not bad, **huh?***
Oh là là!	*Oh! Wow!*	**Oh là là**! Il est trop tard. **Oh! Wow**! It's too late.
Quel ennui!	*How boring!*	J'attends encore. **Quel ennui!** *I'm still waiting. **How boring!***
Quelle horreur!	*How awful!*	C'était mauvais. **Quelle horreur!** *It was bad. **How awful!***
Quel dommage!	*What a pity!*	Nous avons perdu. **Quel dommage!** *We lost. **What a pity!***

Vraiment?!	*For real?!*	**Vraiment?!** C'est arrivé? *For real?! This happened?*
Hourra!	*Hurray!*	Oui, c'est maintenant. **Hourra!** *Yes, it's time.* **Hurray!**
S'il vous plaît!	*Please!*	Apportez-le avec vous, **s'il vous plaît!** *Bring it with you,* **please!**
Évidemment!	*Obviously!*	- Cela te plaît-il? -**Évidemment!** *-Do you like it? -***Obviously!**
Pour l'amour de Dieu!	*For God's sake!*	Que s'est-il passé, **pour l'amour de Dieu?** *What happened,* **for God's sake?**
Va-t'en!	*Go away!*	Je n'ai pas le temps. **Va-t'en!** I don't have time. **Go away!**
Tais-toi! Ferme-la!	*Shut up!*	**Tais-toi!** J'ai du travail à faire. **Shut up!** *I have work to do.*

II. Vocabulary Building

Go over the vocabulary in this section. You could use Anki to study and memorize the new vocabulary efficiently.

1. VERBS IV

Below is a list of verbs that we need at this level:

English	French	Examples
achieve	atteindre réaliser	Il **a atteint** ses objectifs pour ce mois. *He **achieved** his goals for that month.*
act	agir	J'**agis** toujours de manière polie. *I always **act** in a polite manner.*
add	ajouter	J'**ai ajouté** une tasse d'eau au mélange. *I **added** a cup of water to the mixture.*
advise	conseiller	Mon ami m'**a conseillé** sur les universités l'année dernière. *My friend **advised** me about the universities last year.*
apologize	s'excuser	Je m'**excuse**, je l'ai fait involontairement. *I **apologize**, I did it unintentionally.*
avenge	venger	Le héros voulait **venger** la mort de son père. *The hero wanted to **avenge** his father's death.*

avoid	éviter[1]	Je voulais **éviter** de le voir au café. *I wanted to **avoid** seeing him in the café.*
bake	cuire	Je viens de **cuire** cette tarte. *I **have just baked** this pie.*
bathe	prendre un bain	**Prendre un bain** est relaxant. ***Bathing** in the tub is relaxing.*
bounce	rebondir	Les ballons de basket **rebondissent** beaucoup. *Basketballs **bounce** a lot.*
brush	brosser	Vous devez **brosser** le manteau pour vous débarrasser de la saleté et de la poussière. *You have to **brush** the coat to get rid of dirt and dust.*
burn	brûler	Je n'étais pas là quand il **a brûlé** la nourriture. *I wasn't there when he **burned** the food.*
catch up reach	rattraper	Je le **rattraperai** au prochain tour. *I **will catch up** with him in the next round.*
challenge	défier	Je te **défie** en duel. *I **challenge** you to a duel.*
chase pursue	poursuivre	Un chien de la rue m'**a poursuivi** la nuit dernière. *A dog from the street **chased** me last night.*
cheat (in exam)	tricher	Il **a triché** sur les questions du dernier examen. *He **cheated** on the last exam's questions.*
cheat (deceive)	tromper	Les magiciens **trompent** leurs spectateurs. *Magicians **cheat** their spectators.*
check (information)	vérifier	Pouvez-vous **vérifier** vos réponses d'abord? *Can you **check** your answers first?*
claim	réclamer	Je **réclamerai** un remboursement pour le vol manqué. *I **will claim** a reimbursement for the missing flight.*
comb	peigner	Peux-tu **peigner** tes boucles? *Can you **comb** your curls?*
confess	avouer	J'**avou** que j'ai mangé tous les cookies. *I **confess** I ate all the cookies.*
congratulate	féliciter	Elle ne m'a pas **félicité** le jour de ma remise de diplôme. *She didn't **congratulate** me on my graduation day.*
consist	se composer	Le complexe **se compose** de trois châteaux. *The complex **consists** of three castles.*
cut	couper	Je **couperai** mes cheveux très courts. *I **will cut** my hair really short.*

---

[1] The verb "**éviter**" can also mean *"to prevent"* depending on the context.

decrease	diminuer	Si vous dépensez pour cela, vos fonds **diminueront**. *If you spend on that, your funds **will decrease**.*
dedicate devote	consacrer	Je **consacre** mon temps libre à l'écriture. *I **dedicate** my free time to writing.*
delay	retarder	Les expéditions sont **retardées**. *The shipments are **delayed**.*
deserve	mériter	Tu **mérites** cette récompense. *You **deserve** that award.*
dial compose	composer	Il **a composé** le mauvais numéro. *He **dialed** the wrong number.*
digest	digérer	Il est difficile pour moi de **digérer** le lactose. *It's hard for me to **digest** lactose.*
dismantle	démonter	J'ai essayé de **démonter** ma montre. *I tried to **dismantle** my clock.*
doubt	douter	Je **doute** que vous puissiez finir une pizza entière. *I **doubt** you can finish a whole pizza.*
dress	s'habiller se vêtir	C'est bien qu'il **s'habille** sobrement. *It's good that he **dresses** soberly.*
enjoy	profiter apprécier	Je **profiterai** de mes vacances. *I **will enjoy** my vacation.*
entertain	divertir	Cette pièce de théâtre hier soir m'a beaucoup **diverti**. *That play last night **entertained** me a lot.*
erase	effacer	J'ai **effacé** mes messages par accident. *I **erased** my messages by accident.*
escape	s'échapper	Ma souris **s'échappe** de sa cage tout le temps. *My mouse **escapes** from its cage all the time.*
exhibit	exposer	Ils **ont exposé** ses œuvres dans une galerie l'année dernière. *They **exhibited** her works in a gallery last year.*
fall	tomber	La semaine dernière, je **suis tombé** dans l'escalier. *I **fell down** the stairs last week.*
fast (food)	jeûner	Il y a des gens qui **jeûnent** pendant des jours entiers. *There are people who **fast** for whole days.*
feel	se sentir	Je **me sens** heureux et satisfait. *I **feel** happy and content.*
fight struggle wrestle	lutter	Le guerrier **lutte** pour sa liberté. *The warrior **struggles** for his freedom.*

fight **combat**	**se battre**	Les frères et sœurs **se battent** toujours. *Siblings always **fight**.*
float	**flotter**	Le caneton **flotte** dans la baignoire. *The duckling **floats** in the bathtub.*
focus **concentrate**	**se concentrer**	Je **me concentre** mieux si je n'ai pas faim. *I **focus** better if I'm not hungry.*
freeze	**congeler**	N'oublie pas de **congeler** les légumes. *Don't forget to **freeze** the vegetables.*
fry	**frire**	Je **frirai** ces pommes de terre demain. *I **will fry** those potatoes tomorrow.*
gamble	**jouer**	Il **a joué** et perdu. *He **gambled** and lost.*
get up	**se lever**	Peux-tu **te lever**? *Can you **get up**?*
grill **roast**	**griller**	Nous **grillons** des légumes sur le barbecue. *We **grill** vegetables on the barbecue.*
have fun	**s'amuser**	Les gens vont au parc pour **s'amuser**. *People go to the park to **have fun**.*
heal	**guérir**	La brûlure devrait **guérir** rapidement. *The burn should **heal** quickly.*
hide	**cacher**	Je **cache** mon argent dans le placard. *I **hide** my money in the closet.*
hit **strike**	**frapper** **heurter**	Une voiture l'**a heurté** alors qu'il traversait la rue. *A car **hit** him while he was crossing the street.*
hug **embrace**	**embrasser**	Il l'**a embrassé** dès qu'il l'a vu. *He **hugged** him the moment he saw him.*
improve	**améliorer**	J'**ai** beaucoup **amélioré** mon style pendant cette dernière année. *I **improved** my style a lot during this last year.*
increase	**augmenter**	En été, la température **augmente** beaucoup. *In the summer, the temperature **increases** a lot.*
introduce **(oneself)**	**se présenter**	Pouvez-vous **vous présenter**? *Can you **introduce yourself**?*
invade	**envahir**	L'armée craignait d'**envahir** la ville. *The army feared **invading** the city.*
involve	**impliquer**	Je ne veux pas **impliquer** d'autres personnes dans cela. *I don't want to **involve** other people in this.*
launch **throw**	**lancer**	Le 16 juillet 1969, Apollo 11 a été **lancé**. *On July 16, 1969, Apollo 11 was **launched**.*
lift **raise**	**soulever**	Je **souleverai** le canapé pour vérifier. *I **will lift** the couch to check.*

look after	**s'occupier de** **prendre soin de**	Pouvez-vous **vous occuper** de votre neveu aujourd'hui? *Can you **look after** your nephew today?*
lower **reduce**	**baisser** **réduire** **diminuer**	Pouvez-vous **baisser** le volume? *Can you **lower** the volume?*
manage to	**réussir à** **arriver à**	J'**ai réussi** à terminer mon travail à temps. *I **have managed** to finish my work on time.*
maintain	**conserver** **maintenir**	Le réfrigérateur aide à **conserver** les aliments. *The fridge helps in **maintaining** food.*
marry	**se marier**	Mon cousin **s'est marié** au printemps. *My cousin **got married** in the spring.*
measure	**mesurer**	Je **mesurerai** la longueur de ton pied. *I **will measure** your foot's length.*
melt	**fondre**	Tu dois faire **fondre** le chocolat pour l'utiliser. *You have to **melt** the chocolate to use it.*
miss **(emotionally)**	**manquer** [1]	Tu lui **as manqué**, alors il est venu te voir. *He **missed** you, so he came to see you.*
object	**s'objecter** **s'opposer**	Je dois **m'objecter** à ce que vous dites. *I have to **object** to what you're saying.*
obtain	**obtenir**	L'année prochaine, j'**obtiendrai** la certification. *Next year I **will obtain** the certification.*
occur	**se produire** **survenir**	Le crash **se produira** sûrement. *The crash **will surely occur**.*
order	**commander**	Je veux **commander** de la nourriture. *Good evening, I want to **order** food.*
paint	**peindre**	Il aime **peindre** de beaux paysages. *He likes to **paint** beautiful landscapes.*
park (car)	**se garer** **stationner**	Est-il interdit de **se garer** ici? *Is it prohibited to **park** here?*
produce	**produire**	Les abeilles **produisent** du miel. *Bees **produce** honey.*
protect	**protéger**	Les mères ours **protègent** leur progéniture. *Mother bears **protect** their offspring.*
prove	**prouver**	Vous devez **prouver** que vous pouvez le faire. *You must **prove** you can do it.*
publish	**publier**	Je **publierai** ce poème. *I **will publish** this poem.*
punish	**punir**	Je l'**ai puni** en raison de son mauvais comportement hier soir. *I **punished** him due to his bad behavior last night.*

---

[1] Note that the verb "**manquer**" essentially means *"to be missing or lacking,"* e.g., "**Mes amis me manquent**" *(I miss my friends)*. Note here that "**mes amis**" *(my friends)* is the subject.

put up with **endure**	**supporter**	Je déteste devoir **supporter** le froid. *I hate having to put up with the cold.*
recognize **acknowledge**	**reconnaître**	Je ne t'**ai** pas **reconnu** avec cette coiffure. *I didn't recognize you with that hairstyle.*
reduce	**réduire** **diminuer**	Vous devez **réduire** votre vitesse dans les rues du quartier. *You must reduce your speed on neighborhood streets.*
remember	**se souvenir** **se rappeler**	Je **me souviens** du lac que nous avons visité. *I remember the lake we visited.*
replace	**remplacer**	J'**ai remplacé** ma vieille machine à café par une nouvelle. *I replaced my old coffee machine with a new one.*
retire	**se retirer**	Je **me retirerai** dans deux ans. *I will retire in two years.*
return	**retourner** **revenir** **rentrer**	Mon cousin **est revenu** de son voyage hier. *My cousin returned from his trip yesterday.*
review **revise**	**examiner** **réviser**	Nous **examinerons** ce chapitre ensemble. *We will review that chapter together.*
run away	**s'enfuir**	Les enfants aiment **s'enfuir** dans les magasins. *Children like to run away in stores.*
save **rescue**	**sauver**	Je n'ai pas pu **sauver** la tarte après qu'elle a brûlé. *I couldn't save the pie after it burned.*
save **spare**	**économiser**	J'**économiserai** plus d'argent pour ce voyage. *I will save more money for this trip.*
scratch **(oneself)**	**se gratter**	Je **me suis gratté** la piqûre de moustique presque instantanément. *I scratched the mosquito bite almost instantly.*
scratch **(surface)**	**griffer**	Mon chat **griffe** les fauteuils. *My cat scratches the armchairs.*
scream **yell**	**crier**	Ce n'est pas correct que vous **criiez** sur votre fils. *It's not right for you to yell at your son.*
shave	**se raser**	Je **me raserai** demain. *I will shave tomorrow.*
shine	**briller**	Ce diamant **brille** beaucoup! *That diamond shines a lot!*
shoot **fire**	**tirer**	Il **tire** très bien. *He shoots very well.*
sink	**couler**	Je pense que ce jouet ne **coulera** pas. *I think that toy will not sink.*
sit	**s'asseoir**	Tu peux **t'asseoir** à côté de moi. *You can sit next to me.*

skate	patiner	J'adore **patiner** en hiver. *I love to **skate** in winter.*
spend (money)	dépenser	C'est génial que vous ne **dépensiez** pas autant d'argent pour les vêtements. *It's great that you don't **spend** so much on clothes.*
spend (time)	passer	J'adore **passer** du temps sur la plage. *I love to **spend** time on the beach.*
spy	espionner	Ce n'est pas gentil de ta part d'**espionner** tes frères et sœurs. *It's not nice of you to **spy** on your siblings.*
stand	être debout	Je n'aime pas **être debout** dans le bus. *I don't like to **stand** while on the bus.*
stay remain	rester	Veux-tu **rester** dormir? *Do you want to **stay** over?*
stop	arrêter [1]	Tu dois t'**arrêter** au coin. *You have to **stop** at the corner.*
succeed	réussir	J'**ai réussi** après de nombreux essais. *I **succeeded** after many tries.*
suck	aspirer sucer	Tu dois **aspirer** à travers la paille. *You have to **suck** through the straw.*
suggest	suggérer	Il **a suggéré** que je mange quatre fruits par jour. *He **suggested** that I eat four fruits a day.*
survive	survivre	Mes plantes **ont survécu** à l'hiver dernier. *My plants **survived** last winter.*
sustain	soutenir maintenir	Une vie saine est facile à **maintenir**. *A healthy life is easy to **sustain**.*
swear	jurer	Le témoin **a juré** de dire la vérité. *The witness **has sworn** to tell the truth.*
sweat	suer transpirer	Je **sue** beaucoup à la salle de sport. *I **sweat** a lot at the gym.*
switch off	éteindre	Peux-tu **éteindre** la lumière? *Can you **switch off** the light?*
tackle address	aborder s'attaquer	J'**aborderai** de ce sujet dans la prochaine classe. *I **will address** this subject in the next class.*
take a shower	se doucher	Je **me douche** tous les matins. *I **take a shower** every morning.*
take apart	démonter démanteler	Je **démonterai** le placard pour le déménagement. *I **will take apart** the closet for the move.*

---

[1] We can also use the verb "**arrêter de**" to refer to quitting or ceasing an activity, e.g., "**Tu devrais arrêter de fumer**" (*You should stop smoking*).

take out	sortir	Peux-tu **sortir** la poubelle? *Can you **take out** the trash?*
take (photo)	prendre	Peux-tu me **prendre** en photo? *Can you **take** a photo of me?*
throw	lancer jeter	Arrêtez de **lancer** des pierres! *Stop **throwing** rocks!*
throw away	jeter	Je veux **jeter** les vieux meubles. *I want to **throw away** the old furniture.*
tire exhaust	fatiguer	S'occuper des enfants me **fatigue**. *Taking care of children **tires** me.*
tour roam	parcourir	J'aimerais **parcourir** la ville. *I'd like to **tour** the city.*
treat	traiter	Je **traite** toujours les autres avec respect. *I always **treat** others with respect.*
trip stumble	trébucher	Tu dois faire attention de ne pas **trébucher**. *You have to be careful not to **trip**.*
twist	tordre	Je **me suis tordu** la cheville en jouant au tennis. *I **twisted** my ankle while playing tennis.*
upload	télécharger	Je **téléchargerai** les vidéos dans une heure. *I **will upload** the videos in an hour.*
wake up	se réveiller	Il est difficile pour moi de **me réveiller** tôt. *It's hard for me to **wake up** early.*
wear put on	porter s'habiller	N'oublie pas de **porter** une écharpe. *Don't forget to **wear** a scarf.*
weigh	peser	Je me **peserai** lundi. *I **will weigh** myself on Monday.*
wet	mouiller	Tu dois **mouiller** d'abord le sol pour le nettoyer. *You have to **wet** the floor first to clean it.*
whistle	siffler	Je **siffle** toujours pendant que je prends mon bain. *I always **whistle** while I bathe.*
worry	s'inquiéter	Je **m'inquiète** toujours des examens. *I always **worry** about exams.*
worsen	empirer aggraver	La maladie de mon grand-père s'est **aggravée** l'année dernière. *My grandfather's disease **worsened** last year.*

In addition to the above new verbs, we add a few more English cognates that are easy to memorize.

English	French	Examples
adapt	s'adapter	Les enfants **s'adaptent** rapidement à l'école. *Children **adapt** quickly in school.*

adjust	**adjuster**	Il veut **ajuster** la lumière dans la pièce. *He wants to **adjust** the light in the room.*
affirm	**affirmer**	Il **a affirmé** qu'il est là. *He **affirmed** he is there.*
alter	**altérer**	J'**altérerai** la robe un peu. *I **will alter** the dress a bit.*
arrest	**arrêter**	Ils l'**ont arrêté** pour vol. *They **arrested** him for stealing.*
assemble	**assembler**	Nous **assemblerons** la table plus tard. *We **will assemble** the table later.*
assign **allocate**	**assigner**	Ils m'**ont assigné** cette tâche trois fois. *They **assigned** me this task three times.*
capture	**capturer**	Ils **ont capturé** le voleur rapidement hier soir. *They **captured** the thief quickly last night.*
cause	**causer**	Je ne voulais pas **causer** d'histoires. *I didn't want to **cause** a fuss.*
charm	**charmer**	Cela m'a **charmé** dès le début. *It **charmed** me from the beginning.*
communicate	**communiquer**	Il est plus facile de **communiquer** avec Internet. *It's easier to **communicate** with the internet.*
connect	**connecter**	Vous devez **vous connecter** au serveur. *You have to **connect** to the server.*
console	**consoler**	Il a dû la **consoler** quand elle pleurait. *He had to **console** her when she was crying.*
debate	**débattre**	Ils **débattront** du budget. *They **will debate** the budget.*
deteriorate	**détériorer**	Si vous ne prenez pas soin de la peinture, elle peut se **détériorer**. *If you don't take care of the paint, it can **deteriorate**.*
determine	**déterminer**	Le gouvernement **détermine** le budget annuel. *The government **determines** the annual budget.*
develop	**développer**	Récemment, j'**ai développé** un goût pour le café amer. *I recently **developed** a taste for bitter coffee.*
differ	**différer**	Le prix **diffère** de celui indiqué sur l'enseigne. *The price **differs** from that on the sign.*
dispense	**dispenser**	Cette pharmacie **dispense** des ordonnances toute la journée. *This pharmacy **dispenses** prescriptions all day long.*
dispute	**disputer**	Ils sont en train de **disputer** l'héritage. *They **are disputing** the inheritance.*
dissolve	**se dissoudre**	Le sel **se dissout** bien dans l'eau. *The salt **dissolves** well in water.*

embarrass	embarrasser	Mon enfant toujours m'**embarrasse** en public. *My kid always **embarrasses** me in public.*
generate	générer	Le barrage **génère** de l'électricité pour la ville. *The dam **generates** electricity for the city.*
guide	guider	Je me **guiderai** avec la carte. *I **will guide** myself with the map.*
imagine	imaginer	Je ne peux pas **imaginer** comment ça doit être. *I can't **imagine** how it must be.*
incorporate	incorporer	J'essaie d'**incorporer** plus d'exercices dans ma routine. *I try to **incorporate** more exercises into my routine.*
insist	insister	Il **a insisté** tellement, qu'ils l'ont laissé entrer. *He **insisted** so much, they let him in.*
invent	inventer	Qui **a inventé** cette technologie? *Who **invented** this technology?*
negotiate	négocier	Les pays **négocient** un accord commercial. *The countries **negotiate** a trade agreement.*
occupy	occuper	Ils **ont occupé** deux sièges à la table la dernière fois. *They **occupied** two seats at the table last time.*
offend	offenser	Je n'ai pas voulu vous **offenser**. *I didn't mean to **offend** you.*
operate	opérer	Le chirurgien **opère** les patients le jeudi. *The surgeon **operates** on patients on Thursdays.*
prepare	préparer	Je dois me **préparer** pour l'examen de demain. *I have to **prepare** for the exam tomorrow.*
provoke	provoquer	Il n'est pas bon de **provoquer** les animaux sauvages. *It's not good to **provoke** wild animals.*
qualify	se qualifier	Vous ne **vous qualifiez** pas les critères de qualification pour ce programme. *You do not **qualify** for this program.*
refrigerate	réfrigérer	Vous devez **réfrigérer** le soda. *You have to **refrigerate** the soda.*
resist	résister	Je ne peux pas **résister** au gâteau. *I can't **resist** cake.*
reveal disclose	révéler	Il **révèle** comment il est vraiment. *He **reveals** how he truly is.*
ruin	ruiner	Le tabac **ruine** votre santé. *Tobacco **ruins** your health.*
simulate	simuler	La réalité virtuelle tente de **simuler** la vie réelle. *Virtual reality tries to **simulate** real life.*

ski	skier	C'est amusant de **skier** dans les montagnes. *It's fun to **ski** in the mountains.*
suppose	supposer	Je **suppose** que vous n'avez pas de plans aujourd'hui. *I **suppose** you don't have any plans today.*

2. ADJECTIVES IV

Below is a list of adjectives that we need at this level. Adding them to your vocabulary will improve your comprehension of French speech and writing.

English	French	Examples
accustomed	habitué	Je suis **habitué** au temps froid. *I'm **accustomed** to the cold weather.*
advantageous	avantageux	Il est **avantageux** d'être organisé. *It's **advantageous** to be organized.*
alive	vivant	Ce calmar est encore **vivant**! *That squid is still **alive**!*
angry	fâché	J'étais très **fâché**. *I was very **angry**.*
asleep	endormi	Je me suis **endormi** sur le canapé. *I fell **asleep** on the couch.*
confused confusing	confus	Cette question m'a laissé **confus**. *That question left me **confused**.*
conservative	conservateur	Aujourd'hui, le parti **conservateur** a gagné. *Today, the **conservative** party won.*
costly	coûteux	Ce restaurant est très **coûteux**. *That restaurant is very **costly**.*
crushed smashed	écrasé	Vous utilisez de l'ail **écrasé** pour cette recette. *You use **crushed** garlic for this recipe.*
daily	quotidien	Je commence ma routine **quotidienne** avec le petit-déjeuner. *I start my **daily** routine with breakfast.*
dead	mort	Mon arrière-grand-père est **mort** depuis de nombreuses années. *My great-grandfather has been **dead** for many years.*
defeated	battu	J'ai été **battu** au jeu. *I was **defeated** in the game.*
destroyed	détruit	Les empires anciens ont été **détruits**. *The ancient empires were **destroyed**.*

disadvantageous	désavantageux	Il est **désavantageux** de ne pas avoir d'économies. *It's **disadvantageous** to not have savings.*
disappointed	déçu	J'étais **déçu** de voir que tu n'es pas venu. *I was **disappointed** to see you didn't come.*
disgusting	dégoûtant	Ce sac à dos a une odeur **dégoûtante**. *This backpack has a **disgusting** smell.*
dishonest	malhonnête	Je ne lui fais pas confiance car il est **malhonnête**. *I don't trust him because he's **dishonest**.*
distinctive	distinctif	Les vaches ont une odeur **distinctive**. *Cows have a **distinctive** smell.*
doubtful	douteux	J'ai répondu d'une manière **douteuse**. *I answered in a **doubtful** manner.*
efficient	efficace	Il travaille de manière très **efficace**. *He works in a very **efficient** way.*
enormous	énorme	Cet éléphant est **énorme**! *That elephant is **enormous**!*
entertaining	divertissant amusant	Le spectacle était **divertissant**. *The show was **entertaining**.*
enthusiastic	enthousiaste	Ce professeur est très **enthousiaste**. *This teacher is very **enthusiastic**.*
entire	entier	Je veux voir le monde **entier**. *I want to see the **entire** world.*
excited	excité	Je suis **excité** pour le nouveau film. *I'm **excited** for the new movie.*
exciting	excitant	Les montagnes russes sont **excitantes**. *Roller coasters are **exciting**.*
exhausting	épuisant	La randonnée est **épuisante**. *Hiking is **exhausting**.*
fake false	faux	Cette plante est **fausse**. *That plant is **fake**.*
flat	plat	Le sol est très **plat** là-bas. *The floor is very **flat** there.*
foreign	étranger	J'aime les condiments **étrangers**. *I like **foreign** condiments.*
free (liberty)	libre	Vous êtes **libre** de faire ce que vous voulez. *You are **free** to do whatever you want.*
free (money)	gratuit	Obtenez un article **gratuit** avec le coupon de réduction. *Get a **free** item with the discount coupon.*
furnished	meublé	L'appartement est entièrement **meublé**. *The apartment is completely **furnished**.*

grateful	reconnaissant	Je suis **reconnaissant** envers mes parents pour tout. *I am **grateful** to my parents for everything.*
guilty	coupable	Je me sentais **coupable** après avoir mangé le biscuit. *I felt **guilty** after eating the cookie.*
handmade	fait à la main	Cette couverture a été **faite à la main**. *This blanket was **handmade**.*
hated	détesté	Ce personnage est très **détesté**. *That character is very **hated**.*
heavy	lourd	Ce sac à dos est trop **lourd**. *This backpack is too **heavy**.*
hidden	caché	C'était **caché** entre les rochers. *It was **hidden** between the rocks.*
incredible	incroyable	Le spectacle était **incroyable**. *The show was **incredible**.*
jealous	jaloux	La sœur aînée était **jalouse** de la plus jeune. *The older sister was **jealous** of the younger one.*
known	connu	Il est un auteur très **connu**. *He is a very well-**known** author.*
lazy	paresseux	Mon chien est très **paresseux**. *My dog is very **lazy**.*
loved beloved	bien-aimé	C'est mon ours en peluche **bien-aimé**. *This is my **beloved** teddy.*
offended	offensé	Il s'est finalement senti très **offensé** par ce qui s'est passé. *He ended up very **offended** by what happened.*
opposite	opposé	Il est du côté **opposé**. *He's on the **opposite** side.*
picky	exigeant	Ma sœur est très **exigeante**. *My sister is very **picky**.*
pregnant	enceinte	Ma cousine a annoncé qu'elle est **enceinte**. *My cousin announced that she's **pregnant**.*
quiet	tranquille calme	J'aime les endroits **tranquilles** pour me détendre. *I like **quiet** places to relax.*
satisfied	satisfait	Je suis **satisfait** du service à la clientèle de ce magasin. *I'm **satisfied** with customer service of this store.*
silent (person)	silencieux	Il est resté **silencieux** pendant la réunion. *He remained **silent** during the meeting.*
sour	aigre acide	J'adore les bonbons **acides**. *I love **sour** gummies.*
sunny	ensoleillé	C'était très **ensoleillé** hier. *It was very **sunny** yesterday.*

tasty	savoureux délicieux	Ce gâteau est très **savoureux**. *This cake is very **tasty**.*
unknown	inconnu	C'est un restaurant **inconnu**. *It's an **unknown** restaurant.*
used	utilisé usagé	J'achète parfois des vêtements **usagés**. *I sometimes buy **used** clothes.*
various several	divers plusieurs	J'ai **plusieurs** pots de ce style. *I have **several** pots of that style.*
warm tepid	chaud	J'aimerais prendre un café **chaud**. *I would like to have a **warm** coffee.*
weekly	hebdomadaire	Nous aurons des réunions **hebdomadaires**. *We'll have **weekly** meetings.*

In addition to the above new adjectives, we add a few English cognates that are easy to memorize.

English	French	Examples
acceptable	acceptable	La nourriture était **acceptable**. *The food was **acceptable**.*
capable of	capable de	Je suis **capable de** réussir l'examen. *I'm **capable of** passing the exam.*
cellular	cellulaire	Le changement est au niveau **cellulaire**. *The change is at a **cellular** level.*
concise	concis	L'article est **concis**. *The article is **concise**.*
content pleased glad	content	Il était très **content** de te voir en bonne santé. *He was very **pleased** to see you well.*
credible	crédible	Ça me semblait être une histoire **crédible**. *It seemed like a **credible** story to me.*
dangerous	dangereux	Il est **dangereux** de sortir la nuit. *It's **dangerous** to go out at night.*
developed	développé	La trame du livre est bien **développée**. *The book's plot is nicely **developed**.*
effective	effectif	C'est un médicament très **effectif**. *It's a very **effective** medication.*
electrical	électrique	Vous devez être prudent avec la connexion **électrique**. *You must be careful with the **electrical** connection.*
environmental	environnemental	La pollution a un impact **environnemental**. *Pollution has an **environmental** impact.*
exaggerated	exagéré	Je crois que leurs estimations de coûts sont **exagérées**. *I believe that their cost estimates are **exaggerated**.*

existent existing	existant	C'est le seul thermos **existant** ici. *This is the only **existing** thermos here.*
genuine	authentique	Notre amitié est **authentique**. *Our friendship is **genuine**.*
humble	humble	L'acteur était très **humble**. *The actor was very **humble**.*
impressed	impressionné	J'ai été **impressionné** par sa voix. *I was **impressed** with his voice.*
impressive	impressionnant	La taille du bâtiment est **impressionnante**. *The size of the building is **impressive**.*
influenced	influencé	Son style artistique a été **influencé** par d'autres. *His art style was **influenced** by others.*
legal	légal	J'ai besoin de conseil **légal**. *I need **legal** advice.*
lethal	létal mortel	Fumer beaucoup peut être **mortel**. *Smoking a lot can be **lethal**.*
modern	moderne	La technologie **moderne** m'étonne toujours. ***Modern** technology always amazes me.*
nuclear	nucléaire	La ville compte sur une centrale **nucléaire**. *The town relies on a **nuclear** plant.*
obese	obèse	Le vétérinaire m'a dit que mon chat est **obèse**. *The vet told me that my cat is **obese**.*
obligatory mandatory	obligatoire	Ils ont un uniforme **obligatoire**. *They have an **obligatory** uniform.*
offensive	offensant	Je n'utilise jamais de langage **offensant**. *I never use **offensive** language.*
oppressive	oppressif	Il est difficile de vivre sous un régime **oppressif**. *It is difficult to live under an **oppressive** regime.*
pathetic	pathétique	Je me sentais **pathétique** dans cette tenue. *I felt **pathetic** in this outfit.*
portable	portable	C'est une console **portable**. *It's a **portable** console.*
preventive	préventif	Il vaut mieux prendre des mesures **préventives**. *It's better to take **preventive** measures.*
prosperous	prospère	Je crois que cette récolte sera très **prospère**. *I believe this harvest will be very **prosperous**.*
psychological	psychologique	Ses peurs sont toutes **psychologiques**. *His fears are all **psychological**.*
punctual	ponctuel	Il est important d'être **ponctuel** au travail. *It's important to be **punctual** at work.*

pure	**pur**	C'est du miel **pur** provenant des ruches. *This is **pure** honey from the hives.*
realistic	**réaliste**	Je me fixe toujours des objectifs **réalistes**. *I always set **realistic** goals for myself.*
representative	**représentatif**	La statue est **représentative** de la personne réelle. *The statue is **representative** of the real person.*
severe	**sévère**	Les sanctions sont **sévères** dans ce cas. *The punishments are **severe** in this case.*
specific	**spécifique**	J'ai aimé cela dans cette couleur **spécifique**. *I liked it in that **specific** color.*
supreme	**suprême**	Il a fait un effort **suprême** pour réussir. *He has made a **supreme** effort to succeed.*
temporary	**temporaire**	Je dois demander un visa de résidence **temporaire**. *I must apply for a **temporary** residence visa.*
unacceptable	**inacceptable**	Le comportement du chat était **inacceptable**. *His cat's behavior was **unacceptable**.*
unique	**unique**	Son talent est vraiment **unique**. *His talent is truly **unique**.*
vacant	**vacant**[1]	Ce poste est **vacant** depuis des années. *That position has been **vacant** for years.*
visual	**visuel**	La peinture a de bons effets **visuels**. *The painting has good **visual** effects.*

3. PEOPLE II

We go over more vocabulary to describe people in our daily life.

accountant	**comptable**[m,f]	*leader*	**leader**[m] **chef(fe)**
actor	**acteur**[m]	*owner*	**propriétaire**[m,f]
actress	**actrice**[f]	*pharmacist*	**pharmacien(ne)**
architect	**architecte**[m,f]	*philosopher*	**philosophe**[m,f]
artist	**artiste**[m,f]	*poet*	**poète**[m] **poétesse**[f]
author	**auteur(e)**	*police station*	**commissariat**[m] **poste**[m] de police
business partner	**associé(e)**	*policeman*	**policier**

---

[1] The word "**vacant**" often refers to a position. To refer to a vacant seat or apartment, we use "**libre**" *(free)*.

butcher	**boucher**[m]/**bouchère**[f]	*programmer*	**programmeur**[m]/ **programmeuse**[f]
cashier	**caissier**[m]/**caissière**[f]	*reporter*	**reporter**[m, f] **journaliste**[m, f]
chauffeur	**chauffeur**[m]/**chauffeuse**[f]	*researcher*	**chercheur**[m] /**chercheuse**[f]
chef	**chef(fe) (de cuisine)**	*retirement*	**retraite**[f]
chief	**chef(fe)**	*scientist*	**scientifique**[m, f]
colleague	**collègue**[m,f]	*secretary*	**secrétaire**[m, f]
crowd	**foule**[f]	*singer*	**chanteur**[m] /**chanteuse**[f]
dancer	**danseur**[m]/**danseuse**[f]	*society*	**société**[f]
designer	**designer**[m]	*soldier*	**soldat(e)**
director	**directeur**[m]/**directrice**[f]	*speaker*	**orateur**[m] **oratrice**[f] **conférencier**[m]
doctor	**médecin**[m]	*spy*	**espion(ne)**
employee	**employé(e)**	*statue*	**statue**[f]
employer	**employeur**[m]/**employeuse**[f]	*teacher*	**professeur(e)**
engineer	**ingénieur(e)**	*union*	**syndicat**[m]
interview	**entretien**[m]	*veterinarian*	**vétérinaire**[m,f]
journalist	**journaliste**[m, f]	*victim*	**victime**[f]
lawyer	**avocat(e)**	*waiter/waitress*	**serveur**[m]/**serveuse**[f]

4. HEALTH I

Health, or "**la santé**," is always an important topic in any language. Here is some related vocabulary in French:

burn	**brûlure**[f]	*mind*	**esprit**[m]
disorder (medical)	**trouble**[m]	*narcotic*	**narcotique**[m]
drug	**drogue**[f]	*needle*	**aiguille**[f]
fever	**fièvre**[f]	*pain*	**douleur**[f]
floss	**fil dentaire**[m]	*painkiller*	**analgésique**[m]
flu	**grippe**[f]	*pill*	**pilule**[f] **comprimé**[m]
illness	**maladie**[f]	*public health*	**santé publique**[f]
insurance	**assurance**[f]	*surgery*	**chirurgie**[f]
lozenge	**pastille**[f]	*symptom*	**symptôme**[m]
medical coverage	**couverture médicale**[f]	*vaccine*	**vaccin**[m]
medication	**médicament**[m]	*well-being*	**bien-être**[m]

5. LAW

The law, or "**la loi**," usually has its specific set of vocabulary. We go over some important vocabulary here:

acceptance	**acceptation**f	*lawsuit* *trial*	**procès**m
accomplice	**complice**m,f	*lie*	**mensonge**m
background check	**vérification**f **des antécédents**	*murder*	**meurtre**m **assassinat**m
bail *bond*	**caution**f	*murderer*	**meurtrier**m **assassin**m
clue	**indice**m	*offense*	**infraction**f
court	**cour**f **tribunal**m	*pickpocket*	**pickpocket**m **voleur**m **à la tire**
crime	**crime**m	*prosecutor*	**procureur**m
delinquency	**délinquance**f	*lieutenant*	**lieutenant(e)**
evidence	**preuve**f **évidence**f	*meeting*	**réunion**f
fault *guilt*	**culpabilité**f	*mistake*	**erreur**f
fingerprint	**empreinte digitale**f	*patrol*	**patrouille**f
footprint	**empreinte**f	*punishment*	**châtiment**m **peine**f **punition**f
fraud	**fraude**f	*quarrel*	**querelle**f **dispute**f
gang	**gang**m	*report*	**rapport**m
harassment	**harcèlement**m	*request*	**demande**f
hearing	**audience**f	*right*	**droit**m
hit *blow*	**coup**m	*scammer* *swindler*	**escroc**m
judge	**juge**m	*sentence*	**peine**f **sentence**f
jury	**jury**m	*suicide*	**suicide**m
justice	**justice**f	*witness*	**témoin**m

6. MEASUREMENTS

The verb *"to measure"* in French is "**mesurer**," and *measurement* is "**la mesure**." Below is some useful vocabulary related to measurements:

angle	**angle**^m	*meter*	**mètre**^m
average	**moyenne**^f	*mile*	**mile**^m
barrel	**baril**^m **tonneau**^m	*piece*	**pièce**^f **morceau**^m
circle	**cercle**^m	*pound*	**livre**^f
content	**contenu**^m	*quantity* *amount*	**quantité**^f
degree	**degré**^m	*rectangle*	**rectangle**^m
diameter	**diamètre**^m	*sphere*	**sphère**^f
edge	**bord**^m	*square*	**carré**^m
form *shape*	**forme**^f	*step*	**étape**^f **pas**^m
fragment	**fragment**^m	*temperature*	**température**^f
height	**hauteur**^f	*ton*	**tonne**^f
hole	**trou**^m	*unit*	**unité**^f
inch	**pouce**^m	*weight*	**poids**^m
kilometer	**kilomètre**^m	*width*	**largeur**^f
line	**ligne**^f	*yard*	**yard**^m

7. HOUSE II

Here, we add more vocabulary related to *the house*, or "**la maison**."

air conditioner	**climatiseur**^m	*light*	**lumière**^f
ashtray	**cendrier**^m	*lighter*	**briquet**^m
ax	**hache**^f	*lock*	**serrure**^f
bench	**banc**^m	*mattress*	**matelas**^m
blender	**mixeur**^m	*microwave*	**micro-ondes**^f
bucket	**seau**^m	*napkin*	**serviette**^f
calendar	**calendrier**^m	*nail (hardware)*	**clou**^m
candle	**bougie**^f	*pantry*	**garde-manger**^m
chest (container)	**coffre**^m	*paper tissue*	**mouchoir**^m
chores	**corvées**^f	*paper towel*	**essuie-tout**^m
clay	**argile**^f	*patio*	**patio**^m
cleaning *cleanliness*	**nettoyage**^m	*plug*	**prise**^f
cloth	**tissu**^m **chiffon**^m	*plumbing*	**plomberie**^f
coal	**charbon**^m	*plunger*	**débouchoir**^m
column	**colonne**^f	*pool*	**piscine**^f
cottage	**chalet**^m	*porcelain*	**porcelaine**^f
crease	**pli**^m	*portrait*	**portrait**^m

curtain *drape*	**rideau**^m	*pot (cookware)*	**pot**^m
dining room	**salle**^f **à manger**	*project*	**projet**^m
drain	**drain**^m	*property*	**propriété**^f
driveway	**allée**^f	*rice cooker*	**cuiseur**^m **de riz**
dryer	**séchoir**^m **sèche-cheveux**^m	*saw*	**scie**^f
elevator	**ascenseur**^m	*screw*	**vis**^f
fence	**clôture**^f	*shelf*	**étagère**^f
fire (incident)	**incendie**^m	*shower*	**douche**^f
flashlight	**lampe**^f **de poche**	*soap*	**savon**^m
frame	**cadre**^m	*strap*	**sangle**^f
furniture	**meuble**^m	*teaspoon*	**cuillère**^f **à café**
garden	**jardin**^m	*tenant*	**locataire**^m, f
gift	**cadeau**^m	*tent*	**tente**^f
grill	**gril**^m	*tray*	**plateau**^m
hallway	**couloir**^m	*toaster*	**grille-pain**^m
heating	**chauffage**^m	*toilet paper*	**papier toilette**^m
hut	**cabane**^f	*toilet*	**toilettes**^f
instrument	**instrument**^m	*tool*	**outil**^m
ironing board	**planche**^f **à repasser**	*toothbrush*	**brosse**^f **à dents**
iron	**fer**^m **à repasser**	*toothpaste*	**dentifrice**^m
item	**article**^m	*trashcan*	**poubelle**^f
jewelry	**bijou**^m	*tube*	**tube**^m
ladder	**échelle**^f	*utensil*	**ustensile**^m
landlord *owner*	**propriétaire**^m,f	*utilities*	**utilitaires**^m
laundry *dirty clothes*	**lessive**^f **linge sale**^m	*vacuum cleaner*	**aspirateur**^m
lawn	**pelouse**^f **gazon**^m	*view*	**vue**^f
lawn mower	**tondeuse**^f **à gazon**	*wall*	**mur**^m
leak	**fuite**^f	*washing machine*	**machine**^f **à laver**
letter	**lettre**^f	*wax*	**cire**^f
light bulb	**ampoule**^f	*yard*	**cour**^f

8. FOOD II

Here is more vocabulary related to *food*, or "**la nourriture**":

almond	**amande**^f	*melon*	**melon**^m

appetizer	**apéritif**[m]	*nuts*	**noix**[f]
avocado	**avocat**[m]	*onion*	**oignon**[m]
bacon	**bacon**[m]	*peanut*	**cacahuète**[f]
beans	**haricots**[m]	*pear*	**poire**[f]
blueberry	**myrtille**[f]	*pepper*	**poivre**[m]
breakfast	**petit déjeuner**[m]	*pistachio*	**pistache**[f]
burger	**hamburger**[m]	*pomegranate*	**grenade**[f]
butter	**beurre**[m]	*potato*	**pomme**[f] **de terre**
cabbage	**chou**[m]	*raspberry*	**framboise**[f]
cake	**gâteau**[m]	*recipe*	**recette**[f]
can	**boîte**[f]	*sandwich*	**sandwich**[m]
coconut	**noix**[f] **de coco**	*seafood*	**fruits**[m] **de mer**
corn	**maïs**[m]	*shrimp*	**crevette**[f]
cranberry	**canneberge**[f]	*soup*	**soupe**[f]
cucumber	**concombre**[m]	*spice*	**épice**[f]
currant	**groseille**[f]	*straw*	**paille**[m]
dessert	**dessert**[m]	*strawberry*	**fraise**[f]
fries	**frites**[f]	*sweet potato*	**patate douce**[f]
lentil	**lentille**[f]	*takeaway*	**à emporter**
meal	**repas**[m]	*watermelon*	**pastèque**[f]

9. CLOTHES II

Here we add more vocabulary related to *clothes*, or "**les vêtements**[m]":

accessories	**accessoires**[m]	*raincoat*	**imperméable**[m]
attire	**tenue**[f]	*sandals*	**sandales**[f]
blouse	**blouse**[f] **chemisier**[m]	*scarf*	**foulard**[m] **écharpe**[f]
bracelet	**bracelet**[m]	*shoes*	**chaussures**[f]
checkered shirt	**chemise**[f] **à carreaux**	*sideburn*	**favoris**[m]
cleavage	**décolleté**[m]	*size (clothes)*	**taille**[f]
diaper	**couche**[f]	*size (shoes)*	**pointure**[f]
disguise	**déguisement**[m]	*sleeve*	**manche**[f]
dress	**robe**[f]	*socks*	**chaussettes**[f]
fabric	**tissu**[m]	*stain*	**tache**[f]
fitting room	**cabine**[f] **d'essayage**	*stockings*	**bas**[m]
haircut	**coupe**[f] **de cheveux**	*striped shirt*	**chemise**[f] **à rayures**
mask	**masque**[m]	*suit*	**costume**[m]
necklace	**collier**[m]	*sweater*	**pull**[m]
pajamas	**pyjama**[m]	*swimsuit*	**maillot**[m] **de bain**

pattern	**modèle**^m	*tie*	**cravate**^f
perfume	**parfum**^m	*watch*	**montre**^f

10. DIRECTIONS II

Below is some useful vocabulary to describe directions:

alley	**ruelle**^f	*destination*	**destination**^f
around the corner	**dans le coin** **dans les environs**	*downstairs*	**en bas**
arrow	**flèche**^f	*highway*	**autoroute**^f
at the beginning of	**au début de**	*in the middle of*	**au milieu de**
at the corner	**au coin**	*neighborhood*	**quartier**^m
at the end of	**au bout de** **à la fin de**	*next block*	**prochain bloc**^m
avenue	**avenue**^f	*side*	**côté**^m
bottom	**bas**^m **fond**^m	*somewhere*	**quelque part**
corner	**coin**^m	*upstairs*	**en haut** **à l'étage**

I. Introductory Topics & Grammar

As you plow through the language to reach this advanced level, take your time to go over the new topics, which will become a little more challenging but much more interesting. You can use the Anki cards to reinforce these topics in your memory with reviews and exercises.

1. THE PRONOUNS "Y" & "EN"

The two pronouns "**y**" and "**en**" are a constant source of confusion to many learners of French. We will look at the most common uses of these pronominal particles in different contexts.

Uses of "Y"

Here we discuss three important uses of the pronoun "**y**":

1. Meaning *"there"* when referring to a place.

For example, in the sentence: "**Je vais <u>à ce café</u> tous les matins**" *(I go <u>to that coffee shop</u> every morning)*, we can eliminate "**à ce café**" *(to that coffee shop)* and say: "**J'<u>y</u> vais tous les matins**" *(I go <u>there</u> every morning)*.

Notice that "**y**" is placed before the verb. Here are more examples:

Je vais toujours **<u>à la plage</u>** en été.	*I always go **<u>to the beach</u>** in summer.*
J'**<u>y</u>** vais toujours en été.	*I always go **<u>there</u>** in summer.*
Nous habiterons **<u>à Paris</u>** pendant deux ans.	*We will live **<u>in Paris</u>** for two years.*
Nous **<u>y</u>** habiterons pendant deux ans.	*We will live **<u>there</u>** for two years.*
Êtes-vous allé **<u>à Rome</u>**?	*Have you been **<u>to Rome</u>**?*
<u>Y</u> êtes-vous allé?	*Have you been **<u>there</u>**?*

2. Some verbs are usually followed by the preposition "**à**," "**en**," or "**sur**," such as: "**penser à**" *(to think about)*, "**croire en**" *(to believe in)*,

"**compter sur**" *(to count on)*, etc. In this case, the pronoun "**y**" can replace the preposition and the following noun.

For example, in the sentence "**Vous pensez <u>au travail</u>?**" *(Are you thinking <u>about work</u>?)*, we can replace "**au travail**" *(about work)* with "**y**" before the verb, that is, "**Vous <u>y</u> pensez?**" *(Are you thinking <u>about it</u>?)*.

Notice that "**y**" here is placed before the verb and is translated as *"about it."* The inanimate noun (thing or idea) that "**y**" replaces is considered an indirect object because it is preceded by a preposition.

Here are some more examples:

Je vais penser **<u>à ce problème</u>**.	*I will think **<u>about that problem</u>**.*
Je vais **<u>y</u>** penser.	*I will think **<u>about it</u>**.*
Vous pouvez compter **<u>sur leur aide</u>**.	*You can count **<u>on their help</u>**.*
Vous pouvez **<u>y</u>** compter.	*You can count **<u>on it</u>**.*
Je crois en **<u>ce dont il est capable</u>**.	*I believe in **<u>what he is capable of</u>**.*
J'**<u>y</u>** crois.	*I believe **<u>in it</u>**.*

Notice that "**y**" is always placed before the verb. The only exception is if the verb is in the affirmative imperative. In this case, the "**y**" is attached to the end of the verb. For example:

Pensez **<u>à l'offre</u>**.	*Think about **<u>the offer</u>**.*
Pensez-**<u>y</u>**.	*Think about **<u>it</u>**.*
Ne comptez pas **<u>sur leur aide</u>**.	*Don't count **<u>on their help</u>**.*
N'**<u>y</u>** comptez pas.	*Don't count **<u>on it</u>**.*

3. The pronoun "**y**" is used in the expression "**il y a**" which can mean *"there is/are,"* as we have encountered in **Level III, Lesson 6**. For example:

Il y a une façon de résoudre ce problème.	***There is*** *a way to solve this problem.*
Il y a beaucoup de monde ici.	***There are*** *many people here.*
Il n'y a personne ici.	***There is*** *no one here.*
Il n'y a pas assez de chaises dans la salle.	***There aren't*** *enough chairs in the room.*

The expression **"il y a"** has the equivalent meaning of *"ago"* when referring to events that happened in the past, for example:

Le colis est arrivé **il y a** 30 minutes.	*The package arrived 30 minutes **ago.***
Le problème a commencé **il y a** deux ans.	*The problem started two years **ago.***
Il y a deux heures qu'ils ont appelé.	*They called two hours **ago.***
J'ai déménagé ici **il y a** 3 mois.	*I moved here 3 months **ago.***

Uses of "En"

The pronoun **"en"** often precedes the verb unless the verb is in the affirmative imperative. The pronoun **"en"** has the following uses in French:

1. Some verbs and expressions are followed by the preposition **"de,"** such as: **"parler de"** *(to talk about)*, **"avoir besoin de"** *(to need)*, **"content de"** *(happy about)*, **"sûr de"** *(sure of)*, etc. In these expressions, **"en"** can replace the preposition and the following noun.

For example, in the sentence **"Je suis content <u>du résultat</u>"** *(I am happy <u>about the result</u>)*, we can replace **"du résultat"** *(about the result)* with **"en"** and place it before the verb, that is, **"J'<u>en</u> suis content"** *(I am happy <u>about it</u>)*.

Notice that **"en"** here is placed before the verb and is translated as *"about it."* The inanimate noun (thing or idea) that **"en"** replaces is also considered an indirect object.

Here are some more examples:

Il parle **<u>du nouveau projet</u>**. Il **en** parle.	*He is talking **<u>about the new project</u>**.* *He is talking **<u>about it</u>**.*
J'ai besoin **<u>d'argent</u>** pour sortir. J'**en** ai besoin pour sortir.	*I need **<u>the money</u>** to go out.* *I need **<u>it</u>** to go out.*
Es-tu sûr **<u>de la réponse</u>**? **En** es-tu sûr?	*Are you sure **<u>of the answer</u>**?* *Are you sure **<u>of it</u>**?*

There are also some idiomatic expressions that use the pronoun "**en**," even though it may sometimes seem redundant. For example:

Ça **en** vaut la peine.	*It is worth **it**.*
Qui s'**en** soucie de ...?	*Who cares **about** ...?*
Je **en** m'en soucie pas du tout.	*I don't care at all (**about it**).*
Je n'**en** peux plus.	*I can't stand **it** anymore.*

2. The pronoun "**en**" is used with quantities and amounts, and is often translated as *"of it"* or *"of them."* It usually replaces a number or a partitive such as *"some"* or *"a little."*

For example, in the sentence "**Je veux du lait**" (*I want some milk*), we can replace "**du lait**" (*some milk*) with "**en**" and place it before the verb, that is, "**J'en veux**" (*I want some of it*). Notice that "**en**" here is placed before the verb and is translated as *"some of it."*

Similarly, in the sentence "**J'ai deux biscuits**" (*I have two cookies*), we can replace "**biscuits**" (*cookies*) with "**en**" and place it before the verb, that is, "**J'en ai deux**" (*I have two "of them"*). Notice that "**en**" here is placed before the verb and is translated as *"of them."*

Here are some more examples:

Veux-tu **de l'eau**?	*Do you want **some water**?*
En veux-tu?	*Do you want **some**?*
J'ai pris la moitié **du sucre**.	*I took half **the sugar**.*
J'**en** ai pris la moitié.	*I took half **of it**.*
Il y a trois **pommes** sur la table.	*There are three **apples** on the table.*
Il y **en** a trois sur la table.	*There are three **of them** on the table.*

Notice that the noun that "**en**" replaces can be countable or uncountable.

In case there is a reflexive or indirect pronoun in the sentence, the reflexive or indirect pronoun is placed before "**en**." For example:

Je **te** donnerai deux **livres**.	*I will give you two **books**.*
Je **t'en** donnerai deux.	*I will give you two (**of them**).*
Je **lui** donnerai deux **livres**.	*I will give him two **books**.*
Je **lui en** donnerai deux.	*I will give him two (**of them**).*

The pronoun "**en**" is placed after the verb in the case of the affirmative imperative, for example:

Donnez-<u>moi</u> deux **<u>livres</u>**.	*Give <u>me</u> two **<u>books</u>**.*
Donnez-<u>m'**en**</u> deux.	*Give <u>me</u> two (**<u>of them</u>**).*
Donnez-<u>nous</u> **<u>du pain</u>**.	*Give <u>us</u> some **<u>bread</u>**.*
Donnez-<u>nous</u> **en**.	*Give <u>us</u> some (**<u>of it</u>**).*

The pronoun "**en**" is also used in some pronominal verbs, which we will cover in **Level VI, Lesson 4**.

2. IMPERATIVE MOOD & GIVING COMMANDS

The imperative mood is generally used to give commands or instructions in the affirmative or the negative. We have so far encountered the indicative and the subjunctive moods. The imperative is considered a separate mood in French.

The imperative can be in the affirmative or the negative. The imperative can be in the singular informal "**tu**" form, or in the "**vous**" form in the case of plural or singular formal:

1. Singular informal (i.e., "**tu**" **form**)
2. Plural and singular formal (i.e., "**vous**" **form**)

In addition to the above two cases of imperative commands, we will study commands using "**nous**."

Singular Informal Imperative

To give commands to a single person in an informal way, we use the *present indicative* in the second-person singular form, i.e., "**tu**," in both the affirmative and the negative. A minor change is the dropping of the final "**-s**" in the "**-er**" verbs, for example:

Choisis la bonne réponse.	***Choose** the correct answer.*
Marche doucement.	***Walk** slowly.*
Lave-toi les mains.	***Wash** your hands.*
Ne te lave pas le visage.	***Don't wash** your face.*
Ne me mens pas.	***Don't lie** to me.*
Ne parle pas vite.	***Don't speak** fast.*

Notice that if there is a pronoun related to the verb, e.g., a reflexive or indirect object pronoun, it is attached to the end of the verb in the affirmative and placed before the verb in the negative.

There are only four irregular verbs in the singular informal command form.

Infinitive	Command	Example	
être	sois	**Sois** poli.	*Be polite.*
avoir	aie	**Aie** tout.	*Have it all.*
savoir	sache	**Sache** la vérité.	*Know the truth.*
vouloir	veuille	**Veuille** patienter.	*Please wait.*

Notice that the imperative of the verb **"vouloir"** *(to want)* is an invitation to do something and is often roughly translated into English as *"please."*

Plural and Singular Formal Imperative

To give commands to a single person in a formal way or to a group of people in a formal or informal way, we use the **"vous"** form in the present indicative tense in both the affirmative and the negative, for example:

Madame, **entrez** par ici, s'il vous plaît.	*Ma'am, **enter** from here, please.*
Monsieur, **ne fumez pas** ici, s'il vous plaît.	*Sir, **don't smoke** here, please.*

The irregular verbs are the same as the singular informal imperative:

Infinitive	Command	Example	
être	soyez	**Soyez** poli.	*Be polite.*
avoir	ayez	**Ayez** tout.	*Have it all.*
savoir	sachez	**Sachez** la vérité.	*Know the truth.*
vouloir	veuillez	**Veuillez** trouver ci-joint.	*Please find attached.*

Commands using "Nous"

Similar to the expression *"let's do something"* in English, commands using **"nous"** in French express the same idea and can be affirmative or negative. Both use the *present indicative*, for example:

Faisons nos devoirs.	*Let's do our homework.*
Ne fumons pas.	*Let's not smoke.*
Allons-y!	*Let's go!*

The following three verbs are irregular:

Infinitive	Command	Example	
être	soyons	**Soyons** poli.	*Let's be polite.*
avoir	ayons	**Ayons** tout.	*Let's have it all.*
savoir	sachons	**Sachons** la vérité.	*Let's know the truth.*

3. THE CONDITIONAL TENSES

The simple conditional tense is used to describe a hypothetical situation, express wishes, give advice, or make a polite request. It is similar in its use to the simple conditional tense in English, for example, "I *would do the laundry if I had time*."

Similar to the stem formation in the simple future tense, we use the *infinitive* as a stem and drop the final "-e" in the case of "-re" verbs. The endings are the same for the three types of verbs.

	-er ending	-ir ending	-re ending
	parler *(to speak)*	finir *(to finish)*	vendre *(to sell)*
je	parler**ais**	finir**ais**	vendr**ais**
tu	parler**ais**	finir**ais**	vendr**ais**
il/elle/on	parler**ait**	finir**ait**	vendr**ait**
nous	parler**ions**	finir**ions**	vendr**ions**
vous	parler**iez**	finir**iez**	vendr**iez**
ils/elles	parler**aient**	finir**aient**	vendr**aient**

Irregular Verbs

The same verbs that are irregular in the simple future tense are also irregular in the simple conditional tense and use the same stem. Here is a list of irregular verbs in the simple conditional tense:

	je	tu	il/elle	nous	vous	ils/elles
aller *to go*	irais	irais	irait	irions	iriez	iraient
avoir *to have*	aurais	aurais	aurait	aurions	auriez	auraient

courir *to run*	courrais	courrais	courrait	courrions	courriez	courraient
devenir *to become*	deviendrais	deviendrais	deviendrait	deviendrions	deviendriez	deviendraient
devoir *must*	devrais	devrais	devrait	devrions	devriez	devraient
envoyer *to send*	enverrais	enverrais	enverrait	enverrions	enverriez	enverraient
être *to be*	serais	serais	serait	serions	seriez	seraient
faire *to do*	ferais	ferais	ferait	ferions	feriez	feraient
falloir *to have to*	-	-	faudrait	-	-	-
mourir *to die*	mourrais	mourrais	mourrait	mourrions	mourriez	mourraient
pleuvoir *to rain*	-	-	pleuvrait	-	-	-
recevoir *to receive*	recevrais	recevrais	recevrait	recevrions	recevriez	recevraient
revenir *to return*	reviendrais	reviendrais	reviendrait	reviendrions	reviendriez	reviendraient
savoir *to know*	saurais	saurais	saurait	saurions	sauriez	sauraient
tenir *to hold*	tiendrais	tiendrais	tiendrait	tiendrions	tiendriez	tiendraient
valoir *to be worth*	-	-	vaudrait	-	-	-
venir *to come*	viendrais	viendrais	viendrait	viendrions	viendriez	viendraient
voir *to see*	verrais	verrais	verrait	verrions	verriez	verraient
vouloir *to want*	voudrais	voudrais	voudrait	voudrions	voudriez	voudraient

There are some verbs that undergo minor spelling changes. Here are some common examples:

	je	tu	il/elle	nous	vous	ils/elles
employer *to hire*	emploierais	emploierais	emploierait	emploierions	emploieriez	emploieraient
essuyer *to wipe*	essuierais	essuierais	essuierait	essuierions	essuieriez	essuieraient
nettoyer *to clean*	nettoierais	nettoierais	nettoierait	nettoierions	nettoieriez	nettoieraient

acheter *to buy*	ach<u>è</u>terais	ach<u>è</u>terais	ach<u>è</u>terait	ach<u>è</u>terions	ach<u>è</u>teriez	ach<u>è</u>teraient
appeler *to call*	appe<u>ll</u>erais	appe<u>ll</u>erais	appe<u>ll</u>erait	appe<u>ll</u>erions	appe<u>ll</u>eriez	appe<u>ll</u>eraient
jeter *to throw*	je<u>tt</u>erais	je<u>tt</u>erais	je<u>tt</u>erait	je<u>tt</u>erions	je<u>tt</u>eriez	je<u>tt</u>eraient

Examples

Here are some examples that use the simple conditional tense:

Je **voyagerais** chaque année si j'avais de l'argent.	*I **would travel** every year if I had money.*
Si j'étais toi, je **n'irais pas** à la gym aujourd'hui.	*If I were you, I **wouldn't go** to the gym today.*
Si j'avais beaucoup d'argent, j'**achèterais** un palais.	*If I had a lot of money, I **would buy** a palace.*
Vous **pourriez** étudier plus d'heures pour l'examen.	*You **could** study more hours for the exam.*
Pourriez-vous me passer le poivre?	***Could** you pass me the pepper?*
Vivrions-nous dans une petite ville?	***Would** we **live** in a small city?*
Ils **dormiraient** toute la journée s'ils n'avaient pas de travail.	*They **would sleep** all day if they didn't have work.*
Il **dirait** la vérité s'ils le lui demandaient.	*He **would tell** the truth if they asked him.*

The Conditional Perfect: "Would/Could/Should have"

To convey the meaning of *"would/could/should have …"* in French, we resort to the conditional perfect tense.

❖ *"Would have"* + past participle = **"avoir"** or **"être"** in conditional tense + past participle, for example:

Je l'**aurais fait**.	*I **would have done** it.*
Ils **auraient payé**.	*They **would have paid**.*
Nous **serions venus**.	*We **would have come**.*

❖ *"Could have"* + past participle = **"avoir"** or **"être"** in conditional tense + **"pouvoir"** in past participle + infinitive, for example:

J'**aurais pu** le **faire**.	*I **could have done** it.*
Ils **auraient pu payer**.	*They **could have paid**.*

| Nous **aurions pu venir**. | *We **could have come**.* |

❖ *"Should have"* + past participle = **"avoir"** or **"être"** in conditional tense + **"devoir"** in past participle + infinitive, for example:

J'aurais dû le faire.	*I **should have done** it.*
Ils **auraient dû payer**.	*They **should have paid**.*
Nous **aurions dû venir**.	*We **should have come**.*

4. PRESENT SUBJUNCTIVE TENSE II

We discussed some of the uses of the subjunctive mood in **Level IV, Lesson 5**, mainly expressing opinions, possibilities, desires, wishes, feelings, and requests. Here, we will cover other cases in which the subjunctive mood ought to be used.

Expressions Starting with "Que"

The conjunction **"que"** can mean *"whether,"* or can express a wish or hope if placed in the beginning of an expression followed by the subjunctive. For example:

| <u>Que</u> la neige **soit** partout. | <u>*Let*</u> *the snow **be** everywhere.* |
| <u>Que</u> vous y **alliez** ou non, peu importe. | <u>*Whether*</u> *you **go** or not, it doesn't matter.* |

Expressions with Conjunctions ending in "que"

Let us examine the following expressions:

afin que	*so that, in order that*
pour que	
pourvu que	*provided (that)*
à condition que	*on the condition that*
à moins que	*unless*
sans que	*without (that)*
avant que	*before (that)*
bien que	*although, despite that*
quoique	

Such expressions are often followed by the subjunctive, for example:

Donnez-moi la clé <u>pour que</u> je **puisse** entrer.	*Give me the key <u>so that</u> he **can** get in.*
Je ferai de mon mieux <u>pour que</u> vous **vous amusiez**.	*I will do my best <u>so that</u> you **enjoy** your time.*
<u>À moins que</u> vous (ne) **travailliez** dur, il sera difficile de vivre ici.	*<u>Unless</u> you **work** hard, it will be difficult to live here.*
Je laisserai la clé <u>sans</u> qu'il la **voie**.	*I will leave the key <u>without</u> him **seeing**.*
<u>Avant que</u> le jeu (ne) **commence**, allons faire du shopping.	*<u>Before</u> the game **starts**, let's go shopping.*
J'irai à la gym <u>bien que</u> je **sois** fatigué.	*I'll go to the gym <u>although</u> I **am** tired.*

Notice that the **"ne"** after **"à moins que"** and **"avant que"** is redundant and does not affect the meaning. In daily speech, it is often dropped.

In a sense, all the expressions above indicate either doubt or a hypothetical situation, that is, non-fact statements that require the use of the subjunctive mood.

Expressions with Some Conjunctions ending in "-que"

Some conjunctions end in "**-que**," many of which convey the meaning of *"any,"* such as *"whatever," "whenever," "wherever," "whoever,"* etc. Many of these conjunctions require the use of the subjunctive. Examples include:

quel <u>que</u> (soit qui …)	*any, whatever, whichever (it is that …)*
qui <u>que</u> (ce soit)	*whoever (it is)*
quelqu'un (qui)	*someone (who)*
où <u>que</u> (tu sois)	*wherever (you are)*
rien <u>que</u> (je sache)	*nothing that (I know of)*

Superlative Expressions with "que" followed by a Verb

If a superlative expression has a verb in the subordinate clause that follows "**que**," the verb should be in the subjunctive. For example:

| C'est la personne la plus honnête <u>que</u> je **connaisse**. | *He is the most honest person <u>that</u> I* **know.** |
| C'est le maximum <u>que</u> vous **puissiez** faire. | *This is the most <u>that</u> you* **can** *do.* |

Expressions meaning "Although" or "Despite (that)"

The conjunctions "**bien que**," "**malgré que**," "**quoique**," "**encore que**," and "**même si**" all have the meaning of *"although," "even though,"* or *"despite (that),"* and all of them, except "**même si**," require the use of the verb in the subjunctive. Here are some examples:

Il voyage beaucoup <u>bien qu</u>'il ne **soit** pas riche.	
Il voyage beaucoup <u>malgré qu</u>'il ne **soit** pas riche.	
Il voyage beaucoup <u>quoiqu</u>'il ne **soit** pas riche.	*He travels a lot <u>although</u> he* **is** *not rich.*
Il voyage beaucoup <u>encore qu</u>'il ne **soit** pas riche.	
Il voyage beaucoup <u>même s</u>'il n'**est** pas riche.	

Notice that "**même si**" is the only conjunction that requires the indicative to convey the same meaning of *"although"* or *"despite that."*

If "**même si**" is followed by the *imperfect*, the meaning changes to *"even if,"* and the preceding phrase is often in the *conditional tense*, for example:

| Il voyagerait beaucoup <u>même s</u>'il n'**était** pas riche. | *He would travel a lot <u>even if</u> he* **were** *not rich.* |

5. PAST SUBJUNCTIVE TENSE

We have previously studied the subjunctive mood and the present subjunctive tense. The subjunctive mood is used to express opinion, possibilities, and feelings, such as fear, doubt, hope, desire, etc.

We have also studied the compound past tense in the indicative mood. The compound past tense is used to describe events that happened and completed in the past or happened in the past and continue in the present.

Now, we will study the cases when we want to express opinions, possibilities, and feelings, such as fear, doubt, hope, desire, etc., about something that happened and was completed in the past or happened in the past and continues in the present. In other words, we want to describe the compound past but in the subjunctive mood, i.e., the past subjunctive tense.

The past subjunctive, similar to the compound past in the indicative, uses the past participle. However, the only difference is that the auxiliary verb, whether it is **"avoir"** or **"être,"** is conjugated in the subjunctive.

Let us look at some examples of verbs conjugated using the auxiliary **"avoir"**:

		-er ending **parlare**	-ir ending **finir**	-re ending **vendre**
j'	aie			
tu	aies			
il/elle/on	ait			
nous	ayons	parl**é**	fin**i**	vend**u**
vous	ayez			
ils/elles	aient			

Similarly, these are some examples of verbs conjugated using the auxiliary **"être"**:

		-er ending **e.g., aller** *(to go)*	-ir ending **e.g., partir** *(to leave)*	-re ending **e.g., descender** *(to go down)*
je	sois	all**é**(e)	parti(e)	descendu(e)
tu	sois	all**é**(e)	parti(e)	descendu(e)
il/on	soit	all**é**	parti	descendu
elle	soit	all**ée**	parti**e**	descend**ue**
nous	soyons	all**é**(e)s	parti(e)s	descendu(e)s
vous	soyez	all**é**(e)s	parti(e)s	descendu(e)s
ils/elles	soient	all**é**(e)s	parti(e)s	descendu(e)s

Here are some more examples in context:

Examples	
C'est bien que vous **vous soyez détendu** après le match.	*It is good that you **have relaxed** after the match.*
Je suis content que tu **aies apprécié** ton voyage.	*I'm glad that you **have enjoyed** your trip.*
Ça me rend triste qu'il ne m'**ait** pas **appelé**.	*It makes me sad that he **hasn't called** me.*
Je doute que nous **ayons vu** votre maison avant aujourd'hui.	*I doubt that we **have seen** your house before today.*
Je suis content que tu **sois arrivé**.	*I am happy that you **have arrived**.*
Je ne crois pas qu'ils **aient vécu** ici.	*I don't believe they **have lived** here.*

6. IMPERFECT INDICATIVE TENSE

The imperfect indicative tense is used to describe:

1. Habitual or repeated actions in the past, e.g., *"I used to play volleyball when I was young."*
2. Actions that continued in the past for an undefined period, especially those interrupted by or in the background of another action, e.g., *"While you were studying, I was watching TV."*
3. Descriptions of people, places, and objects in the past, e.g., *"Da Vinci was a famous painter and scientist."*
4. Time and age in the past, e.g., *"When I was 15 years old, I lived in a village."*

Notice that, depending on the context, the imperfect indicative tense can correspond to the simple past tense or the past progressive tense in English. In some contexts, it can also be translated to *"used to"* + *infinitive* or *"would"* + *infinitive*.

Conjugation

To conjugate verbs in the imperfect for all forms, we begin from the *first-person plural in the present indicative*, that is, the "**nous**" form, e.g., "**parlons**," "**finissons**," "**buvons**," "**partons**," etc., and we extract the stem "**parl-**," "**finiss-**," "**buv-**," "**part-**," etc., by dropping the last "**-ons**."

The suffixes are the same for all three types of verbs.

	parler *(to speak)* nous <u>parl</u>ons	**finir** *(to finish)* nous <u>finiss</u>ons	**boire** *(to drink)* nous <u>buv</u>ons
je	parl**ais**	finiss**ais**	buv**ais**
tu	parl**ais**	finiss**ais**	buv**ais**
il/elle/on	parl**ait**	finiss**ait**	buv**ait**
nous	parl**ions**	finiss**ions**	buv**ions**
vous	parl**iez**	finiss**iez**	buv**iez**
ils/elles	parl**aient**	finiss**aient**	buv**aient**

Irregular Verbs

In essence, the verb "**être**" *(to be)* is the only irregular verb in the imperfect.

	je	tu	il/elle/on	nous	vous	ils/elles
être *to be*	étais	étais	était	étions	étiez	étaient

Some verbs in the imperfect undergo minor spelling changes similar to those encountered in conjugation in other tenses to maintain the proper pronunciation, for example:

	je	tu	il/elle/on	nous	vous	ils/elles
manger *to eat*	mangeais	mangeais	mangeait	mangions	mangiez	mangeaient
menacer *to threaten*	menaçais	menaçais	menaçait	menacions	menaciez	menaçaient

Examples

Let us now look at some examples of the imperfect in different contexts:

*As a child, I **used to live** in a village.* Enfant, je **vivais** dans un village.	Habit in the past, indicated by *"used to"*
*In the past, I **would sleep** only a few hours.* Autrefois, je ne **dormais** que quelques heures.	Habit in the past, indicated by *"would"*

My school professor **was** *tall.* Mon professeur d'école **était** grand.	Description in the past
When I **was** *15 years old, I* **used to play** *tennis.* Quand **j'avais** 15 ans, je jouais au tennis.	Time and age in the past
I **was** *at work when you called me.* J'**étais** au travail quand tu m'as appelé.	Actions continuously happening in the past when interrupted by another action

In general, use the imperfect when the sentence is in the *past* and you see words such as: **"habituellement"** *(usually)*, **"toujours"** *(always)*, **"pendant"** *(while)*, **"tous les jours"** *(every day)*, **"de temps en temps"** *(every so often)*, etc., or phrases such as: **"en tant qu'enfant"** *(as a child)*, **"quand j'étais jeune"** *(when I was young)*, **"quand j'avais 15 ans"** *(when I was 15 years old)*, etc.

Quand j'**étais** jeune, je **pouvais** beaucoup courir.	*When I* **was** *young, I* **could** *run a lot.*
Quand j'**étais** enfant, j'**aimais** les fruits.	*When I* **was** *a child, I* **used to like** *fruits.*
Quand j'**étais** adolescent, je **buvais** du café.	*When I* **was** *a teenager, I* **used to drink** *coffee.*

Also, use the imperfect when comparing the present to the past, for example:

Aujourd'hui, il est facile de voyager, <u>mais avant</u>, c'**était** difficile.	*Today it is easy to travel, <u>but before</u>, it* **used to be** *difficult.*

Another important use of the imperfect tense is to express a past intention of doing something that does not end up being done in the present. These are expressions such as *"I was going to …,"* *"I was thinking of …,"* and *"I wanted to …."*

The general formula of such expressions is as follows:

Imperfect tense of (**"aller,"** **"penser,"** or **"vouloir"**) + *infinitive*

For example:

J'**allais** t'appeler, mais je me suis endormi.	*I was going to call you, but I fell asleep.*
Je **pensais** sortir, mais il est déjà trop tard.	*I was thinking of going out, but it's already too late.*

| Je **voulais** venir, mais j'ai eu un accident. | *I **wanted to*** *come, but I had an accident.* |

On the other hand, use the compound past if you are talking about actions with a defined time or period in the past. Look for expressions such as: *yesterday, last night, last week, ago, in 1994, from… to…, two times, for three hours, the other day*, etc. These expressions may not be explicitly used, but the meaning can implicitly refer to a defined time or period in the past, which necessitates the use of the compound past.

*I **visited*** *my mother last night.* J'**ai rendu** visite à ma mère hier soir.	Action with defined time in the past (last night)
*I **talked*** *to her the other day.* Je lui **ai parlé** l'autre jour.	Action with defined time in the past (the other day [1])
*In 1922, Alexander Bell **invented*** *the telephone.* En 1922, Alexander Bell **a inventé** le téléphone.	Action with defined time in the past (in 1922)

Special Constructions in the Imperfect

One special use of the imperfect is the construction:

"**si**" + "**on**" + imperfect indicative

Expressions that contain the above structure are often translated as *"what about …?"*, that is, suggesting or inviting someone to do something. Here are some examples:

Si on **sortait** ce soir?	*What about **going out*** *tonight?*
Si on **achetait** quelque chose à manger?	*What about **buying*** *something to eat?*
Si on y **mangeait** aujourd'hui?	*What about **eating*** *there today?*
Si on **jouait** au football demain?	*What about **playing*** *soccer tomorrow?*

Another expression that uses the imperfect is:

"**si**" + "**seulement**" + subject pronoun + imperfect indicative

---

[1] Although *"the other day"* may seem vague and undefined, it is considered a defined time from a grammatical viewpoint. In addition, the sentence does not imply any habit or continuous action in the past.

The above expression is often translated as *"if only ..."* Here are some examples:

Si seulement je **savais**.	*If only I **knew**.*
Si seulement il **était** là.	*If only he **was** there.*
Si seulement nous **avions** assez d'argent.	*If only we **had** enough money.*
Si seulement ils **venaient** avec nous.	*If only they **came** with us.*

7. TIME EXPRESSIONS: "EN TRAIN DE," "VENIR DE," "DEPUIS," & "ÇA FAIT"

In this lesson, we will learn more advanced time expressions that are common in French.

1. "En train de"

The French language does not have a present or past continuous tense equivalent to that in English, e.g., *"I am/was speaking."* It is common to use the simple present tense in French to talk about actions that are happening right now, e.g., **"Je parle"** *(I am talking)*, **"Qu'est-ce que tu fais?"** *(What are you doing?)*, etc. We have also seen in **Lesson 6** of this level how the imperfect can be used sometimes to describe the past continuous in English, e.g., **"Pendant que tu étudiais, je regardais la télé"** *(While you were studying, I was watching TV)*.

To emphasize the continuous state of an action, one could use the expression **"être en train de"** *(to be in the process of)*. Here are some examples:

Je **suis en train de parler**.	*I am speaking.*
Il **est en train de manger**.	*He is eating.*
Nous **sommes en train de jouer**.	*We are playing.*

The verb **"être"** *(to be)* can be used in the *imperfect* to describe actions that were happening continuously in the past, for example:

J'**étais** en train de parler.	*I **was speaking**.*
Il **était** en train de manger.	*He **was eating**.*
Nous **étions** en train de jouer.	*We **were playing**.*

Similarly, the conditional continuous tense can be expressed by using the verb "**être**" in the simple conditional tense, for example:

Je **serais** en train de parler.	*I **would be speaking**.*
Il **serait** en train de manger.	*He **would be eating**.*
Nous **serions** en train de jouer.	*We **would be playing**.*

Unless you want to stress the continuous nature of an action, simple tenses are often used instead of the expression "**être en train de**" in most situations.

2. "Venir de"

The verb "**venir**" *(to come)* is used in the expression "**venir de**" to express the recent past, often described in English as *"having just done something."* In this case, the verb "**venir**" is conjugated in the simple present indicative tense. Let us take some examples:

Je **viens de finir** de manger.	*I **have just finished** eating.*
Il **vient d'arriver** il y a peu de temps.	*He **has just arrived** a while ago.*
Nous **venons d'atterrir** à Londres.	*We **have just landed** in London.*

If the verb "**venir**" is in the *imperfect*, it can be used to describe something that *"had just happened"* before something else happened next, for example:

Je **venais de terminer** avant que tu appelles.	*I **had just finished** before you called.*
Il **venait d'arriver** quand je m'apprêtais à sortir.	*He **had just arrived** when I was about to go out.*
J'ai appris la nouvelle après que nous **venions d'atterrir** à Londres.	*I heard the news after we **had just landed** in London.*

3. "Depuis"

Depending on the context, "**depuis**" can mean *"since"* or *"for."*

If used to indicate a point in time in the past, it is usually translated as *"since,"* for example:

J'habite ici **depuis** avril dernier.	*I have been living here **since** last April.*
Je joue au football **depuis** que je suis enfant.	*I have played football **since** I was a child.*
Je n'ai pas voyagé **depuis** 2019.	*I haven't traveled **since** 2019.*

On the other hand, "**depuis**" is translated as *"for"* when describing a duration of time, for example:

J'habite ici **depuis** deux ans.	*I have been living here **for** two years.*
Je n'ai pas voyagé **depuis** trois ans.	*I haven't traveled **for** three years.*

Notice that in both sets of examples, when the statement is in the *affirmative*, the sentence preceding "**depuis**" is in the *present simple* tense in French although the English equivalent is in the present perfect or present perfect continuous.

If the sentence preceding "**depuis**" is in the *past* tense in French, it is often translated into the past perfect in English, for example:

Je n'avais pas mangé **depuis** ton arrivée.	*I hadn't eaten **since** you arrived.*
Nous te cherchions **depuis** des heures quand tu as appelé.	*We had been looking for you **for** hours when you called.*

Alternatively, "**pour**" or "**pendant**" can replace "**depuis**" when used meaning *"for"* if the French verb is in the past, for example:

Nous te cherchions **pour** des heures quand tu as appelé.	*We had been looking for you **for** hours when you called.*
Nous te cherchions **pendant** des heures quand tu as appelé.	*We had been looking for you **for** hours when you called.*

4. "Ça fait"

The expression **"ça fait … que …"** using the verb **"faire"** is often used in informal speech. It is often translated as *"it's been … that …"* Let us take some examples:

Ça fait deux ans **que** j'habite ici.	*I have been living here **for** two years.*
Ça fait trois ans **que** je n'ai pas voyagé.	*I haven't traveled **for** three years.*

Alternatively, **"il y a"** or **"voilà"** can replace **"ça fait"** in the previous examples, for instance:

Il y a deux ans **que** j'habite ici.	*I have been living here **for** two years.*
Voilà trois ans **que** je n'ai pas voyagé.	*I haven't traveled **for** three years.*

II. Vocabulary Building

Go over the vocabulary in this section. You could use Anki to study and memorize the new vocabulary efficiently.

1. VERBS V

Below is a list of some important verbs that we need at this level:

English	French	Examples
accomplish	accomplir réaliser	J'**ai accompli** mon objectif de devenir en bonne santé. *I **have accomplished** my goal of becoming healthy.*
admonish	admonester	J'ai dû **admonester** mes élèves aujourd'hui. *I had to **admonish** my students today.*
advertise	annoncer promouvoir	Vous pouvez **annoncer** pour votre entreprise à la télévision. *You can **advertise** your business on TV.*
afford	se permettre	Il est riche et peut **se permettre** n'importe quelle dépense. *He is rich and can **afford** any expense.*
age	vieillir	Cette viande **a** très bien **vieilli**. *This meat **has aged** very well.*

agree	**être d'accord** **convenir**	J'**ai été d'accord** avec son discours en l'écoutant. *I **agreed** with his speech upon listening to him.*
amaze	**émerveiller** **étonner**	La technologie moderne m'**émerveille** toujours. *Modern technology always **amazes** me.*
anger	**fâcher** **mettre en colère**	Son traitement des clients me **met en colère**. *His treatment of customers **angers** me.*
announce	**annoncer**	Ma tante **annoncera** sa grossesse samedi. *My aunt **will announce** her pregnancy on Saturday.*
approach (motion)	**s'approcher**	J'ai vu comment l'écureuil **s'approchait** de mes plantes. *I saw how the squirrel **approached** my plants.*
assure **ensure**	**assurer**	Je vous **assure** que vous allez aimer cela. *I **assure** you that you will like it.*
attract	**attirer**	Les pôles opposés **s'attirent** l'un l'autre. *Opposite poles **attract** one another.*
bark	**aboyer**	Mon chien **aboie** beaucoup. *My dog **barks** a lot.*
be born	**naître**	Mon neveu **naîtra** par césarienne. *My nephew **will be born** through a C-section.*
be worth	**valoir**	Cette version du livre **vaut** une fortune. *That version of the book **is worth** a fortune.*
beg	**mendier** **supplier**	Je n'aimerais pas devoir **mendier**. *I wouldn't like to have **to beg**.*
bend	**plier**	Il **a plié** involontairement la fourchette avec sa main. *He inadvertently **bent** the fork with his hand.*
benefit	**bénéficier**	Vous pouvez **bénéficier** de cet arrangement. *You can **benefit** from that arrangement.*
bet	**parier** **miser**	Il **pariait** toujours beaucoup d'argent. *He **used to** always **bet** a lot of money.*
bite	**mordre**	Il **a mordu** le fromage car il avait faim. *He **bit off** the cheese because he was hungry.*
blackmail	**faire du chantage**	Il **a fait du chantage** à ses amis quand ils l'ont confronté. *He **blackmailed** his friends when they confronted him.*
blame	**blâmer** **en vouloir**	Je ne lui **en veux** pas de vouloir partir. *I don't **blame** him for wanting to leave.*
bleed	**saigner**	Je n'aime pas voir les gens **saigner**. *I don't like to see people **bleed**.*

blink	clinger clignoter	Il faut **cligner** des paupières pour hydrater vos yeux. *You have to **blink** to hydrate your eyes.*
bloom blossom	fleurir	Les roses **fleurissent** au printemps. *Roses **bloom** in the spring.*
boil	bouillir	L'eau **bout** à 100 degrés Celsius. *The water **boils** at 100 degrees Celsius.*
borrow	emprunter	Puis-je **emprunter** votre brosse? *Can I **borrow** your brush?*
bow	s'incliner	Au Japon, il est d'usage de **s'incliner** en saluant. *In Japan, it's customary to **bow** when saluting.*
break down	tomber en panne	Ma voiture est **tombée en panne** hier. *My car **broke down** yesterday.*
breastfeed	allaiter	La chatte **allaite** ses bébés. *The cat **is breastfeeding** its babies.*
bribe	soudoyer corrompre	Vous ne devriez jamais **corrompre** la police. *You should never **bribe** the police.*
burst	éclater	La bouteille **a éclaté** à cause de la pression. *The bottle **burst** because of the pressure.*
cage	mettre en cage	Au cirque, ils **mettent** les animaux **en cage**. *In the circus they **cage** the animals.*
carry out	effectuer réaliser	Vendredi, ils **effectueront** les tâches restantes. *On Friday, they **will carry out** the remaining tasks.*
catch	attraper rattraper	La police a réussi à **attraper** le voleur. *The police managed to **catch** the thief.*
chew	mâcher mastiquer	Il est impoli de **mâcher** du chewing-gum en classe. *It's bad manners to **chew** gum in class.*
clap applaud	applaudir	Tout le monde **a applaudi** quand il a fini de chanter. *Everyone **applauded** when he finished singing.*
clarify	clarifier	Pouvez-vous **clarifier** cette réponse? *Can you **clarify** this answer?*
classify sort	classer	Pouvez-vous **classer** ces dossiers? *Can you **classify** these folders?*
climb	monter grimper	Ne **grimpe** pas à l'arbre! *Don't **climb** the tree!*
complain	se plaindre	Ne **te plains** pas autant. *Don't **complain** so much.*
conceal	dissimuler	Son ami a essayé de **dissimuler** ce qu'il avait volé. *His friend tried to **conceal** what he had stolen.*

cool down	refroidir	Vous devez laisser le pain **refroidir**. *You have to let the bread **cool down**.*
cough	tousser	J'**ai** beaucoup **toussé** avec la grippe le mois dernier. *I **coughed** a lot with the flu last month.*
crack	craquer se fissure	Ça **se fissurera** si vous y versez de l'eau chaude. *It **will crack** if you pour hot water into it.*
crawl	ramper	Il a appris à **ramper** quand il était tout petit. *He learned how to **crawl** when he was very little.*
curl	se boucler	Je **me bouclerai** les cheveux pour sortir. *I **will curl** my hair to go out.*
dare	oser	J'**oserai** parler devant un public. *I **will dare** to talk in front of an audience.*
deal with	traiter avec	Il est difficile de **traiter avec** des personnes cruelles. *It is difficult to **deal with** cruel people.*
demand require	exiger	Mon précédent travail **exigeait** que je porte un uniforme. *My previous job **demanded** that I wear a uniform.*
dent	cabosser enfoncer	L'accident **a enfoncé** ma voiture. *The accident **dented** my car.*
deprive	priver	Ce n'est pas bon de se **priver** tout le temps. *It's not good to **deprive** yourself all the time.*
discourage	décourager	Je ne veux pas te **décourager** de continuer. *I don't want to **discourage** you from continuing.*
disturb	déranger	Tu ne devrais pas **déranger** les chiens du voisin. *You shouldn't **disturb** the neighbor's dogs.*
download	télécharger	Dans le passé, je **téléchargeais** de la musique illégalement. *In the past, I **would download** music illegally.*
drag	glisser traîner	J'**ai** accidentellement **traîné** une boîte avec ma voiture. *I accidentally **dragged** a box with my car.*
drag & drop	glisser et déposer	Faites **glisser et déposer** les éléments sur la page. ***Drag and drop** the elements on the page.*
drop	tomber	La pluie **est** soudainement **tombée** du ciel. *The rain suddenly **dropped** from the sky.*
empty	vider	Pouvez-vous **vider** vos poches? *Can you **empty** your pockets?*
enrich	enrichir	Je ne crois pas que je **m'enrichirai**, mais je vais essayer. *I don't believe I **will enrich myself**, but I'll try.*

erupt	**éclater** entrer en éruption	Le volcan **est entré en éruption** le mois dernier. *The volcano **erupted** last month.*
evaluate **assess**	**évaluer**	Je dois **évaluer** les dégâts. *I have to **assess** the damages.*
exhaust **deplete**	**épuiser**	Je dois **épuiser** toutes les chances. *I have to **exhaust** all the chances.*
explode	**exploser** **éclater**	J'ai entendu comment les grains de maïs **explosaient**. *I heard how the popcorn kernels **were exploding**.*
extract	**extraire**	Ils **ont extrait** mes dents de sagesse. *They **extracted** my wisdom teeth.*
familiarize **acquaint**	**se familiariser**	Vous devez **vous familiariser** avec les étapes. *You have to **familiarize yourself** with the steps.*
flow	**couler**	L'eau **coule** dans la conduite pour générer de l'énergie. *The water **flows** in the duct to generate power.*
graduate	**obtenir son diplôme**	J'**obtiendrai mon diplôme** cette année. *I **will graduate** this year.*
grant	**accorder**	Ils m'**accorderont** une bourse complète. *They **will grant** me a full scholarship.*
greet	**saluer**	Vous devez **saluer** vos invités quand ils arrivent. *You have to **greet** your guests when they arrive.*
haggle **bargain**	**marchander**	J'**ai marchandé** le prix de ma voiture quand je l'ai achetée. *I **haggled** over the price of my car when I bought it.*
heat	**chauffer** **réchauffer**	Le poêle à bois **chauffait** mieux dans le passé. *The wood stove **heated** better in the past.*
hinder	**entraver** **empêcher**	La hauteur de la colline **entrave** l'atterrissage. *The height of the hill **hinders** landing.*
hold	**tenir**	Pouvez-vous **tenir** mon bébé pendant une seconde? *Can you **hold** my baby for a second?*
hook	**accrocher**	Il **a accroché** un poisson du premier coup hier. *He **hooked** a fish on the first try yesterday.*
hunt	**chasser**	Je n'aime pas **chasser**. *I don't like to **hunt**.*
induce	**induire** **provoquer**	Les médecins ont décidé de **provoquer** l'accouchement. *The doctors decided to **induce** the labor.*
inhabit	**habiter**	Beaucoup d'ours **habitent** cette zone. *Many bears **inhabit** this zone.*

inherit	hériter	Il **a hérité** de la maison de sa grand-mère. *He **inherited** his grandmother's house.*
interrupt	interrompre	Ne m'**interrompez** pas quand je parle. *Do not **interrupt** me when I'm talking.*
invest	investir	N'**investissez** pas d'argent du budget du ménage. *Don't **invest** money from the household's budget.*
judge	juger	Je n'aime pas qu'on me **juge** sans me connaître. *I don't like that they **judge** me without knowing me.*
kidnap	kidnapper séquestrer	J'ai entendu dire qu'ils **ont kidnappé** une autre personne. *I heard they **kidnapped** another person.*
knock (door)	frapper	**Frappez** à la porte avant d'entrer. ***Knock** on the door before you enter.*
land	atterrir	L'avion **a atterri** tôt. *The airplane **landed** early.*
legislate	légiférer	Ils essaient de **légiférer** sur cette question. *They are trying to **legislate** on this issue.*
lend	prêter	Pouvez-vous me **prêter** de l'argent? *Can you **lend** me money?*
lie down	s'allonger se coucher	Je dois **m'allonger** pour me reposer. *I have to **lie down** to rest.*
locate	localiser	As-tu pu **localiser** ta mère? *Were you able to **locate** your mom?*
make a mistake	se tromper faire une erreur	Je **me suis trompé** en achetant cette marque de thé. *I **made a mistake** buying this brand of tea.*
make sense	avoir du sens	Maintenant, tout cela **a du sens** pour moi. *It all **makes sense** to me now.*
mature	mûrir	Cet avocat a besoin de **mûrir** davantage. *That avocado needs to **mature** more.*
misinterpret	mal interpréter	Il **a mal interprété** ce que j'ai dit la dernière fois. *He **misinterpreted** what I said last time.*
moan	gémir	Mon chat me fait peur quand elle **gémit**. *My cat scares me when she **moans**.*
move (emotionally)	toucher	Ce film me **touche** toujours. *That movie always **moves** me.*
move (direction)	déplacer bouger	Pouvez-vous **vous déplacer** d'une place? *Can you **move** a spot?*
move (residence)	déménager	Mon voisin **déménagera** le mois prochain. *My neighbor **will move** next month.*
obey	obéir	Mon chien m'**obéit** toujours. *My dog always **obeys** me.*

obstruct	obstruer	Ce poteau **obstrue** le passage. *That post **obstructs** the way.*
oppose to	s'opposer à	Il **s'oppose** toujours à mes propositions. *He always **opposes** my proposals.*
overcome surpass exceed	**surpasser** **dépasser**	Je veux **surpasser** ma meilleure note. *I want to **surpass** my best mark.*
pardon	**pardonner** **excuser**	Il faudra **excuser** ses manières. *You'll have to **pardon** his manners.*
paste	coller	**Collez** ce bord avec l'autre. ***Paste** that edge with the other one.*
play (instrument)	jouer	Enfant, je **jouais** de la flûte. *As a child, I **played** the flute.*
polish	polir	Elle **a poli** tous les couverts l'année dernière. *She **polished** all the cutlery last year.*
pour	verser	Elle **a versé** le jus dans sa tasse et est partie. *She **poured** the juice in her cup and left.*
preach	prêcher	Nous devons **prêcher** la paix entre les gens. *We must **preach** peace among people.*
prevent	**prévenir** **éviter** [1]	Être prudent **évite** beaucoup d'accidents. *Being cautious **prevents** lots of accidents.*
promise	promettre	Il m'**a promis** qu'il se comporterait bien cette fois-ci. *He **promised** me he'd behave well this time.*
quit	quitter	Elle a dit qu'elle veut **quitter** le groupe. *She said she wants to **quit** the band.*
recover	**récupérer** **recouvrer** **se mettre**	Je dois **récupérer** après avoir couru. *I have to **recover** after running.*
reflect	refléter	C'est tellement propre que ça **reflète** tout. *It's so clean it **reflects** everything.*
refresh freshen up	rafraîchir	J'ai dû **rafraîchir** l'air plusieurs fois. *I had to **refresh** the air several times.*
reimburse	rembourser	La société ne **rembourse** pas les frais d'expédition. *The company doesn't **reimburse** the shipping costs.*
reinforce	renforcer	Son livre a aidé à **renforcer** le nouveau concept. *His book helped **reinforce** the new concept.*
release	**relâcher** **libérer**	Il **a relâché** son papillon de compagnie hier soir. *He **released** his pet butterfly last night.*

---

[1] The verb "**éviter**" can also mean *"to avoid"* depending on the context.

repent	**se repentir**	Il est important de **se repentir** pour apprendre. *It's important to **repent** in order to learn.*
resign	**démissionner**	Il **a démissionné** de son poste dans l'entreprise. *He **resigned** from his position in the company.*
restrict	**restreindre**	L'accès à cette zone est **restreint**. *Access to that zone is **restricted**.*
rhyme	**rimer**	J'essaie de faire **rimer** mes poèmes. *I try to make my poems **rhyme**.*
roll	**rouler**	Il **a roulé** en bas de la colline par accident. *He **rolled** down the hill by accident.*
rub	**frotter**	Il faut **frotter** la crème pour qu'elle fonctionne. *You have to **rub** the cream on for it to work.*
sail **navigate**	**naviguer**	Il aimait **naviguer** à travers la mer. *He loved to **sail** across the sea.*
scan **(computer)**	**numériser**	Pouvez-vous **numériser** ces pages, s'il vous plaît? *Can you **scan** these pages, please?*
scare	**effrayer** **faire peur**	Les fantômes me **font peur**. *Ghosts **scare** me.*
scatter	**disperser**	Le vent **a dispersé** tous mes papiers. *The wind **scattered** all of my papers.*
schedule	**programmer** **planifier**	Je vous **programmerai** pour la semaine prochaine. *I **will schedule** you for next week.*
scold	**gronder** **réprimander**	Ils **grondent** leur fils tout le temps. *They **scold** their son all the time.*
sew	**coudre**	Je **coudrai** mes chaussettes. *I **will sew** my socks.*
slim down	**maigrir** **mincir**	Il **a** beaucoup **maigri** cette année. *He **slimmed down** a lot this year.*
sneeze	**éternuer**	Au printemps, j'**éternue** beaucoup. *In the spring I **sneeze** a lot.*
spin	**tourner**	Les roues ont commencé à **tourner** tout de suite. *The wheels started to **spin** right away.*
stroll **go for a walk**	**se promener**	Je me sens calme quand je vais **me promener** sur la plage. *I feel calm when I **go for a walk** on the beach.*
subscribe	**s'abonner** **souscrire**	Ils **se sont abonnés** à la salle de sport pendant un an. *They **subscribed** to the gym for a year.*
subtract	**soustraire**	Il faut **soustraire** 100 dollars de la dette. *You have to **subtract** $100 from the debt.*

sue	**poursuivre**	Ils veulent **poursuivre** l'entreprise. *They want to **sue** the company.*
suspect	**soupçonner** **suspecter**	J'**ai soupçonné** que le vieil homme était le tueur. *I **suspected** the old man was the killer.*
swing **oscillate**	**osciller**	Le pendule de l'horloge **oscille** correctement. *The clock's pendulum **swings** correctly.*
take advantage of	**profiter de** **bénéficier de**	Je **profiterai de** l'offre et j'en acheterai trois. *I **will take advantage of** the offer and I'll buy three.*
take off	**décoller**	Nous **décollerons** dans une demi-heure. *We **will take off** in half an hour.*
tempt	**tenter**	Ces gâteaux me **tentent** toujours. *Those cakes always **tempt** me.*
tie	**lacer** **attacher** **nouer**	Il faut savoir **nouer** ses lacets tout seul. *You have to know how to **tie** your shoelaces by yourself.*
trap	**piéger**	Il a utilisé une nouvelle technique pour **piéger** son adversaire. *He used a new technique to **trap** his opponent.*
turn	**tourner**	**Tournez** à droite, puis continuez tout droit. ***Turn** right and then keep going straight ahead.*
update	**mettre à jour** **actualiser**	Je dois **mettre à jour** le système d'exploitation. *I have to **update** the operating system.*
welcome	**accueillir**	Les conseillers nous **ont accueillis** hier. *The advisors **welcomed** us yesterday.*
whisper	**chuchoter**	S'il vous plaît, **chuchotez** pour ne pas réveiller le bébé. *Please **whisper** to not wake up the baby.*
witness	**témoigner** **assister**	J'**ai assisté** à l'accident en personne. *I **witnessed** the accident in person.*
wrap	**emballer** **envelopper**	Je suis mauvais pour **emballer** les cadeaux. *I'm bad at **wrapping** gifts.*
yield	**céder**	Tu dois **céder** ta place dans ce coin. *You have to **yield** your spot in that corner.*

In addition to the above new verbs, we add a few more English cognates that are easy to memorize.

English	**French**	**Examples**
absorb	**absorber**	Le sol **a absorbé** toute l'eau immédiatement. *The soil **absorbed** all the water immediately.*
administer	**administrer**	Je dois **administrer** un groupe de 10. *I have to **administer** a group of 10.*

authorize	**autoriser**	Elle **a autorisé** l'utilisation de son image. *She **authorized** the use of her image.*
automate	**automatiser**	Je cherche à **automatiser** les processus. *I am seeking to **automate** the processes.*
coincide	**coïncider**	Nos emplois du temps **coïncident** tous les jours. *Our schedules **coincide** every day.*
collaborate	**collaborer**	Ils **ont collaboré** pour acheter cette voiture. *They **collaborated** to buy this car.*
compile	**compiler**	J'**ai compilé** des photos de mon enfance l'autre jour. *I **compiled** photos of my childhood the other day.*
cooperate	**coopérer**	Ils **ont coopéré** pour construire cette maison. *They **cooperated** to build that house.*
coordinate	**coordonner**	Nous devons **coordonner** la sortie. *We have to **coordinate** the outing.*
declare	**déclarer**	Ils **ont déclaré** leur indépendance il y a 50 ans. *They **declared** their independence 50 years ago.*
denote	**dénoter**	Ce résultat **dénote** un échec général. *This result **denotes** a general failure.*
derive	**dériver**	Ce mot **dérive** du latin. *This word **derives** from Latin.*
deviate	**dévier**	Il est dangereux de **dévier** du sentier. *It's dangerous to **deviate** from the trail.*
disperse	**se disperser**	Le groupe **s'est dispersé** immédiatement. *The group **dispersed** immediately.*
distinguish	**distinguer**	Il ne peut pas **distinguer** le vert du rouge. *He can't **distinguish** between green and red.*
emerge	**émerger**	Il **a émergé** après des mois d'isolement. *He **emerged** after months isolated.*
emit	**émettre**	Ils **ont émis** une alerte concernant les mauvaises conditions météorologiques hier soir. *They **emitted** an alert about the bad weather last night.*
encourage	**encourager**	Ma maman m'**encourage** beaucoup dans ma vie. *My mom **encourages** me a lot in my life.*
envy	**envier**	J'**envie** son style. *I **envy** her style.*
err	**errer**	Il préfère **errer** par prudence. *He prefers to **err** for being cautious.*
execute	**exécuter**	Le soldat **a exécuté** l'ordre immédiatement. *The soldier **executed** the order right away.*
exploit	**exploiter**	Dans cette entreprise, ils **exploitent** leurs employés. *In that company, they **exploit** their employees.*
flirt	**flirter**	Ce n'est pas bien de **flirter** avec des collègues. *It's not good to **flirt** with colleagues.*

forge	**forger**	Mon grand-père **forge** des épées. *My grandfather **forges** swords.*
improvise	**improviser**	Je n'aime pas **improviser** sur le moment. *I don't like to **improvise** on the fly.*
inhale	**inhaler**	J'adore **inhaler** de l'air frais. *I love to **inhale** fresh air.*
inhibit	**inhiber**	Ils sont **inhibés** en public. *They **get inhibited** when in public.*
insert	**insérer**	C'était une fente pour **insérer** des disques. *That was a slot to **insert** disks.*
insinuate	**insinuer**	Vous **insinuez** quelque chose que je n'ai pas dit. *You **are insinuating** something I didn't say.*
inspect	**inspecter**	Il **a inspecté** ma voiture en détail. *He **inspected** my car in detail.*
inspire	**inspirer**	Il a été **inspiré** par les grands écrivains. *He was **inspired** by the great writers.*
interview	**interviewer**	J'**interviewerai** la célébrité. *I **will interview** the celebrity.*
mark	**marquer**	Ils **ont marqué** son passeport à l'aéroport à son entrée. *They **marked** his passport at the airport upon entering.*
mobilize	**mobiliser**	La résistance **s'est mobilisée** contre l'occupation immédiatement. *The resistance **mobilized** against the occupation immediately.*
narrate	**narrer**	J'aime **narrer** des histoires. *I like to **narrate** stories.*
oblige **compel**	**obliger**	Les lois nous **obligent** à nous comporter. *Laws **oblige** us to behave.*
participate	**participer**	J'aimerais **participer** au défilé. *I'd like to **participate** in the parade.*
pedal	**pédaler**	Je **pédale** toujours beaucoup quand j'utilise le vélo. *I always **pedal** a lot when I use the bicycle.*
persist	**persister**	Ces mauvaises herbes **persistent** même si je les coupe. *These weeds **persist** even if I cut them.*
personalize	**personnaliser**	Je **personnalise** toujours mes cahiers. *I always **personalize** my notebooks.*
persuade	**persuader**	Tu dois **persuader** maman pour qu'elle me laisse. *You have to **persuade** mom so she'll let me.*
present	**présenter**	L'entreprise **a présenté** son nouveau projet. *The company **presented** its new project.*
proceed	**procéder**	**Procédez** avec prudence. ***Proceed** with caution.*

prolong	prolonger	J'ai essayé de **prolonger** ma routine. *I tried to **prolong** my routine.*
propose	proposer	Je **propose** qu'ils installent un feu de signalisation. *I **propose** they put a stoplight.*
recite	réciter	Elle devra **réciter** un poème complet. *She will have to **recite** a complete poem.*
refuse reject	refuser	Je **refuse** de payer cette somme. *I **refuse** to pay that amount.*
refute	réfuter	Dans le débat, il **a réfuté** tout ce que j'ai dit. *In the debate, he **refuted** everything I said.*
reprimand	réprimander	Je n'aime pas devoir le **réprimander**. *I don't like having to **reprimand** him.*
sculpt	sculpter	Il a appris à **sculpter** des figures de son père. *He learned to **sculpt** figures from his father.*
stimulate	stimuler	Le café me **stimule** pour travailler davantage. *Coffee **stimulates** me to work more.*
subsist	subsister	J'ai réussi à **subsister** dans la nature. *I've managed to **subsist** in nature.*
substitute	substituer	Je **substituerai** le sucre par de l'édulcorant. *I **will substitute** the sugar for sweetener.*
theorize	théoriser	Les experts **ont théorisé** la solution possible l'année dernière. *The experts **theorized** the possible solution last year.*
transform	transformer	Il **s'est transformé** presque en une autre personne récemment. *He **transformed** almost into another person recently.*
transplant	transplanter	Ils **ont transplanté** un rein dans son corps. *They **transplanted** a kidney into his body.*
validate	valider	Elle doit **valider** son diplôme. *She has to **validate** her diploma.*

2. ADJECTIVES V

Below is a list of some common adjectives that we need at this level. You could use Anki to study and memorize the new vocabulary efficiently. Notice that an adjective must agree with the noun in number and gender.

English	French	Examples
acute sharp	aigus	Je déteste les bruits **aigus**. *I hate **sharp** noises.*
aggregate	aggloméré	Il indique qu'il n'a pas de sucre **aggloméré**. *It says it doesn't have **aggregated** sugar.*
alleged	présumé	C'est un voleur **présumé**. *He's an **alleged** thief.*

astonished	étonné stupéfait	J'ai été **étonné** par ma note. *I was **astounded** by my grade.*
astonishing	étonnant stupéfiant	C'était **étonnant**! *That was **astonishing**!*
balanced	équilibré	J'ai un régime **équilibré**. *I have a **balanced** diet.*
bald	chauve	Mon professeur d'université était **chauve**. *My university teacher was **bald**.*
based on	basé sur	Le livre était **basé sur** des événements réels. *The book was **based on** real events.*
beaten (defeated)	battu	Je me sentais **battu** après le combat. *I felt **beaten** after the fight.*
blurry	flou	Je vois tout **flou** sans mes lunettes. *I see everything **blurry** without my glasses.*
brief	bref	Je m'excuse pour un **bref** moment. *I'll excuse myself for a **brief** moment.*
brunette	brune	Cette femme est **brune**. *That woman is a **brunette**.*
cautious	prudent	Je suis toujours **prudent** dans la rue. *I'm always **cautious** on the street.*
challenging	difficile exigeant	La course est très **difficile**. *The race is very **challenging**.*
clumsy awkward	maladroit	Enfant, j'étais très **maladroit**. *As a child I was very **clumsy**.*
committed	engagé	Ils sont maintenant **engagés** envers la cause. *They're **committed** to the cause now.*
cruel	cruel	Il est difficile de traiter avec des personnes **cruelles**. *It is difficult to deal with **cruel** people.*
curved	courbé	Ma maison a un mur **courbé**. *My house has a **curved** wall.*
deaf	sourd	Mon cousin est né **sourd**. *My cousin was born **deaf**.*
dear	cher	C'était une personne très **chère** pour moi. *He was a very **dear** person to me.*
dented	cabossé bosselé	La voiture était **cabossée** après l'accident. *The car was **dented** after the accident.*
dizzy	étourdi vertigineux	Les montagnes russes me rendent **étourdi**. *Roller coasters leave me **dizzy**.*
edible	comestible	Crois-le ou non, ces fleurs sont **comestibles**. *Believe it or not, those flowers are **edible**.*
embarrassed	gêné embarrassé	J'étais très **gêné** par ce qu'il a dit. *I was very **embarrassed** by what he said.*

embarrassing	gênant embarrassant	C'était un moment un peu **gênant**. *It was a moment that was a bit **embarrassing**.*
envious	envieux	C'est très moche d'être **envieux**. *It's very ugly to be **envious**.*
fidgety agitated restless	agité	Tu es **agité** aujourd'hui. *You're **fidgety** today.*
flattered	flatté	Je suis **flatté** de votre intérêt. *I am **flattered** by your interest.*
flawed	défectueux	J'ai dû le retourner car il était **défectueux**. *I had to return it because it was **flawed**.*
floating	flotant	J'aimais ce canard **flottant**. *I loved that **floating** duck.*
following	prochain	Je suis impatient d'attendre le **prochain** épisode. *I can't wait for the **following** episode.*
former	ancien ex	L'**ancien** propriétaire de la maison l'a peinte. *The **former** owner of the house painted it.*
grated	râpé	J'utilise beaucoup de fromage **râpé**. *I use a lot of **grated** cheese.*
hospitable	hospitalier accueillant	Mon cousin est toujours très **hospitalier**. *My cousin is always very **hospitable**.*
immersed	immergé	J'étais complètement **immergé** dans l'intrigue. *I was completely **immersed** in the plot.*
immigrant	immigrant	Je suis l'enfant de parents **immigrants**. *I'm the child of **immigrant** parents.*
injured	blessé	Il a été **blessé** pendant la course. *He was **injured** during the race.*
intimate	intime	Ils viennent d'avoir un mariage **intime**. *They just had an **intimate** wedding.*
in order	en ordre	J'aime maintenir ma maison **en ordre**. *I like to keep my house **in order**.*
linked	lié	Il est **lié** à de nombreuses rumeurs. *He is **linked** to many rumors.*
long-lasting durable	durable	Ils ont une relation très **durable**. *They have a very **long-lasting** relationship.*
loose	lâche ample	J'aime les vêtements **amples** et confortables. *I like **loose** and comfortable clothes.*
luxurious	luxueux	Le restaurant était très **luxueux**. *The restaurant was very **luxurious**.*
pale	pâle	Tu as l'air très **pâle**. *You look very **pale**.*
picturesque	pittoresque	C'est un paysage **pittoresque**. *It's a **picturesque** landscape.*

populated	peuplé	Cette ville n'est pas très **peuplée**. *This town isn't very **populated**.*
reliable	fiable	Tu sais qu'il est une personne **fiable**. *You know he's a **reliable** person.*
remote	à distance	J'ai un bureau **à distance**. *I have a **remote** office.*
round	rond	La bulle semble **ronde**. *The bubble looks **round**.*
sacred	sacré	Ce sol est **sacré** pour beaucoup de gens. *This ground is **sacred** to many people.*
safe	sûr en sécurité	Il se sent **en sécurité** avec vous. *He feels **safe** with you.*
scared frightened	effrayé terrifié	Mon chiot était **effrayé** quand je l'ai vu. *My puppy was **scared** when I saw him.*
scary frightening	effrayant terrifiant	Les zombies sont **effrayants**. *Zombies are **scary**.*
shredded	déchiqueté	J'ai vu des papiers **déchiquetés** dans la corbeille. *I saw **shredded** papers in the basket.*
square	carré	J'ai essayé de rendre la serre **carrée**. *I tried to make the greenhouse **squared**.*
steep	raide escarpé	La montagne est très **raide**. *The mountain is very **steep**.*
stingy	avare radin	Une personne **avare** n'est pas un bon ami. *A **stingy** person is not a good friend.*
subtle	subtil	J'aime porter un maquillage **subtil**. *I like to wear **subtle** makeup.*
sudden	soudain brusque	Le changement a été très **soudain**. *The change was very **sudden**.*
suitable	approprié adapté adéquat	Il est un enseignant **approprié** pour ces enfants. *He's a **suitable** teacher for those children.*
surprised	surpris étonné	Il a pris un visage **surpris**. *He put on a **surprised** face.*
surprising	surprenant étonnant	C'était un événement **surprenant**. *It was a **surprising** event.*
suspicious	suspect suspicieux	Son comportement est très **suspect**. *His behavior is very **suspicious**.*
theoretical	théorique	Je ne suis pas doué en sciences **théoriques**. *I'm not good at **theoretical** sciences.*
tight	étroit serré	L'intérieur de cette voiture est très **étroit**. *The interior of this car is very **tight**.*

trivial	trivial banal	Ne t'inquiète pas pour des choses **triviales**. *Don't worry over **trivial** things.*
unbearable	insupportable insoutenable intolérable	La douleur était **insupportable**. *The pain was **unbearable**.*
unbeatable	imbattable	Il était **imbattable** pendant longtemps. *He was **unbeatable** for a long time.*
unprecedented	sans précédent	C'était un résultat **sans précédent**. *It was an **unprecedented** result.*
unworthy	indigne	Il est **indigne** de ma confiance. *He's **unworthy** of my trust.*
veiled	voilé	La mariée est allée à l'autel **voilée**. *The bride walked to the altar **veiled**.*
wavy	ondulé	L'arrière-plan a une apparence **ondulée**. *The background has a **wavy** appearance.*
wicked evil	méchant	Le personnage était très **méchant**. *The character was very **wicked**.*
wild savage	sauvage	Cette plante est une fleur **sauvage**. *This plant is a **wild** flower.*
willing to	prêt à disposé à	Je suis **prêt à** vous aider avec tout. *I'm **willing to** help you with everything.*
wooden	en bois	Il avait beaucoup de jouets **en bois**. *He had a lot of **wooden** toys.*
worthy of	digne de	Il est **digne du** titre qu'il a obtenu. *He's **worthy of** the title he earned.*
woven	tissé	C'est un joli cardigan **tissé**. *It's a nice **woven** cardigan.*
wrinkled	froissé ridé	Cette chemise est très **froissée**. *That shirt is very **wrinkled**.*
zealous	zélé	Il était très **zélé** dans son idéologie. *He was very **zealous** in his ideology.*

In addition to the above new adjectives, we add a few English cognates that are easy to memorize.

English	French	Examples
absurd	absurde	Le complot me semblait **absurde**. *The plot seemed **absurd** to me.*
adequate	adéquat	Il a un prix **adéquat**. *It has an **adequate** price.*
agitated	agité	Es-tu **agité**? *Are you feeling **agitated**?*

ambitious	**ambitieux**	Mon frère a toujours été **ambitieux**. *My brother has always been **ambitious**.*
anonymous	**anonyme**	Cette peinture a été réalisée par un artiste **anonyme**. *That painting was made by an **anonymous** artist.*
appropriate	**appropriée**	Cette tenue vous semble-t-elle **appropriée**? *Does this outfit seem **appropriate** to you?*
archeological	**archéologique**	Cette relique **archéologique** provient d'une autre époque. *This **archeological** relic is from another era.*
charitable	**charitable**	C'est un travail **charitable**. *It's a **charitable** job.*
conscientious	**consciencieux**	Mon père est très **consciencieux**. *My father is very **conscientious**.*
consecutive	**consécutif**	Ils sont en ordre **consécutif**. *They are in **consecutive** order.*
cosmopolitan	**cosmopolite**	Je ne me considère pas comme une personne **cosmopolite**. *I don't consider myself a **cosmopolitan** person.*
deliberate	**délibéré**	Il l'a fait de manière **délibérée**. *He did it in a **deliberate** manner.*
delicate	**délicat**	Je lave les vêtements **délicats** à la main. *I wash **delicate** clothes by hand.*
desperate	**désespéré**	J'étais **désespéré** d'obtenir le travail. *I was **desperate** to obtain the job.*
erroneous	**erroné**	La première fois, il a obtenu un résultat **erroné**. *The first time, he had an **erroneous** result.*
essential	**essentiel**	L'eau est **essentielle** à la vie. *Water is **essential** for life.*
explicit	**explicite**	Le film a de la violence **explicite**. *The movie has **explicit** violence.*
federal	**fédéral**	L'infraction au droit d'auteur est une infraction **fédérale**. *Copyright infraction is a **federal** offense.*
homogeneous	**homogène**	Remuer jusqu'à ce que la pâte soit **homogène**. *Stir until the dough is **homogeneous**.*
humanitarian	**humanitaire**	Je participe à divers travaux **humanitaires**. *I participate in various **humanitarian** works.*
immune	**immunisé**	Aujourd'hui, personne n'est **immunisé** contre la critique. *Today no one is **immune** to criticism.*

individual [1]	individuel	Voici un dessert **individuel**. *Here you have an **individual** dessert.*
involuntary inadvertent	involontaire	Un hoquet est un réflexe **involontaire**. *A hiccup is an **involuntary** reflex.*
legitimate	légitime	Au final, il a eu un héritier **légitime**. *In the end, he had a **legitimate** heir.*
meticulous	méticuleux	Je suis très **méticuleux** quand je cuisine. *I am very **meticulous** when I cook.*
metropolitan	métropolitain	C'est dans la zone **métropolitaine** du pays. *It's in the **metropolitan** area of the country.*
pertinent relevant	pertinent	J'ai besoin d'informations **pertinentes**. *I need **pertinent** information.*
pioneer	pionnier	Il était un **pionnier** dans son domaine. *He was a **pioneer** in his field.*
privileged	privilégié	Il n'est pas une personne **privilégiée**. *He's not a **privileged** person.*
reciprocal	réciproque	L'amour qu'ils avaient était **réciproque**. *The love they had was **reciprocal**.*
sinister	sinistre	Son rire **sinistre** m'a effrayé. *His **sinister** laugh scared me.*
spontaneous	spontané	J'aime prendre des photos **spontanées**. *I like to take **spontaneous** photos.*
sterile	stérile	Il faut le nettoyer avec une compresse **stérile**. *You have to clean it with a **sterile** gauze.*
synthetic	synthétique	Je préfère utiliser des tissus **synthétiques**. *I prefer to use **synthetic** fabrics.*
tremendous formidable	formidable	L'éducation a un impact **formidable** sur nos vies. *Upbringing has a **tremendous** impact on our lives.*
urban	urbain	Cette zone a plusieurs légendes **urbaines**. *This zone has various **urban** legends.*
vague	vague	La description du livre est trop **vague**. *The book's description is too **vague**.*
vigorous	vigoureux	J'ai fait un entraînement **vigoureux**. *I did **vigorous** training.*
visionary	visionnaire	Da Vinci est considéré comme un penseur **visionnaire**. *Da Vinci is considered a **visionary** thinker.*

---

[1] The adjective *"individual"* in English is referred to using the adjective **"individuel"** in French, whereas the noun *"individual"* referring to a person uses the French word **"individu**m**."**

3. ANIMALS II

Here we add more animal vocabulary to our list.

alligator	**alligator**[m]	*hunting*	**chasse**[f]
ant	**fourmi**[f]	*insect*	**insecte**[m]
bark (of a dog)	**aboiement**[m]	*ivory*	**ivoire**[m]
bat (animal)	**chauve-souris**[f]	*kangaroo*	**kangourou**[m]
bear	**ours**[m]	*lion*	**lion**[m]
beaver	**castor**[m]	*monkey*	**singe**[m]
bee	**abeille**[f]	*octopus*	**poulpe**[m] **pieuvre**[f]
beehive	**ruche**[f]	*ostrich*	**autruche**[f]
breed	**race**[f]	*owl*	**hibou**[m]
cage	**cage**[f]	*oyster*	**huître**[f]
camel	**chameau**[m]	*parrot*	**perroquet**[m]
caterpillar	**chenille**[f]	*paw*	**patte**[f]
cattle	**bétail**[m]	*peacock*	**paon**[m]
cheetah	**guépard**[m]	*penguin*	**manchot**[m] **pingouin**[m]
chick	**poussin**[m]	*petting*	**caresse**[f]
cockroach	**cafard**[m]	*pigeon*	**pigeon**[m]
creature	**créature**[f]	*poaching*	**braconnage**[m]
crocodile	**crocodile**[m]	*predator*	**prédateur**[m]
deer	**cerf**[m]	*prey*	**proie**[f]
dinosaur	**dinosaure**[m]	*seagull*	**mouette**[f]
dove	**colombe**[f]	*seal*	**phoque**[m]
eagle	**aigle**[m]	*shark*	**requin**[m]
elephant	**éléphant**[m]	*slaughterhouse*	**abattoir**[m]
extinction	**extinction**[f]	*snake*	**serpent**[m]
falcon	**faucon**[m]	*spider*	**araignée**[f]
feather	**plume**[f]	*spiderweb*	**toile**[f] **d'araignée**
fishing rod	**canne**[f] **à pêche**	*squirrel*	**écureuil**[m]
fox	**renard**[m]	*tail*	**queue**[f]
frog	**grenouille**[f]	*tiger*	**tigre**[m]
gill	**branchie**[f]	*turtle* *tortoise*	**tortue**[f]
giraffe	**girafe**[f]	*vulture*	**vautour**[m]
goat	**chèvre**[f]	*wasp*	**guêpe**[f]
goose	**oie**[f]	*whale*	**baleine**[f]
herd	**troupeau**[m]	*wing*	**aile**[f]

hippopotamus	**hippopotame**^m	*wolf*	**loup**^m
howl (of a wolf)	**hurlement**^m	*worm*	**ver**^m

4. POLITICS

Politics, in French, is "**la politique**," and it is singular. Below is some related vocabulary:

agenda	**ordre**^m **du jour**	*governor*	**gouverneur**^m
ambassador	**ambassadeur**^m	*grant subsidy*	**subvention**^f
anthem	**hymne**^m	*heritage*	**patrimoine**^m
awareness	**conscience**^f	*mayor*	**maire**^{m,f}
ballot box	**urne électorale**^f	*measures*	**mesures**^f
bill (law)	**projet**^m **de loi**	*minister*	**ministre**^{m,f}
candidate	**candidat(e)**	*ministry*	**ministère**^m
citizen	**citoyen(ne)**	*monarchy*	**monarchie**^f
citizenship	**citoyenneté**^f	*nomination*	**nomination**^f
congress	**congrès**^m	*official (government employee)*	**fonctionnaire**^{m,f}
constitution	**constitution**^f	*parliament*	**parlement**^m
controversy	**controverse**^f **polémique**^f	*podium*	**podium**^m
council (committee)	**conseil**^m	*policy*	**politique**^f
coup d'état	**coup**^m **d'État**	*political party*	**parti politique**^m
crown	**couronne**^f	*political post*	**poste politique**^m
democracy	**démocratie**^f	*power*	**pouvoir**^m
demonstration	**manifestation**^f	*prince*	**prince**^m
dictatorship	**dictature**^f	*princess*	**princesse**^f
donor	**donateur**^m/**donatrice**^f	*protocol*	**protocole**^m
dual-citizenship	**double nationalité**^f	*province*	**province**^f
dynasty	**dynastie**^f	*rebel*	**rebelle**^{m,f}
election	**élection**^f	*referendum*	**référendum**^m
electoral campaign	**campagne électorale**^f	*republic*	**république**^f
embassy	**ambassade**^f	*senate*	**sénat**^m
emperor	**empereur**^m	*senator*	**sénateur**^m **sénatrice**^f
empire	**empire**^m	*skeptic*	**sceptique**^{m,f}
ethics	**éthique**^f	*slip of the tongue*	**lapsus**^m

exit polls	**sondages**^m **sortie des urnes**	*trick*	**truc**^m **astuce**^f
flag	**drapeau**^m	*unrest*	**trouble**^m **agitation**^f
government	**gouvernement**^m	*vote*	**vote**^m

5. COUNTRIES & NATIONALITIES II

More vocabulary to expand our knowledge about countries and nationalities is in the table below:

Algeria	**Algérie**^f	*Algerian*	**algérien(ne)**
Austria	**Autriche**^f	*Austrian*	**autrichien(ne)**
Belarus	**Biélorussie**^f	*Belarusian*	**biélorusse**^{m,f}
Belgium	**Belgique**^f	*Belgian*	**belge**^{m,f}
Belize	**Bélize**^m	*Belizean*	**bélizien(ne)**
Central America	**Amérique centrale**^f	*Central American*	**centre-américain(e)**
Chile	**Chili**^m	*Chilean*	**chilien(ne)**
Costa Rica	**Costa Rica**^m	*Costa Rican*	**costaricain(e)**
Denmark	**Danemark**^m	*Danish*	**danois(e)**
Ecuador	**Équateur**^m	*Ecuadorian*	**équatorien(ne)**
Finland	**Finlande**^f	*Finnish*	**finlandais(e)**
Greece	**Grèce**^f	*Greek*	**grec(que)**
Guatemala	**Guatemala**^m	*Guatemalan*	**guatémaltèque**^{m,f}
Haiti	**Haïti**^m	*Haitian*	**haïtien(ne)**
Honduras	**Honduras**^m	*Honduran*	**hondurien(ne)**
Hungary	**Hongrie**^f	*Hungarian*	**hongrois(e)**
India	**Inde**^f	*Indian*	**indien(ne)**
Ireland	**Irlande**^f	*Irish*	**irlandais(e)**
Lebanon	**Liban**^m	*Lebanese*	**libanais(e)**
Middle East	**Moyen-Orient**^m	*Middle Eastern*	**du Moyen-Orient**
Netherlands	**Pays-Bas**^m	*Dutch*	**néerlandais(e)**
Nicaragua	**Nicaragua**^m	*Nicaraguan*	**nicaraguayen(ne)**
North America	**Amérique**^f **du Nord**	*North American*	**nord-américain(e)**
Norway	**Norvège**^f	*Norwegian*	**norvégien(ne)**
Peru	**Pérou**^m	*Peruvian*	**péruvien(ne)**
Philippines	**Philippines**^f	*Filipino*	**philippin(e)**
Romania	**Roumanie**^f	*Romanian*	**roumain(e)**
South Korea	**Corée**^f **du Sud**	*South Korean*	**sud-coréen(ne)**
Sweden	**Suède**^f	*Swedish*	**suédois(e)**
Switzerland	**Suisse**^f	*Swiss*	**suisse**^{m,f}

Syria	**Syrie**[f]	*Syrian*	**syrien(ne)**
Thailand	**Thaïlande**[f]	*Thai*	**thaïlandais(e)**
Ukraine	**Ukraine**[f]	*Ukrainian*	**ukrainien(ne)**
United Kingdom	**Royaume-Uni**[m]	*British*	**britannique**[m,f]
United States	**États-Unis**[m]	*American*	**américain(e)**
Venezuela	**Vénézuela**[m]	*Venezuelan*	**vénézuélien(ne)**
Wales	**Pays**[m] **de Galles**	*Welsh*	**gallois(e)**

6. TRANSPORTATION II

We continue to add more vocabulary related to transportation.

anchor	**ancre**[f]	*ride (bike)*	**balade**[f] **à vélo** **promenade**[f] **à vélo**
bus stop	**arrêt**[m] **de bus**	*ride (car)*	**trajet**[m] **en voiture**
chassis	**châssis**[m]	*rush hour*	**heure**[f] **de pointe**
cobblestone	**pavé**[m]	*sailing boat*	**bateau**[m] **à voile** **voilier**[m]
convertible (car)	**voiture décapotable**[f]	*scratch*	**rayure**[f]
curb *sidewalk*	**trottoir**[m]	*seat*	**siège**[m]
dashboard	**tableau**[m] **de bord**	*seat belt*	**ceinture**[f] **de sécurité**
dent	**bosse**[f]	*ship*	**navire**[m]
flat tire	**pneu crevé**[m]	*shipwreck*	**naufrage**[m]
fuel	**carburant**[m] **combustible**[m]	*speed bump*	**ralentisseur**[m]
glove *compartment*	**boîte**[f] **à gants**	*speed limit*	**limitation**[f] **de vitesse**
gravel	**gravier**[m]	*steering wheel*	**volant**[m]
hood (car)	**capot**[m]	*toll*	**péage**[m]
landing	**atterrissage**[m]	*traffic jam*	**embouteillage**[m]
lane	**voie**[f]	*traffic light*	**feu**[m] **de circulation**
notice (warning)	**avis**[m]	*truck*	**camion**[m]
pedestrian	**piéton**[m]	*tunnel*	**tunnel**[m]
postage stamp	**timbre**[m]	*undocumented*	**sans papiers**
pothole	**nid**[m] **de poule**	*van*	**van**[m] **camionnette**[f]
railway	**chemin**[m] **de fer**	*warning*	**avertissement**[m]
rearview mirror	**rétroviseur**[m]	*wheel*	**roue**[f]

7. NATURE II

Let us go over more vocabulary related to nature.

ash	**cendre**^f	*mountain range*	**chaîne**^f **de montagne**
bank (river)	**rive**^f	*mud*	**boue**^f
bay	**baie**^f	*passage*	**passage**^m
beauty	**beauté**^f	*path*	**chemin**^m
branch	**branche**^f	*peak*	**sommet**^m
brook	**ruisseau**^m	*pearl*	**perle**^f
bush	**buisson**^m	*pollution*	**pollution**^f
carbon dioxide	**dioxide**^m **de carbone**	*pond*	**étang**^m
cliff	**falaise**^f	*puddle*	**flaque**^f
darkness gloom	**obscurité**^f	*rainbow*	**arc-en-ciel**^m
dawn	**aube**^f	*ranch*	**ranch**^m
dew	**rosée**^f	*ravine*	**ravin**^m
dusk nightfall	**crépuscule**^m **tombée**^f **de la nuit**	*ray beam*	**rayon**^m
earthquake	**séisme**^m **tremblement**^m **de terre**	*reef*	**récif**^m
eclipse	**éclipse**^f	*rock*	**roche**^f
environment	**environnement**^m	*seashell*	**coquillage**^m
flood	**inondation**^f	*slope*	**pente**^f **versant**^m
fog	**brouillard**^m	*soil*	**sol**^m
forecast	**prévisions**^f	*sound*	**son**^m
forest	**forêt**^f	*species*	**espèce**^f
frost	**gel**^m	*spectrum*	**spectre**^m
fumes smoke	**fumée**^f	*stick*	**bâton**^m
galaxy	**galaxie**^f	*stone*	**pierre**^f
gap	**écart**^m	*storm*	**tempête**^f **orage**^m
geology	**géologie**^f	*strength force*	**force**^f
grove	**bosquet**^m	*sunrise*	**lever**^m **du soleil**
heat	**chaleur**^f	*sunset*	**coucher**^m **du soleil**
heatwave	**canicule**^f **vague**^f **de chaleur**	*surface*	**surface**^f
hemisphere	**hémisphère**^m	*swamp*	**marais**^m
hill	**colline**^f	*thorn*	**épine**^f

horizon	**horizon**[m]	*thunder*	**tonnerre**[m]
humidity	**humidité**[f]	*trail*	**sentier**[m] **piste**[f]
hurricane	**ouragan**[m]	*trench*	**tranchée**[f]
hydrogen	**hydrogène**[m]	*trunk (tree)*	**tronc**[m]
instinct	**instinct**[m]	*twilight*	**crépuscule**[m]
jungle	**jungle**[f]	*vacuum*	**vide**[m]
leaf (tree)	**feuille**[f]	*valley*	**vallée**[f]
lightning	**foudre**[f] **éclair**[m]	*vine*	**vigne**[f]
marvel	**merveille**[f]	*volcano*	**volcan**[m]
mist	**brume**[f] **brouillard**[m]	*waterfall*	**cascade**[f] **chute**[f] **d'eau**
molecule	**molécule**[f]	*wave*	**vague**[f] **onde**[f]

8. HEALTH II

We add more vocabulary related to health.

allergy	**allergie**[f]	*injection*	**injection**[f]
ambulance	**ambulance**[f]	*microbe*	**microbe**[m]
antibiotic	**antibiotique**[m]	*migraine*	**migraine**[f]
arthritis	**arthrite**[f]	*operating room*	**salle**[f] **d'opération**
bandage	**bandage**[m]	*outbreak*	**épidémie**[f]
bee sting	**piqûre**[f] **d'abeille**	*pandemic*	**pandémie**[f]
cholesterol	**cholestérol**[m]	*paralysis*	**paralysie**[f]
cough	**toux**[f]	*plague*	**peste**[f]
cramp	**crampe**[f]	*pneumonia*	**pneumonie**[f]
cream	**crème**[f]	*prescription*	**ordonnance**[f]
diabetes	**diabète**[m]	*pulse (health)*	**pouls**[m]
diagnosis	**diagnostic**[m]	*remedy*	**remède**[m]
dizziness	**vertiges**[m]	*rupture*	**rupture**[f]
dose	**dose**[f]	*scar*	**cicatrice**[f]
drop	**goutte**[f]	*seizure*	**crise**[f] **d'épilepsie**
emergency room	**salle**[f] **d'urgence**	*shiver* / *chill*	**frisson**[m]
epilepsy	**épilepsie**[f]	*side effect*	**effet secondaire**[m]
first aid	**premiers soins**[m] **premiers secours**[m]	*smallpox*	**variole**[f]
food poisoning	**intoxication alimentaire**[f]	*sneeze*	**éternuement**[m]

fracture	**fracture**[f]	*stroke*	**accident vasculaire cérébral**[m]
heart attack	**crise cardiaque**[f] **infarctus**[m]	*stitches*	**points**[m] **de suture**
heart burn	**brûlures**[f] **d'estomac**	*stuffy nose*	**nez bouché**[m]
blood pressure	**pression artérielle**[f]	*sunstroke*	**insolation**[f]
hygiene	**hygiène**[f]	*syringe*	**seringue**[f]
immunity	**immunité**[f]	*vomit*	**vomi**[m]

9. FOOD III

We continue to add to our set of vocabulary related to food.

all-you-can-eat buffet	**buffet**[m] **à volonté**	*ginger*	**gingembre**[m]
asparagus	**asperge**[f]	*jam*	**confiture**[f]
beet	**betterave**[f]	*layer*	**couche**[f]
bite	**bouchée**[f]	*leftovers*	**les restes**[m]
blackberry	**mûre**[f]	*mushroom*	**champignon**[m]
carbohydrate	**glucides**[m]	*oat*	**avoine**[f]
cashew	**noix**[f] **de cajou**	*peach*	**pêche**[f]
cauliflower	**chou-fleur**[m]	*peas*	**pois**[m]
chewing gum	**chewing-gum**[m]	*pine nut*	**pignon**[m] **de pin**
chickpea	**pois chiche**[m]	*plum*	**prune**[f]
cookie	**biscuit**[m]	*potion*	**potion**[f]
crust	**croûte**[f]	*pumpkin*	**citrouille**[f] **potiron**[m]
dairy	**produits laitiers**[m]	*quince*	**coing**[m]
date	**datte**[f]	*radish*	**radis**[m]
fat	**gras**[m] **graisse**[f]	*sausage*	**saucisse**[f]
fig	**figue**[f]	*seed*	**graine**[f]
flour	**farine**[f]	*soy*	**soja**[m]
garlic	**ail**[m]	*slice*	**tranche**[f]
glucose	**glucose**[m]	*spinach*	**épinard**[m]
grain	**grain**[m]	*starch*	**amidon**[m]
green beans	**haricots verts**[m]	*turnip*	**navet**[m]
harvest crop	**récolte**[f]	*wheat*	**blé**[m]
hazelnut	**noisette**[f]	*zucchini*	**courgette**[f]

10. ANATOMY II

Below is some more advanced vocabulary related to anatomy:

armpit	**aisselle**[f]	*lung*	**poumon**[m]
blood vessel	**vaisseau sanguin**[m]	*nail*	**ongle**[m]
bone	**os**[m]	*neck*	**cou**[m]
cell	**cellule**[f]	*nerve*	**nerf**[m]
chest	**poitrine**[f]	*reflex*	**réflexe**[m]
chin	**menton**[m]	*skeleton*	**squelette**[m]
elbow	**coude**[m]	*skull*	**crâne**[m]
dimple	**fossette**[f]	*spine*	**colonne vertébrale**[f]
forehead	**front**[m]	*spleen*	**rate**[f]
hip	**hanche**[f]	*tear*	**larme**[f]
intestine	**intestin**[m]	*throat*	**gorge**[f]
joint	**articulation**[f]	*tongue*	**langue**[f]
kidney	**rein**[m]	*vein*	**veine**[f]
liver	**foie**[m]	*waist*	**taille**[f]

LEVEL VI: FLUENT

I. Introductory Topics & Grammar

Congratulations on reaching the fluent level. It must feel great to have achieved this accomplishment. At this level, all you need is to perfect a few concepts that are preventing you from achieving full fluency.

1. THE PAST INFINITIVE

The past infinitive is formed as follows:

"avoir" or **"être"** + past participle

It is equivalent to the English combination of *"having"* followed by the past participle, e.g., *"having finished," "having eaten," "having seen,"* etc.

One common use of the past infinitive in French is when there are two actions in the past and the subject is the same. For example:

Après **avoir terminé** son travail, il a pris une semaine de repos.	*After **having finished** his work, he took a week off.*
On lui a demandé de quitter les lieux pour **avoir violé** les règles.	*He was told to leave the place for **having violated** the rules.*
Après **être parti** tard hier soir, j'ai dû rentrer à pied.	*After **having left** late last night, I had to walk home.*

Notice that the above example can be rephrased using the present participle of the verb **"avoir"** or **"être,"** followed by the past participle, that is:

Ayant terminé son travail, il a pris une semaine de repos.	***Having finished*** *his work, he took a week off.*
Ayant violé les règles, on lui a demandé de quitter les lieux.	***Having violated*** *the rules, he was told to leave the place.*
Étant parti tard hier soir, j'ai dû rentrer à pied.	***Having left*** *late last night, I had to walk home.*

Remember that the past participle must agree with the gender and number of the noun in the case of verbs conjugated with "**être**."

We can also use the past infinitive in cases where we would normally use the infinitive in English, if the action referred to by the infinitive is in the past. For example:

Merci de m'**avoir invité**.	*Thank you for **inviting** me.*
Je suis désolé d'**être parti** tôt hier soir.	*I'm sorry for **leaving** early last night.*

Notice that the actions that the past infinitive refers to in both examples are understood to be in the past.

2. SIMPLE PAST TENSE

The simple past tense is often used in literary French to relate past or historical events. It is often used in reference to past events or narrations. In general, the simple past is not used in daily spoken language except in formal speech. Nevertheless, it is important to recognize this special tense, especially in writing.

Conjugation

To conjugate a verb, we use the stem from the *infinitive*. We remove the final "-**er**," "-**ir**," or "-**re**," and attach the conjugation suffix. The suffixes are the same for "-**ir**" and "-**re**" verbs.

	-er ending parler *(to speak)*	-ir ending finir *(to finish)*	-re ending vendre *(to sell)*
je	parl**ai**	fin**is**	vend**is**
tu	parl**as**	fin**is**	vend**is**
il/elle/on	parl**a**	fin**it**	vend**it**
nous	parl**âmes**	fin**îmes**	vend**îmes**
vous	parl**âtes**	fin**îtes**	vend**îtes**
ils/elles	parl**èrent**	fin**irent**	vend**irent**

Irregular Verbs

The verbs "**être**" *(to be)* and "**avoir**" *(to have)* are irregular in the simple past:

	être	avoir
je/j'	fus	eus
tu	fus	eus
il/elle/on	fut	eut
nous	fûmes	eûmes
vous	fûtes	eûtes
ils/elles	furent	eurent

Other irregular verbs include the following:

	je	tu	il/elle	nous	vous	ils/elles
boire *to drink*	bus	bus	but	bûmes	bûtes	burent
conduire *to drive*	conduisis	conduisis	conduisit	conduisîmes	conduisîtes	conduisirent
connaître *to know*	connus	connus	connut	connûmes	connûtes	connurent
courir *to run*	courus	courus	courut	courûmes	courûtes	coururent
couvrir *to cover*	couvris	couvris	couvrit	couvrîmes	couvrîtes	couvrirent
craindre *to fear*	craignis	craignis	craignit	craignîmes	craignîtes	craignirent
croire *to believe*	crus	crus	crut	crûmes	crûtes	crurent
devoir *must*	dus	dus	dut	dûmes	dûtes	durent
écrire *to write*	écrivis	écrivis	écrivit	écrivîmes	écrivîtes	écrivirent
éteindre *to turn off*	éteignis	éteignis	éteignit	éteignîmes	éteignîtes	éteignirent
faire *to do*	fis	fis	fit	fîmes	fîtes	firent
falloir *to have to*	-	-	fallut	-	-	-
introduire *to introduce*	introdusis	introdusis	introdusit	introdusîmes	introdusîtes	introdusirent
lire *to read*	lus	lus	lut	lûmes	lûtes	lurent
mettre *to put*	mis	mis	mit	mîmes	mîtes	mirent
mourir *to die*	mourus	mourus	mourut	mourûmes	mourûtes	moururent

naître *to be born*	naquis	naquis	naquit	naquîmes	naquîtes	naquirent
obtenir *to obtain*	obtins	obtins	obtint	obtînmes	obtîntes	obtinrent
offrir *to offer*	offris	offris	offrit	offrîmes	offrîtes	offrirent
peindre *to paint*	peignis	peignis	peignit	peignîmes	peignîtes	peignirent
plaire *to please*	plus	plus	plut	plûmes	plûtes	plurent
pleuvoir *to rain*	-	-	plut	-	-	-
pouvoir *can*	pus	pus	put	pûmes	pûtes	purent
prendre *to take*	pris	pris	prit	prîmes	prîtes	prirent
recevoir *to receive*	reçus	reçus	reçut	reçûmes	reçûtes	reçurent
rire *to laugh*	ris	ris	rit	rîmes	rîtes	rirent
savoir *to know*	sus	sus	sut	sûmes	sûtes	surent
sourire *to smile*	souris	souris	sourit	sourîmes	sourîtes	sourirent
tenir *to hold*	tins	tins	tint	tînmes	tîntes	tinrent
valoir *to be worth*	valus	valus	valut	valûmes	valûtes	valurent
venir *to come*	vins	vins	vint	vînmes	vîntes	vinrent
vivre *to live*	vécus	vécus	vécut	vécûmes	vécûtes	vécurent
vouloir *to want*	voulus	voulus	voulut	voulûmes	voulûtes	voulurent

Examples

Let us look at some examples:

La guerre **se termina** par une victoire nette.	*The war **ended** with a clear victory.*
Cette invention **eut** un grand impact sur la vie des gens.	*That invention **had** a great impact on people's lives.*
Il **remporta** de nombreux prix pour ses recherches sur le sujet.	*He **won** many awards for his research on the topic.*

| Les événements de cette année **changèrent** notre mode de vie. | *The events of that year **changed** our way of life.* |
| Il **parla** de ce qu'il avait appris lors de sa dernière visite en Afrique. | *He **spoke** about what he had learned in his last visit to Africa.* |

3. PLUPERFECT INDICATIVE TENSE

The pluperfect tense, literally meaning *the more than perfect* tense, describes the past before the simple past. If two actions took place in the past, the one that occurred before is often described in the pluperfect.

The pluperfect indicative is formed as follows:

> **"avoir"** or **"être"** in the imperfect indicative + past participle

Depending on the verb, the pluperfect indicative uses the auxiliary **"avoir"** or **"être"** in the imperfect, which are conjugated as follows:

	"avoir" in the imperfect indicative	**"être"** in the imperfect indicative
je	avais	étais
tu	avais	étais
il/elle/on	avait	était
nous	avions	étions
vous	aviez	étiez
ils/elles	avaient	étaient

For example:

Avant notre rencontre, je n'**étais** jamais **allé** en Espagne.	*Before we met, I **had** never **been** to Spain.*
Quand je suis allé voir ma mère, ma sœur **était** déjà **arrivée**.	*When I visited my mom, my sister **had** already **arrived**.*
Après que la sécurité **avait fermé** la porte, la foule est rentrée chez elle.	*After the security **had closed** the door, the crowd went home.*

Hypothetical Expressions in the Past

Hypothetical expressions in the past generally use the pluperfect. The pluperfect tense in such expressions is often preceded by the conditional **"si"** *(if)*. Here are some examples:

> Si j'**avais étudié** la médecine, …   *If I **had studied** medicine, …*
> Si mon grand-père n'**était** pas **mort**, … *If my grandfather **hadn't died**, …*

The conditional statements above are usually followed by

❖ a verb in simple conditional, or

❖ *"would have"* + past participle

> Si j'**avais étudié** la médecine, je **serais** riche aujourd'hui.   *If I **had studied** medicine, I **would be** rich today.*
> Si mon grand-père n'**était** pas **mort**, j'**aurais passé** du temps avec lui.   *If my grandfather **hadn't died**, I **would have spent** time with him.*

Another way to describe a hypothetical or impossible past is using the expression "**comme si**," translated as *"as if,"* for example:

> Il parle comme s'il **avait étudié** la médecine.   *He talks as if he **had studied** medicine.*
> Il a pleuré comme si son grand-père **était mort**.   *He cried as if his grandfather **had died**.*

Although the *pluperfect subjunctive* tense exists in formal written French, it remains mostly a literary tense.

4. Idiomatic Pronominal Verbs

A pronominal verb is a verb that is accompanied by at least one pronoun. An example of pronominal verbs is reflexive verbs, which are preceded with "**se**" in the infinitive, indicating that the action of the verb is performed on oneself.

Not all pronominal verbs are reflexive. Some verbs simply change their meaning when attached to pronouns to form new idiomatic meanings that do not often make complete sense if translated literally into English.

Take, for example, the verb "**aller**" *(to go)*. If preceded by the pronouns "**se**" and "**en**," we obtain the pronominal verb "**s'en aller**," which means *"to go away."* For example, "**s'en aller**" in the informal command form is "**Va-t'en!**" *(Go away!)*, that is: "**va**" + "**te**" + "**en.**"

Similarly, if the verb "**passer**" *(to passer)* is preceded with the pronoun "**se**," we obtain the pronominal verb "**se passer**," which means *"to happen."*

There are many similar idiomatic pronominal verbs in French. Some are formed using one pronoun, while others are formed by using two pronouns. In general, a pronominal verbs uses a reflexive pronoun and/or the special pronouns "**y**" and "**en.**"

To conjugate a pronominal verb, the pronouns are placed in the same order before the conjugated verb. If the conjugation needs a past participle, as in the present perfect tense, the auxiliary "**être**" is used, and the past participle takes the treatment of an adjective, meaning it must follow the subject in gender and number. Here is the conjugation of the pronominal verbs "**s'en aller**" *(to go away)* and "**s'y prendre**" *(to set about doing something)* in the present perfect:

	s'en aller	s'y prendre
je	m'en suis allé(e)	m'y suis pris(e)
tu	t'en es allé(e)	t'y es pris(e)
il/ on	s'en est allé	s'y est pris
elle	s'en est allée	s'y est prise
nous	nous en sommes allé(e)s	nous y sommes pris(es)
vous	vous en êtes allé(e)s	vous y êtes pris(e)(s)
il	s'en sont allés	s'y sont pris
elles	s'en sont allées	s'y sont prises

The following table lists some of the most common idiomatic pronominal verbs:

Verb	Meaning	Example
s'en aller	*to go away*	**Va-t'en!** Je ne veux pas parler. **Go away!** *I do not want to talk.*
s'amuser	*to have a good time*	Ils **se sont amusés** sur la plage. *They **had a good time** on the beach.*
s'apercevoir	*to notice*	Je **me suis aperçu** que le travail était difficile. *I **noticed** that the work was difficult.*

s'attendre	*to expect*	Ils **s'attendent** à ce que l'économie s'améliore. *They **expect** the economy to improve.*
se demander	*to wonder*	Je **me demandais** ce qui s'était passé. *I **was wondering** what had happened.*
se dépêcher	*to hurry*	**Dépêche-toi!** Nous sommes en retard. ***Hurry up!** We are late.*
se dérouler	*to unfold or happen*	Les événements **se sont déroulés** si vite. *The events **unfolded** so fast.*
se douter	*to suspect*	Je crois qu'il **se doute** de quelque chose. *I think he **suspects** something.*
s'éclater	*to have a blast*	Ils **se sont éclatés** pendant leurs vacances. *They **had a blast** during their vacation.*
s'enfuir	*to run away*	Il **s'est enfui** des lieux en quelques minutes. *He **ran away** from the scene within minutes.*
s'ennuyer	*to be bored*	Je **me suis ennuyé** devant la télé hier soir. *I **was bored** watching TV last night.*
s'entendre	*to get along*	Les deux voisins ne **s'entendent** pas. *The two neighbors don't **get along**.*
s'évanouir	*to faint*	Elle **s'est évanouie** quand elle a vu le sang. *She **fainted** when she saw the blood.*
se figurer	*to imagine*	Je peux **me figurer** la beauté du paysage. *I can **imagine** the beauty of the landscape.*
s'habituer à	*to get used to*	Je **me suis habitué à** la vie en ville. *I **got used to** life in the city.*
s'installer	*to settle in*	J'ai besoin de temps pour **m'installer** ici. *I need some time to **settle in** here.*
se mettre à	*to begin to*	Je rentrerai chez moi si la pluie **se met à** tomber. *I will go home if the rain **begins to** fall.*
se moquer de	*to make fun of*	Ne **te moque** pas **de** ton amie. *Don't **make fun of** your friend.*
se passer	*to happen*	Que **s'est**-il **passé** hier soir? *What **happened** last night?*
se perdre	*to get lost*	Nous **nous sommes perdus** au parc hier. *We **got lost** at the park yesterday.*
se plaindre	*to complain*	Ils **se plaignent** toujours des règles. *They always **complain** about the rules.*
s'y prendre	*to set about or do something*	Comment on **s'y prend** n'est pas important. *How we **do** it is not important.*
se refuser à	*to deny oneself*	Il **s'est refusé** à accepter le pot-de-vin. *He **refused** to take the bribe.*
se rendre à	*to go to*	Il **se rendra à** Paris le mois prochain. *He will **go to** Paris next month.*
se rendre compte de	*to realize*	Il **s'est rendu compte** qu'il avait tort. *He **realized** that he was wrong.*

s'en retourner	*to go back*	Il sauva ses hommes avant de **s'en retourner** en Espagne. *He saved his men before **going back** to Spain.*
se réunir	*to meet or get together*	Nous **nous réunirons** demain matin. *We will **get together** tomorrow morning.*
se saisir de	*to take up*	Il **s'est saisi d**u pouvoir il y a 20 ans. *He **took up** power 20 years ago.*
se servir de	*to make use of*	Ce site **se sert de** cookies. *This site **makes use of** cookies.*
se tromper	*to be mistaken*	Elle **s'est trompée** l'autre jour. *She **was wrong** the other day.*
se trouver	*to be located*	L'entrée **se trouve** de l'autre côté. *The entrance **is located** on the other side.*

5. PREPOSITIONAL VERBS

A prepositional verb is a verb that is followed by a preposition. Many verbs in French are followed by a preposition. A prepositional verb often has a similar meaning to the original verbs. However, a new meaning is sometimes obtained when using the prepositional verb. For example, when the verb "**donner**" *(to give)* is followed by the preposition "**sur**" *(on)*, the prepositional verb "**donner sur**" means *"to face"* or *"to overlook,"* e.g., "**La maison donne sur la mer**" *(The house overlooks the sea).*

Here is a list of some common prepositional verbs in French:

Verb	Meaning	Example
arriver	*to arrive*	Je vais **arriver** à Madrid la semaine prochaine. *I am going to **arrive** in Madrid next week.*
arriver à	*to manage to* *to succeed*	Il **est arrivé à** résoudre le problème hier. *He **managed to** solve the problem yesterday.*
chercher	*to look for* *to pick up*	Il **cherche** un emploi dans son domaine. *He is **looking for** a job in his field.*
chercher à	*to attempt* *to try*	Tu dois **chercher à** changer ton plan. *You have to **try to** change your plan.*
commence	*to start*	Les cours **commencent** mercredi prochain. *Classes **start** next Wednesday.*
commence à	*to start (to)*	Il **a commencé à** pleurer quand je le lui ai dit. *He **started to** cry when I told him.*

commence par	*to start by* / *to start with*	On **commence par** se présenter. / *We **start by** introducing ourselves.*
compter	*to count*	Mon fils sait **compter** jusqu'à dix. / *My son can **count** to ten.*
compter pour	*to count for* / *to be worth*	Cela ne **compte pour** rien dans le calcul. / *This **counts for** nothing in the calculation.*
compter sur	*to count on*	Vous pouvez **compter sur** moi pour le faire. / *You can **count on** me to do it.*
croire	*to believe* / *to think*	Je ne **crois** pas ce qu'il a dit. / *I don't **believe** what he said.*
croire à	*to believe (in) (something)*	Je **crois à** la tentative honnête qu'il a faite. / *I **believe** the honest attempt he made.*
croire en	*to believe in*	Je **crois en** une solution pacifique à cela. / *I **believe in** a peaceful solution to this.*
être	*to be*	Il **est** étudiant dans cette université. / *He **is** a student at this university.*
être à	*to belong to*	Ce document **est à** moi. / *This document **belongs to** me.*
être pour	*to be in favor of*	Il **est pour** la loi et nous sommes contre. / *He **is for** the law and we are against it.*
finir	*to finish* / *to complete*	Il **a fini** toute la pizza tout seul. / *He **finished** the entire pizza by himself.*
finir de	*to finish* / *to be done with*	Il **a fini de** manger et est parti tout de suite. / *He **finished** eating and left right away.*
finir par	*to end up*	Elle **a fini par** refuser l'offre d'emploi. / *She **ended up** refusing the job offer.*
jouer	*to play*	Les enfants **jouent** dans le jardin. / *The children **are playing** in the garden.*
jouer de	*to play (an instrument)*	Il **jouait de** la guitare quand il était jeune. / *He **used to play** the guitar when he was young.*
jouer à	*to play (a sport or game)*	Il **jouait** au tennis à l'école. / *He **used to play** tennis at school.*
parler	*to speak* / *to talk*	Nous attendons tous qu'il **parle**. / *We are all waiting for him to **speak**.*
parler à	*to talk to*	Il voulait **parler à** sa mère. / *He wanted to **talk to** his mother.*
parler de	*to talk about*	Je ne veux pas **parler de** ce sujet maintenant. / *I don't want to **talk about** this subject now.*
parler pour	*to speak for*	Il **parle pour** nous tous sur cette question. / *He **speaks for** all of us on this issue.*

rêver	to dream	Je ne **rêve** pas beaucoup ces temps-ci. *I don't **dream** much these days.*
rêver à	*to dream of*	**J'ai rêvé à** ce bruit d'oiseaux. *I **dreamed of** this sound of birds.*
rêver de	*to dream about*	**J'ai rêvé de** lui l'autre jour. *I **dreamed about** him the other day.*
tenir	*to hold*	La mère **tient** son bébé dans ses mains. *The mother **holds** her baby in her hands.*
tenir à	*to want (eagerly)* *to be attached to*	Je **tiens à** tous vous remercier. *I **want to** thank all of you.*
tenir de	*to take after*	Je pense qu'il **tient de** son père. *I think he **takes after** his father.*

6. PASSIVE VOICE

One way to describe something in the passive voice in French is by moving the noun acted upon to the beginning of the sentence to emphasize it and using a *"to be"* verb followed by the adjective or the past participle. For example:

| Le tissu a été **fabriqué** à partir de matériaux recyclés (par l'usine). | *The textile was **made** from recycled material (by the factory).* |
| Le contrat sera **signé** (par l'entreprise). | *The contract will be **signed** (by the company).* |

The performer of the action in the above two examples, denoted by **"par ..."** (*by ...*), can be omitted because it is deemed not to be of great significance.

In some cases, the preposition **"de"** is used to denote the agent if the agent plays a less active role, for example:

| Le bâtiment est encerclé **d'**un mur. | *The building is surrounded **by** a wall.* |
| Le bâtiment est encerclé **par** des soldats. | *The building is surrounded **by** soldiers.* |

In the two examples above, notice that the agent plays a less active role in the first example. Thus, we use the proposition **"de."** On the other hand, we use **"par"** in the second example to highlight the active role of the agent.

The preposition **"de"** is commonly used to denote the agent with verbs that express emotion or opinion.

Il est <u>aimé</u> **de** tous ses voisins.	*He is <u>liked</u> **by** all his neighbors.*
Cette idée est <u>appréciée</u> **des** élèves.	*This idea is <u>appreciated</u> **by** the students.*

Using the Pronoun "On"

It is common to use the third-person singular pronoun **"on"** to construct the passive voice in French, especially in daily speech. In this context, the subject pronoun **"on"** can mean *"we," "one,"* or *"they,"* e.g., **"On parle francais ici"** *(We/They speak French here)* means *"French is spoken here."*

Passive Reflexive Constructions

Some pronominal verbs are used in a manner similar to reflexive verbs to convey the passive voice. The following are some examples:

Ça **se voit**.	*It **shows**.*
Ça ne **se fait** pas.	*That is not **done** (We don't do that).*
Ça ne **se dit** pas.	*That is not **said** (We don't say that).*
La porte **s'ouvre** facilement.	*The door is easy to **open**.*
Comment ça **se répare**?	*How is this **repaired**?*

7. DIMINUTIVES & AUGMENTATIVES

In French, diminutives and augmentatives are sometimes used to exaggerate descriptions or show certain emotions such as endearment or affection. Understanding some rules and familiarity with some vocabulary in this category will help you enhance your understanding of the French language.

Diminutives

In the English language, we sometimes form the diminutive by suffixing *"-ie"* or *"-y,"* as in *"doggie"* for *"dog"* and *"kitty"* for *"kitten,"* indicating small size and sometimes the state or quality of being familiarly known, lovable, pitiable, or contemptible. Sometimes other suffixes are used, such as *"-ette"* in *"kitchenette"* and *"novelette,"* *"-let"* in *"booklet"* and *"droplet,"* and *"-ling"* in *"duckling"* and *"gosling" (a young goose)*.

In French, the purpose of using the diminutive is often similar to that in English. In fact, many diminutives have found their way into English from French.

The most common diminutive suffixes in French are "**-et**" for masculine and "**-ette**" for feminine. If the word ends with a vowel, the final vowel is dropped before adding the suffix. Here are some nouns in diminutive forms:

livre[m] *(boy)*	livre	+	-et	=	livret[m] *(booklet)*
jardin[m] *(garden)*	jardin	+	-et	=	jardinet[m] *(little garden)*
fille[f] *(girl)*	fille	+	-ette	=	fillette[f] *(little girl)*
cigare[m] *(cigar)*	cigare	+	-ette	=	cigarette[f] *(cigarette)*
maison[f] *(house)*	maison	+	-ette	=	maisonette[f] *(little house)*

The suffixes "**-et**" and "**-ette**" can also be used with adjectives. In this context, the suffix has a similar function to the "**-ish**" suffix in English. The suffix is usually added to the feminine form of the adjective, for example:

gentille[f] *(nice)*	gentille	+	-et -ette	=	gentillet[m] gentillette[f] *(somewhat nice)*
jaune[m,f] *(yellow)*	jaune	+	-et -ette	=	jaunet[m] jaunette[f] *(yellowish)*
molle[f] *(soft)*	molle	+	-et -ette	=	mollet[m] mollette[f] *(somewhat soft)*

In addition, some verbs take on the suffix "**-et**" or "**-ette**" to form a noun that is related to the verb, for example:

jouer *(to play)*	jouer	+	-et	=	jouet[m] *(toy)*
sonner *(to ring)*	sonner	+	-ette	=	sonnette[m] *(bell)*
fumer *(to smoke)*	fumer	+	-et	=	fumet[m] *(aroma)*

Finally, some given names, especially female names, take the suffix "**-et**" or "**-ette**" to form diminutive forms, for example:

Marie	Marie	+	-ette	=	Mariette

| Anne | Anne | + | -ette | = | Annette |
| Jeanne | Jeanne | + | -ette | = | Jeannette |

Other less common diminutives in French include: "**-ot**," "**-otte**," and "**-on.**" Here are some examples:

Pierre	Pierre	+	-ot	=	Pierrot
chat^m *(cat)*	chat	+	-on	=	chaton^m *(kitten)*
ours^m *(bear)*	ours	+	-on	=	ourson^m *(cub)*

Although these are not all the suffixes used to form diminutives in French, most other suffixes are either of mainly regional use or rarely encountered in daily life.

Augmentatives

Augmentatives are the opposite of diminutives. They indicate that something is large or intense, sometimes in an undesirable way. Augmentatives can apply to nouns and adjectives. In the English language, although not versatile and common, augmentatives are formed by using prefixes rather than suffixes. You can think of the prefix *"super-"* in *"superpower"* and *"supernatural,"* the prefix *"mega-"* in *"megaphone"* and *"megastore,"* the prefix *"grand-"* in *"grandmaster"* and *"grandfather,"* the prefix *"over-"* in *"overgrown"* and *"overqualified,"* and the prefix *"arch-"* in *"archrival"* and *"archenemy."*

In French, it is also uncommon to use augmentative suffixes. Instead, similar prefixes to the ones used in English are sometimes used with some words, such as: "**supermarché**" *(supermarket)*, "**surhumain**" *(superhuman)*, "**hyperactif**" *(hyperactive)*, etc.

II. Vocabulary Building

Go over the vocabulary in this section. You could use Anki to study and memorize the new vocabulary efficiently.

1. VERBS VI

Below is a list of some important verbs that we need at this level:

English	French	Examples
acquire	acquérir	Il **a acquis** l'appartement sans problème l'année dernière. *He **acquired** the apartment with no problems last year.*
adore worship	adorer	Ma fille **adorait** sa grand-mère quand elle était jeune. *My daughter **adored** her grandma when she was young.*
align	aligner	J'aime **aligner** correctement les bocaux. *I like to **align** the jars correctly.*
ally	allier	Les gouvernements **se sont alliés** les uns aux autres pendant de nombreuses années. *The governments **allied** with one another for many years.*
approve	approuver	Je ne peux pas **approuver** de telles mesures. *I can't **approve** of such measures.*
attack	attaquer	Le chien du voisin **attaque** toujours le facteur. *My neighbor's dog always **attacks** the mailman.*
attend	assister à	Si j'avais su, j'**aurais assisté à** la réunion. *Had I known, I **would've attended** the meeting.*
behave	se comporter	J'espère que vous **vous comporterez** en gentleman. *I hope you **will behave** like a gentleman.*
betray	trahir	Ne **trahissez** pas la confiance de vos amis. *Don't **betray** your friend's trust.*
bless	bénir	Le prêtre **a béni** le couple. *The priest **blessed** the couple.*
blush	rougir	Il **a rougi** en entendant l'histoire. *He **blushed** upon hearing the story.*
brag boast	se vanter	Je l'apprécierais s'il ne **se vantait** pas de tout. *I'd like him if he **would** not **brag** about everything.*
brake (vehicle)	freiner	Si je n'**avais** pas **freiné**, j'aurais eu un accident. *If I **had** not **braked**, I would have crashed.*
broadcast transmit	diffuser	Ils **diffusent** en direct. *They **are broadcasting** live.*
bury	enterrer	Nous avons dû **enterrer** le poisson rouge. *We had to **bury** the pet fish.*
charge (fee)	facturer faire payer	Ils **facturent** beaucoup d'argent pour les billets. *They **charge** a lot for tickets.*
check in	s'enregistrer	Je **me suis enregistré** à l'hôtel voisin hier soir. *I **checked in** at a nearby hotel last night.*

chop down	**abattre** **couper**	Ils **abattent** les arbres dans le parc. *They are chopping down the trees in the park.*
cite	**citer**	Ils **ont cité** beaucoup de preuves dans leur dernière recherche. *They cited a lot of evidence in their latest research.*
collapse	**s'effondrer** **s'écrouler**	Ce bâtiment est sur le point de **s'effondrer**. *That building is about to collapse.*
collect or raise (money)	**recueillir**	Ils **recueillent** de l'argent pour la charité. *They are raising money for the charity.*
commit	**commettre**	Il ne voulait pas **commettre** un crime. *He didn't want to commit a crime.*
compose	**composer**	Elle **a composé** cette belle chanson. *She composed that beautiful song.*
compress	**compresser**	J'ai dû **compresser** les fichiers. *I had to compress the files.*
compromise	**compromettre**	Ils ont décidé de **compromettre** certaines idées. *They decided to compromise some ideas.*
confuse	**confondre**	Son explication nous **a confondus**. *His explanation has confused us.*
conquer	**conquérir**	Ils ont essayé de **conquérir** cette île. *They tried to conquer that island.*
contain	**contenir**	Ce tube peut **contenir** un liquide dangereux. *This tube may contain a dangerous liquid.*
contaminate	**contaminer**	La rivière est **contaminée** par les déchets. *The river is contaminated by waste.*
contradict	**contredire**	Je ne veux pas te **contredire**. *I don't want to contradict you.*
correspond	**correspondre**	Les chaussettes ne **correspondent** pas à la même paire. *The socks don't correspond to the same pair.*
cram	**bourrer** **entasser**	C'était **bourré** de mes affaires. *It was crammed with my stuff.*
crease	**plier** **froisser**	**Pliez** les bords du papier. *Crease the edges of the paper.*
curse	**jurer**	Tu sais que tu ne devrais pas **jurer**. *You know you shouldn't curse.*
damage **harm**	**endommager** **léser** **nuire**	Il était très prudent de ne pas **endommager** la peinture. *He was very careful not to damage the paint.*
dazzle	**éblouir**	Le spectacle vous **éblouira**. *The show will dazzle you.*
defeat	**battre** **vaincre**	Il m'**a battu** dans cette manche. *He defeated me in this round.*

deliver turn in	livrer rendre	Ils sont en train de le **livrer** en ce moment. *They **are delivering** it right now.*
deny	**refuser** nier	Personne ne devrait **refuser** de l'eau aux autres. *No one should **deny** water to others.*
deplete	épuiser	La guerre **a épuisé** les ressources du pays. *The war **has depleted** the country's resources.*
detain	détenir	La police l'**aurait détenu** de toute façon. *The police **would have stopped** him anyway.*
diagnose	diagnostiquer	Le médecin sera celui qui me **diagnostiquera**. *The doctor will be the one who will **diagnose** me.*
dig	creuser excaver	Ils sont en train de **creuser** dans la grotte. *They **are digging** in the cave.*
dive	plonger	Il **plonge** dans l'eau sans regarder. *He **dives** into the water without looking.*
dribble (soccer)	dribbler	L'attaquant **a dribblé** en déjouant trois défenseurs et a marqué un but. *The striker **dribbled** past three defenders and scored a goal.*
drip	goutter	Le robinet **gouttait** pendant qu'ils dormaient. *The faucet **was dripping** while they were asleep.*
drizzle	bruiner	Il **bruine** en ce moment. *It **is drizzling** right now.*
drown	se noyer	Je **me serais noyé** sans le gilet de sauvetage. *I **would have drowned** without the life jacket.*
embellish	embellir	Ils **embellissent** toujours leurs histoires d'aventure. *They always **embellish** their adventure stories.*
emphasize	souligner	J'ai essayé de **souligner** ce point. *I tried to **emphasize** that point.*
engrave	graver	Ils **ont gravé** leurs noms sur la bague avant le mariage. *They **engraved** their names on the ring before the wedding.*
enlarge extend	agrandir	Elle **a agrandi** la pièce en abattant ce mur. *She **extended** the room by knocking down that wall.*
enroll (school)	s'inscrire enrôler	Je dois **m'inscrire** le mois prochain. *I have to **enroll** next month.*
entail	impliquer entraîner	Il ne savait pas ce que cela **impliquerait**. *He didn't know what it **would entail**.*
equate (put on the same level)	assimiler	Nous ne pouvons pas **assimiler** les différentes idées et solutions. *We cannot **equate** the different ideas and solutions.*
evict	expulser évincer	Ils **ont expulsé** toute la famille le mois dernier. *They **evicted** the entire family last month.*

expel	expulser	Ils l'**auraient expulsé** s'ils l'avaient découvert. *They **would have expelled** him if they'd found out.*
expose	exposer	J'**exposerai** l'ensemble de la thèse. *I **will expose** the entire thesis.*
face confront	affronter	Tu dois **affronter** tes peurs. *You have to **face** your fears.*
fade	s'estomper s'effacer	La tache **s'est** complètement **estompée**. *The stain completely **faded away**.*
faint	s'évanouir	Il **s'est évanoui** en voyant le sang après l'accident. *He **fainted** when he saw blood after the accident.*
fall behind	prendre du retard	Il **prendra du retard** s'il ne se dépêche pas. *He **will fall behind** if he doesn't hurry.*
feed	nourrir alimenter	Mon voisin **nourrit** parfois mon chat. *My neighbor sometimes **feeds** my cat.*
find out	découvrir savoir	Je savais qu'il le **découvrirait** tôt ou tard. *I knew he **would find out** sooner or later.*
fire dismiss	licencier	Ils ont dû **licencier** de nombreux employés. *They had to **fire** many employees.*
fit	convenir s'intégrer	Je pense que ça **convient** dans cette pièce. *I think it **fits** in that room.*
flatter	flatter	Il **flatte** le patron pour obtenir une augmentation. *He **flatters** the boss to give him a raise.*
flicker	scintiller vaciller clignoter	La lumière **scintille**. *The light **is flickering**.*
foil thwart	contrecarrer déjouer faire échec	Le mauvais temps **a contrecarré** ses plans. *The bad weather **thwarted** her plans.*
found	fonder	Ils **fonderont** une association pour aider les gens. *They **will found** an association to help people.*
frown	froncer les sourcils	Il **a froncé les sourcils** en voyant le tableau. *He **frowned** when he saw the painting.*
get along	s'entendre	Mes filles ne **s'entendent** pas. *My daughters don't **get along**.*
get involved	se mêler s'impliquer s'engager	Il vaut mieux ne pas **se mêler** de ces questions. *It's best to not **get involved** in those matters.*
govern	gouverner	Il a abusé du pouvoir lorsqu'il **gouvernait**. *He abused power when he **governed**.*

grab grasp seize	saisir attraper	**Saisis** le dernier avant que quelqu'un d'autre ne le fasse. *Grab the last one before someone else does.*
grind	moudre broyer	Il faut bien **moudre** le poivre. *You have to grind the pepper well.*
hang	accrocher	Peux-tu **accrocher** les vêtements? *Can you hang the clothes?*
hang on	s'accrocher	Tu ne devrais pas **t'accrocher** au passé. *You shouldn't hang on to the past.*
harmonize	harmoniser	J'ai essayé d'**harmoniser** les couleurs. *I tried to harmonize the colors.*
have to do with	avoir à voir avec	Cela **a à voir avec** ce qui s'est passé hier. *This has to do with what happened yesterday.*
hesitate	hésiter	Tu ne devrais pas **hésiter** après avoir commencé. *You shouldn't hesitate after you've started.*
highlight stand out	se démarquer	Il cherchait toujours à **se démarquer**. *He'd always try to stand out.*
hire contract	embaucher engager	J'**embaucherai** un charpentier pour cela. *I will hire a carpenter for that.*
house accommodate	loger	Ils **logeront** toute la famille. *They will house the entire family.*
hurry rush	se dépêcher se presser	Peux-tu **te dépêcher**? *Can you hurry up?*
hurt	blesser faire du mal	Il **s'est blessé** par accident. *He hurt himself by accident.*
impose	imposer	Ils **ont imposé** une nouvelle loi récemment. *They imposed a new law recently.*
imprison	emprisonner incarcérer	Ils **ont emprisonné** le criminel qui a commis le crime. *They imprisoned the felon who committed the crime.*
intend	avoir l'intention de	J'**ai l'intention de** commencer un régime. *I intend to start a diet.*
iron	repasser	Je n'aime pas **repasser** les vêtements. *I don't like to iron clothes.*
irrigate water	arroser irriguer	S'ils les **avaient arrosées**, elles ne seraient pas mortes. *If they had watered them, they wouldn't have died.*
jump hop	sauter	Nous **sautions** partout quand nous étions enfants. *We would jump everywhere when we were kids.*
kneel	s'agenouiller	**Agenouille-toi** pour regarder sous le comptoir. *Kneel down to see under the counter.*

knock over	**renverser** **faire tomber**	Il **a renversé** le vase l'autre jour. *He knocked over the vase the other day.*
lease	**louer**	Mes parents **louent** leur maison. *My parents are leasing their house.*
light **illuminate**	**éclairer** **illuminer**	Une lampe là-bas **éclairerait** toute la pièce. *A lamp there would light the entire room.*
load	**charger**	Pourrais-tu m'aider à **charger** la voiture? *Would you help me load the car?*
make fun of	**se moquer de**	C'est désagréable que tu **te sois moqué** de lui de cette façon. *It's unpleasant that you made fun of him like this.*
manage **handle**	**gérer**	Je **gérais** toujours l'argent de la maison. *I used to always handle the house's money.*
manifest	**se manifester**	J'ai pensé qu'un fantôme **s'était manifesté**. *I thought a ghost had manifested.*
manufacture	**fabriquer**	Ils **fabriquent** des voitures là-bas. *They manufacture cars there.*
meet up	**se retrouver** **se rencontrer**	Nous **nous retrouverons** dans la salle de classe. *We will meet up in the classroom.*
murmur	**murmurer**	Je parviens seulement à **murmurer** quand je suis somnolent. *I only manage to murmur when I'm sleepy.*
nail	**clouer**	J'ai dû le **clouer** au mur. *I had to nail it to the wall.*
neglect	**négliger** **oublier**	J'**oublie** toujours mes plantes par accident. *I always neglect my plants by accident.*
nourish **nurture**	**nourrir**	Tu devrais bien te **nourrir**. *You should nourish yourself well.*
pack	**emballer**	J'**ai** tout **emballé** en cinq minutes. *I packed everything in five minutes.*
pamper **spoil**	**gâter**	Je **gâte** toujours mon animal de compagnie. *I always pamper my pet.*
pave	**paver**	Ils sont en train de **paver** la rue. *They are paving the street.*
penalize	**pénaliser** **sanctionner**	Jeter des déchets est **sanctionné** par des amendes. *Throwing trash is penalized with fines.*
perceive	**percevoir**	Je peux **percevoir** le sarcasme dans sa réponse. *I can perceive the sarcasm in his answer.*
pet **stroke** **fondle**	**caresser**	Mon chat adore être **caressé**. *My cat loves being petted.*

pick up	**chercher** **ramasser**	Peux-tu aller **chercher** ta sœur? *Can you go **pick up** your sister?*
pinch	**pincer**	Ne me **pince** pas! *Don't **pinch** me!*
please	**plaire** **satisfaire**	Il est difficile à **satisfaire**. *He is hard to **please**.*
pollute	**polluer**	Tu ne devrais pas **polluer** l'environnement. *You shouldn't **pollute** the environment.*
portray	**dépeindre** **représenter**	Je pense qu'ils **ont** bien **représenté** sa personnalité dans le film. *I think they **portrayed** her persona very well in the movie.*
pose (photo)	**poser**	Ils **posent** déjà pour la photo. *They are already **posing** for the photo.*
postpone	**reporter** **repousser** **retarder**	Ils **ont reporté** l'événement à cause de la pluie. *They **postponed** the event because of the rain.*
praise	**louer** **louanger**	Ils **ont loué** son jeu d'actrice dans ce film. *They **praised** her acting in that movie.*
pray	**prier**	Ils **priaient** tous les jours. *They **used to pray** every day.*
predict	**prédire**	Ils ne **prédisent** jamais correctement la météo. *They never correctly **predict** the weather.*
prescribe	**prescrire**	Ils lui **ont prescrit** des vitamines pour sa maladie de l'année dernière. *They **prescribed** him some vitamins for his last year's illness.*
preserve	**préserver** **conserver**	La nourriture **se conserve** mieux au réfrigérateur. *Food **is preserved** best in the fridge.*
press	**appuyer** **presser**	Il **aurait appuyé** sur le bouton pour entrer. *He **would have pressed** the button to go in.*
pretend	**faire semblant** **prétendre**	Ne **fais** pas **semblant** de dormir. *Don't **pretend** to be asleep.*
prevail	**prévaloir** **prédominer**	Les couleurs froides **prédominent** dans la peinture. *Cold colors **prevail** in the painting.*
prohibit ban	**interdire** **empêcher** **prohiber**	Le gouvernement **a interdit** certaines importations l'année dernière. *The government **prohibited** certain imports last year.*
promote	**promouvoir**	La société **a promu** son nouveau produit pendant des mois. *The company **promoted** its new product for months.*

provide	fournir	Les bananes **fournissent** beaucoup de potassium. *Bananas **provide** a lot of potassium.*
put together	assembler rassembler	Il **a rassemblé** tous les matériaux et a commencé le projet. *He **put together** all the materials and started the project.*
rally behind	se rallier derrière	Ils **se sont ralliés derrière** le président lors de sa dernière campagne. *They **rallied behind** the president in his last campaign.*
ransack	saccager piller	Ils **ont saccagé** tout l'endroit quand ils sont entrés. *They **ransacked** the entire place when they broke in.*
rape violate	violer	Le suspect a été accusé de **violer** quelqu'un. *The suspect was accused of **raping** someone.*
recruit	recruter	On s'attendrait à ce qu'ils **recrutent** plus de personnes. *One would expect them to **recruit** more people.*
refine	affiner raffiner	Vous devez **affiner** votre recherche sur Internet. *You have to **refine** your search on the internet.*
register sign up	s'inscrire s'abonner	Je savais que vous auriez besoin de **vous inscrire** pour entrer. *I knew you'd need to **register** to get in.*
regret	regretter	Je **regretterais** de le manquer toute ma vie. *I **would regret** missing it all my life.*
rehearse	répéter	Ils ont dû **répéter** la pièce plusieurs fois. *They had to **rehearse** the play many times.*
remove	enlever supprimer éliminer	J'essaierai d'**enlever** cette tache immédiatement. *I'll try to **remove** that stain immediately.*
rescue	sauver secourir	Tu l'**aurais sauvé** si tu y avait été. *You **would have rescued** him had you been there.*
restart reboot	redémarrer	Je **redémarrerai** l'ordinateur. *I **will restart** the computer.*
restore (order or connection)	rétablir	Nous **rétablirons** la paix pour prévenir les conflits. *We **will restore** peace to prevent conflicts.*
restore (repair)	restaurer	J'**ai restauré** les vieux meubles. *I **restored** the old furniture.*
resume	reprendre	Ils **reprendront** les négociations demain. *They **will resume** the negotiations tomorrow.*

reverberate	réverbérer résonner	Le bruit **résonne** dans toute la maison. *The noise **reverberates** through the entire house.*
reward	récompenser rémunérer	Ils l'**auraient récompensé** pour son travail. *They **would have rewarded** him for his work.*
rise	augmenter monter lever	Les prix **ont** beaucoup **augmenté** l'année dernière. *Prices **rose** a lot last year.*
risk	risquer	Je ne voudrais pas qu'il **risque** tout son salaire. *I wouldn't want him to **risk** all his salary.*
rot decay	pourrir	Ça **pourrira** si tu ne l'utilises pas bientôt. *It **will rot** if you don't use it soon.*
run out	manquer épuiser	Il est difficile de **manquer** d'économies. *It's hard to **run out** of savings.*
run over	écraser	Ça l'**aurait écrasé** s'il n'avait pas couru. *It **would have run** him **over** if he hadn't run.*
sacrifice	sacrifier	Parfois, il faut **sacrifier** un peu de son temps. *Sometimes you have to **sacrifice** a bit of your time.*
sadden	attrister	La nouvelle de la mort de son oncle l'**a attristé**. *The news of his uncle's death **saddened** him.*
scorn	mépriser	Elle **méprise** toujours sa belle-fille. *She always **scorns** her daughter-in-law.*
scrap (car)	mettre à la ferraille	Ils **mettent à la ferraille** les vieilles voitures là-bas. *They **scrap** old cars there.*
scribble doodle	griffonner gribouiller	Les enfants **griffonnent** beaucoup. *Children **scribble** a lot.*
scrub	récurer frotter	Je **récurerai** la vaisselle après le dîner. *I **will scrub** the dishes after dinner.*
seal	sceller	Ils **scelleront** l'enveloppe. *They **will seal** the envelope.*
shake	secouer	**Secouez** bien la bouteille. ***Shake** the bottle very well.*
sharpen	affûter aiguiser	Vous devez bien **affûter** vos couteaux de cuisine. *You have to **sharpen** your kitchen knives well.*
shove	fourrer	Ils **fourreront** tout ça dans le coffre? *They **will shove** all that into the trunk?*
shovel	pelleter	Ils **pelletaient** toujours la neige quand ils habitaient là-bas. *They always **shoveled** the snow when they lived there.*
sigh	soupirer	Je **soupire** à chaque fois que je vois mon grand-père. *I **sigh** every time I see my grandfather.*

sin	pécher	L'homme croyait qu'ils **avaient péché**. *The man believed that they **had sinned**.*
skimp	lésiner	Ils **ont lésiné** sur les décorations lorsqu'ils ont emménagé. *They **skimped** on the decorations when they moved in.*
skip over	sauter	Il a réussi à **sauter** une année. *He managed to **skip over** a year.*
slap	gifler	Il **a giflé** le méchant sur la scène de crime. *He **slapped** the villain at the crime scene.*
slide slip	glisser	Il **glisse** comme il peut. *He **is sliding** the way he can.*
smash crush	écraser	Ça l'**aurait écrasé** s'il n'avait pas bougé. *It **would have crushed** him if he hadn't moved.*
sneak	se faufiler	Nous avons réussi à **nous faufiler** à l'intérieur. *We managed to **sneak** into the place.*
snore	ronfler	Mon chien **ronfle** très fort. *My dog **snores** very loudly.*
soak	tremper	J'**ai trempé** les haricots secs pendant cinq heures. *I **soaked** the dry beans for five hours.*
sow	semer	Je **semerai** les graines au printemps. *I **will sow** the seeds in spring.*
specify	spécifier	Il **a spécifié** exactement dans quelle salle de classe c'était. *He **specified** exactly what classroom it was.*
spill shed	renverser répandre	Le thé **se serait renversé** si je n'avais pas arrêté la tasse. *The tea **would have spilled** if I hadn't stopped the cup.*
splash	éclabousser	L'encre **a éclaboussé** le mur par accident. *The ink **splashed** on the wall by accident.*
sponsor	parrainer	Je pense que c'est une excellente idée que vous les **parrainiez**. *I think it's a great idea that you **sponsor** them.*
spread (extend)	étaler	Vous devez **étaler** les draps sur le matelas. *You have to **spread** the bed sheets over the mattress.*
spread (propagate)	se propager	La maladie **s'est propagée** très rapidement. *The disease **spread** very quickly.*
squander fritter	gaspiller dilapider	Arrête de **gaspiller** ton argent. *Stop **squandering** your money.*
squeeze	presser appuyer sur	Tu dois bien **presser** les citrons. *You have to **squeeze** the lemons well.*

stain taint	tacher	Je **tachais** toujours mes vêtements avec de la nourriture. *I **used to** always **stain** my clothes with food.*
stamp	timbrer	Tu dois **timbrer** le colis. *You have to **stamp** the package.*
stir	remuer	Peux-tu **remuer** le ragoût, s'il te plaît? *Can you **stir** the stew, please?*
stray get lost	se perdre	Il **se serait perdu** sans la carte. *He **would have gotten lost** without the map.*
stretch	s'étirer	Je **m'étire** toujours quand je me réveille. *I always **stretch** when I wake up.*
stun	étourdir stupefier étonner	Le bruit fort m'**a stupéfié** alors que je lisais. *The loud noise **stunned** me as I was reading.*
stutter	bégayer bafouiller	J'**ai bégayé** beaucoup pendant ce discours. *I **stuttered** a lot during that speech.*
summarize	résumer récapituler	Je dois **résumer** les textes dans ces livres. *I have to **summarize** the texts in these books.*
support back up	soutenir appuyer	Pouvez-vous **soutenir** votre frère? *Can you **support** your brother?*
suppress	supprimer réprimer	Ils **ont supprimé** de nombreux thèmes du spectacle hier soir. *They **suppressed** many themes from the show last night.*
surrender give up	se rendre abandonner	**Abandonne** pour que je remporte cette manche! ***Give up** so I win this round!*
surround encircle	entourer encercler	Ils l'**auraient entouré** s'ils avaient pu. *They **would have surrounded** him if they could.*
survey poll	interroger sonder	Ils **ont sondé** cent individus la semaine dernière. *They **surveyed** a hundred individuals last week.*
swallow	avaler	Vous devez **avaler** votre médicament. *You have to **swallow** your medication.*
swell	enfler gonfler	Mon pied **a enflé** très rapidement après le match. *My foot **swelled** up really fast after the game.*
take for granted	tenir pour acquis	Il **a tenu pour acquis** qu'il remporterait cette course. *He **took for granted** that he'd win that race.*
tangle	s'emmêler s'enchevêtrer	Mes cheveux **se sont emmêlés** pendant que je les coiffais hier soir. *My hair **got tangled** while I was styling it last night.*

tear **rip**	**déchirer** **arracher**	Mon chien **déchirait** tous les papiers qu'il voyait. *My dog **would rip** all the papers he saw.*
terrify	**terrifier**	Quand j'étais enfant, les poupées me **terrifiaient**. *When I was a child, dolls **terrified** me.*
threaten	**menacer**	Ce ne serait pas acceptable s'il **menaçait** ses enfants. *It wouldn't be okay if he **threatened** his children.*
thunder	**tonner**	Il **tonne** en ce moment. *It **is thundering** now.*
tickle	**chatouiller**	Ses parents avaient l'habitude de **chatouiller** leurs enfants. *His parents used to **tickle** their kids.*
toast	**trinquer**	**Trinquons** à ton succès! *Let's **toast** to your success!*
touch	**toucher**	Ça **aurait touché** mon visage si je n'avais pas bougé. *It **would have touched** my face if I hadn't moved.*
transfer	**transférer**	Je **transférerai** l'argent directement dans votre compte. *I **will transfer** the money directly into your account.*
trigger	**déclencher**	Ce mouvement **a déclenché** une avalanche. *That movement **triggered** an avalanche.*
twinkle	**scintiller**	Les étoiles **scintillent** et les planètes ne le font pas. *Stars **twinkle** and planets don't.*
uncover	**découvrir**	Quelqu'un **découvrira** le mystère un jour. *Someone **will uncover** the mystery one day.*
unleash	**déchaîner** **libérer**	Ils **ont déchaîné** le dragon quand la guerre a commencé. *They **unleashed** the dragon when the war started.*
waste	**gaspiller** **gâcher**	Vous **gaspillez** les ressources. *You **are wasting** the resources.*
watch over	**surveiller**	**Surveillez** le four pour qu'il ne brûle pas. ***Watch over** the oven so that it doesn't burn.*
withdraw **retreat**	**se retirer**	La tortue **s'est retirée** dans sa carapace en me voyant. *The turtle **withdrew** into its shell upon seeing me.*
withdraw **(money)**	**retirer**	Il **retirera** de l'argent à la banque. *He **will withdraw** money from the bank.*
wrinkle	**froisser** **rider**	Faites attention à ne pas **froisser** vos vêtements. *Be careful not to **wrinkle** your clothes.*

yawn	bâiller	Ne **baillez** pas en public. *Don't **yawn** in public.*

2. ADJECTIVES VI

Below is a list of some important adjectives that we need at this level:

English	French	Examples
abnormal	anormal	Ce fromage a une couleur **anormale**. *This cheese has an **abnormal** color.*
advocate (defender)	défenseur	Il est un **défenseur** des droits des enfants. *He's an **advocate** for children's rights.*
affectionate	affectueux	Mon grand-père est très **affectueux**. *My grandfather is very **affectionate**.*
agricultural	agricole	Il s'est intéressé au travail **agricole**. *He's become interested in **agricultural** work.*
anxious	anxieux	Mon chat devient **anxieux** au parc. *My cat gets **anxious** in the park.*
appetizing	appétissant	Ce steak a l'air très **appétissant**. *That steak looks very **appetizing**.*
arctic	arctique	Je n'aime pas ces froids **arctiques**. *I don't like these **arctic** colds.*
attached (file)	attaché	Tu peux trouver le fichier **attaché** à l'e-mail. *You can find the file **attached** to the mail.*
audacious	audacieux	Elle finit par être très **audacieuse**. *She ended up being very **audacious**.*
bankrupt	en faillite	À la fin du mois, je suis **en faillite**. *By the end of the month, I'm **bankrupt**.*
bent	tordue plié coudé	La fourchette a finie **tordue**. *The fork ended up **bent**.*
broken down (vehicle)	en panne	La voiture était à la maison car elle était **en panne**. *The car was at home because it had **broken down**.*
cheerful	joyeux	L'enseignant est très **joyeux** avec les enfants. *The teacher is very **cheerful** with the children.*
chemical	chimique	Faites attention aux réactions **chimiques**. *Be careful with **chemical** reactions.*
civilian	civil	Il a quitté l'armée et est redevenu **civil**. *He left the army and went back to being a **civilian**.*
compassionate	compatissant compassionnel	Il est très **compatissant** envers les animaux. *He's very **compassionate** with animals.*
corny	ringard cucul	Il m'a écrit un poème **ringard**. *He wrote me a **corny** poem.*

creepy	effrayant	Avec ce masque, il a l'air **effrayant**. *With that mask he looks **creepy**.*
crispy	croustillant croquant	J'aime mon toast très **croustillant**. *I like my toast very **crispy**.*
crowded	bondé ecombré surpeuplé	Le cinéma était trop **bondé**. *The cinema was too **crowded**.*
deceased	décédé défunt	Il appartenait à mon grand-père **décédé**. *It belonged to my **deceased** grandfather.*
deceptive	trompeur	Cette publicité était **trompeuse**. *That advertisement was **deceptive**.*
devoid of	dépourvue de	Cette région est **dépourvue de** matière première. *This region is **devoid of** raw material.*
disabled	handicapé	Cette place de parking est réservée aux personnes **handicapées**. *That parking space is for **disabled** people.*
dissatisfied	insatisfait	J'étais **insatisfait** du service. *I was **dissatisfied** with the service.*
elementary	élémentaire	Il est **élémentaire** de savoir cuisiner. *It's **elementary** to know how to cook.*
empty-handed	les mains vides	Il est venu **les mains vides**. *He came **empty-handed**.*
even & odd	pair et impair	Ils ont commandé les choses en **pairs et impairs**. *They ordered the things in **evens and odds**.*
expected	attendu prévu	C'était un résultat **attendu**. *It was an **expected** result.*
fierce	féroce	Le lion au zoo a l'air **féroce**. *The lion at the zoo looks **fierce**.*
giant	géant	Ils ont un éléphant **géant** dans ce zoo. *They have a **giant** elephant in this zoo.*
gigantic	gigantesque	La montagne était **gigantesque**. *The mountain was **gigantic**.*
gratifying	gratifiant	C'est **gratifiant** de faire du travail caritatif. *It is **gratifying** to do charity work.*
greedy	avide cupide	Éloignez-vous des gens **avides**. *Stay away from **greedy** people.*
hasty	pressé hâtif	Il était très **pressé** de partir. *He was very **hasty** to leave.*
hollow	creux	Cet arbre est **creux**. *That tree is **hollow**.*
homeless roofless	sans-abri	Il était un jeune homme **sans-abri**. *He was a **homeless** young man.*

hooked	accroché	C'est **accroché** au mur. *It's **hooked** to the wall.*
impolite	impoli	Le serveur était un peu **impoli**. *The waiter was a bit **impolite**.*
in a hurry	pressé	Elle était **pressée** d'y arriver. *She was **in a hurry** to get there.*
in open-air outdoors	à l'extérieur	Il est permis de fumer **à l'extérieur**. *Smoking is allowed **outdoors**.*
indebted	endetté	Il était très **endetté** pendant un an. *He was very **indebted** for a year.*
inebriated	ivre enivré	Il était **ivre** hier soir. *He was **inebriated** last night.*
inner internal	intérieure	Ma voix **intérieure** me dit de ne pas le faire. *My **inner** voice tells me not to do it.*
juristic	juridique	Il aime vraiment le champ **juridique**. *He really likes the **juristic** scope.*
last	dernier	Nous avons pris le **dernier** bus. *We took the **last** bus.*
led by	dirigé par	Ils étaient **dirigés par** le plus âgé d'entre eux. *They were **led by** the oldest one of them.*
lower	inférieure	Sa lèvre **inférieure** a enflé. *His **lower** lip got swollen.*
loyal	fidèle loyal	J'ai beaucoup d'amis **fidèles**. *I have a lot of **loyal** friends.*
mature ripe	mûr	Cet avocat n'est pas encore **mûr**. *That avocado isn't **ripe** yet.*
merciful	miséricordieux clément	Il a été très **clément** avec l'amende. *He was very **merciful** with the fine.*
needy	nécessiteux dans le besoin	Il y a beaucoup de personnes **dans le besoin** ici. *There are many **needy** people here.*
negligible	négligeable	La quantité de sucre qu'il contient est **négligeable**. *The amount of sugar it has is **negligible**.*
ongoing in progress	en cours	L'écran indique que le téléchargement est **en cours**. *The screen says the download is **in progress**.*
opponent adversary	adversaire opposant	Il était un bon **adversaire** dans le jeu. *He was a good **opponent** in the game.*
ostentatious	ostentatoire	Cette demeure est très **ostentatoire**. *That mansion is very **ostentatious**.*
outstanding exceptional	exceptionnel	Il a toujours été un étudiant **exceptionnel**. *He's always been an **outstanding** student.*

overcrowded	**surpeuplé** **bondé**	Le stade était **surpeuplé**. *The stadium was **overcrowded**.*
overweight	**en surpoids**	L'exercice est très utile pour les personnes **en surpoids**. *Exercise is very useful for **overweight** people.*
overwhelming	**accablant** **écrassant**	L'arôme était **accablant**. *The aroma was **overwhelming**.*
pending	**en attente** **en suspens**	Le statut indique toujours **en attente**. *It's still in **pending** status.*
poisonous	**vénéneux** **venimeux** **toxique**	Cette plante est très **toxique**! *That plant is very **vénéneuse**!*
predicted	**prédite** **prévu**	La fin était **prédite**. *The ending was **predicted**.*
profitable	**rentable** **profitable**	C'est une entreprise assez **rentable**. *It's a pretty **profitable** business.*
rear	**arrière** **postérieur**	Le feu **arrière** ne fonctionne pas. *The **rear** light isn't working.*
reluctant	**réticent**	Il a cuisiné, bien qu'il était **réticent** à le faire. *He cooked, although he was **reluctant** to do so.*
replete with full of	**remplie de** **plein de**	L'armoire est **remplie de** tasses. *The cabinet is **replete with** mugs.*
reputable respectable	**réputé**	Je l'ai obtenu d'un fournisseur **réputé**. *I got it from a **reputable** provider.*
rooted	**enraciné**	Il a une culture profondément **enracinée**. *He has a deeply-**rooted** culture.*
rotten	**pourri**	La moitié des œufs était **pourrie**. *Half of the eggs were **rotten**.*
rough	**rugueux**	Ce papier de verre est très **rugueux**. *That sandpaper is very **rough**.*
seasonal	**saisonnier**	Ce travail est seulement **saisonnier**. *That job is just **seasonal**.*
second-hand	**d'occasion**	Ils vendent des vêtements **d'occasion** ici. *They sell **second-hand** garments here.*
secure safe	**en sécurité**	L'argent sera **en sécurité** ici. *The money will be **safe** here.*
shallow (water)	**peu profond**	La piscine est très **peu profonde**. *The pool is very **shallow**.*
sharp (knife)	**tranchant** **pointu**	Vous l'avez coupé avec un couteau **tranchant**. *You cut it with a **sharp** knife.*
slippery	**glissant**	Fais attention! Le sol est **glissant** là-bas. *Be careful! The floor is **slippery** there.*

smooth	lisse	La surface est sortie très **lisse**. *The surface came out very **smooth**.*
sold out	épuisés	Les billets étaient **épuisés**. *The tickets were **sold out**.*
stranded	échoué bloqué	Ils l'ont trouvé **échoué** sur une île. *They found him **stranded** on an island.*
stray	errant	J'ai trouvé un chat **errant**. *I found a **stray** cat.*
stubborn	têtu obstiné	Parfois je suis un peu **têtu**. *Sometimes I'm a bit **stubborn**.*
stuck	coincé bloqué	Le chien était **coincé** dans le trou. *The dog was **stuck** in the hole.*
subsequent	subséquent suivant	Je suivrai les étapes **suivantes**. *I will follow the **subsequent** steps.*
tanned	bronzé	Elle est revenue **bronzée** de ses vacances. *She came back **tanned** from her vacation.*
terrified	terrifié	Le film m'a laissé **terrifié**. *The movie left me **terrified**.*
tidy	bien rangé	J'aime garder mon bureau **bien rangé**. *I like to keep my desk **tidy**.*
tied	lié attaché	Les carottes viennent **attachées** ensemble. *The carrots come **tied** together.*
tiny	petit miniscule	Elle a acheté une **petite** maison. *She bought a **tiny** house.*
trustworthy	fiable	Est-ce que ce chèque a l'air **fiable**? *Does this check look **trustworthy**?*
unexpected	inattendu imprévu inespéré	J'ai eu une visite **inattendue**. *I had an **unexpected** visit.*
unpleasant	désagréable	Cela a dégagé une odeur très **désagréable**. *It released a very **unpleasant** smell.*
unscathed	indemne	Il a survécu à l'accident **indemne**. *He survived the accident **unscathed**.*
upper	supérieur	C'est dans le tiroir **supérieur**. *It's in the **upper** drawer.*
upstairs	à l'étage en haut	Vous pouvez le trouver dans la salle de bains **à l'étage**. *You can find it in the **upstairs** bathroom.*
waterproof	imperméable étanche	La veste était **imperméable**. *The jacket was **waterproof**.*
widespread	répandu généralisé	Maintenant, c'est une tendance **répandue**. *Now it's a **widespread** trend.*

3. CONCEPTS & BEHAVIORS

A more abstract topic is related to *concepts and behaviors*, or "**les concepts**[m] **et les comportements**[m]." The table below covers some related vocabulary:

ability *capacity*	**capacité**[f]	*legacy*	**héritage**[m]
affection	**affection**[f]	*legend*	**légende**[f]
anxiety	**anxiété**[f]	*leisure*	**loisirs**[m]
apology	**excuse**[f]	*luxury*	**luxe**[m]
applause	**applaudissement**[m]	*mentality*	**mentalité**[f]
attitude	**attitude**[f]	*mercy*	**miséricorde**[f]
birth	**naissance**[f]	*mischief*	**méfait**[m] **malice**[m] **bêtises**[m]
certainty	**certitude**[f]	*mood*	**humeur**[f][1]
chance (accident)	**hasard**[m]	*motive*	**motif**[m]
charm	**charme**[m]	*myth*	**mythe**[m]
choice	**choix**[m]	*nap*	**sieste**[f]
comfort	**confort**[m]	*nightmare*	**cauchemar**[m]
common sense	**bon sens**[m] **sens commun**[m]	*novelty*	**nouveauté**[f]
compliment (praise)	**compliment**[m]	*nuisance*	**nuisance**[f]
concern	**préoccupation**[f] **inquiétude**[f]	*objective*	**objectif**[m]
contrast	**contraste**[m]	*opportunity*	**opportunité**[f]
courage	**courage**[m]	*pat*	**tape**[f]
courtesy	**courtoisie**[f]	*perspective* *outlook*	**perspective**[f]
craziness	**folie**[f]	*pinch*	**pincement**[m]
cycle	**cycle**[m]	*plagiarism*	**plagiat**[m]
death	**mort**[f] **décès**[m]	*praise*	**louange**[f] **éloge**[m]
deception	**tromperie**[f]	*prejudice*	**préjudice**[m]
deterioration	**détérioration**[f]	*pride*	**fierté**[f] **orgueil**[m]
difficulty	**difficulté**[f]	*privilege*	**privilège**[m]

---

[1] For instance, "**être de bonne humeur**" means *"to be in a good mood"* and "**être de mauvaise humeur**" means *"to be in a bad mood."*

disrespect	**manque**[m] **de respect** **irrespect**[m]	*promise*	**promesse**[f]
dream	**rêve**[m]	*purpose*	**but**[m] **objectif**[m]
ethnicity	**ethnicité**[f]	*race (ethnicity)*	**race**[f]
ease	**facilité**[f]	*rage*	**rage**[f] **colère**[f]
encouragement	**encouragement**[m]	*randomness*	**hasard**[m]
fable	**fable**[f]	*reach*	**portée**[f] **atteinte**[f]
failure	**échec**[m]	*recognition acknowledgment*	**reconnaissance**[f]
fate	**destin**[m] **sort**[m]	*refusal*	**refus**[m] **rejet**[m]
focus	**focus**[m] **accent**[m]	*renaissance*	**renaissance**[f]
feeling	**sentiment**[m]	*respect*	**respect**[m]
foolishness	**bêtise**[f] **folie**[f]	*responsibility*	**responsabilité**[f]
freedom *liberty*	**liberté**[f]	*rest* *remainder*	**reste**[m]
friendship	**amitié**[f]	*rhythm*	**rythme**[m]
gender *sex*	**genre**[m] **sexe**[m]	*scientific research*	**recherche scientifique**[f]
goal (aim)	**but**[m] **objectif**[m]	*self-esteem*	**estime**[f] **de soi** **amour-propre**[m]
goodwill	**bonne volonté**[f]	*shadow*	**ombre**[f]
greed	**avidité**[f] **cupidité**[f]	*silence*	**silence**[m]
glance *gaze*	**coup**[m] **d'œil**	*snore*	**ronflement**[m]
habit	**habitude**[f]	*solidarity*	**solidarité**[f]
hatred	**haine**[f]	*solitude loneliness*	**solitude**[f]
heaviness	**lourdeur**[f]	*slap*	**gifle**[f] **claque**[f]
hobby	**passe-temps**[m] **hobby**[m]	*slavery*	**esclavage**[m]
homage (tribute)	**hommage**[m]	*spirit*	**esprit**[m]

hope *expectation*	**espoir**^m	*spite* *grudge*	**rancune**^f
hunch (feeling)	**intuition**^f	*stupidity*	**stupidité**^f
hypothesis	**hypothèse**^f	*subtlety*	**subtilité**^f
idiocy	**idiotie**^f	*suggestion*	**suggestion**^f
impulse	**impulsion**^f	*sympathy*	**sympathie**^f
inequality	**inégalité**^f	*term*	**terme**^m
intelligence	**intelligence**^f	*thirst*	**soif**^f
interchange	**échange**^m	*thought* *thinking*	**pensée**^f
joy	**joie**^f	*tip* *gratuity*	**pourboire**^m
knowledge	**connaissance**^f	*virtue*	**vertu**^f
language	**langue**^f	*weakness*	**faiblesse**^f
laughter	**rire**^m	*wisdom*	**sagesse**^f
leadership	**leadership**^m **direction**^f	*whisper*	**chuchotement**^m
learning	**apprentissage**^m **formation**^f	*yawn*	**bâillement**^f

4. Economy & Business

The economy is "**l'économie**^f" in French, and *business* is "**les affaires**^f."
Some important vocabulary is in the following list:

achievement	**réalisation**^f	*index*	**indice**^m **index**^m
acquaintance	**connaissance**^f	*industrial waste*	**déchets industriels**^m
advantage	**avantage**^m	*installment*	**versement**^m
agriculture	**agriculture**^f	*interest*	**intérêt**^m
apprenticeship	**apprentissage**^m	*internship*	**stage**^m
asset	**actif**^m **bien**^m	*investment*	**investissement**^m
auction	**enchères**^f	*investor*	**investisseur**^m
audit	**audit**^m	*living standard*	**niveau**^m **de vie**
banknote	**billet**^m	*loan*	**prêt**^m
bankruptcy	**faillite**^f **banqueroute**^f	*mailing list*	**liste**^f **de diffusion** **liste**^f **d'envoi**
barter	**troc**^m	*making decisions*	**prendre des décisions**

benefit	**bénéfice**ᵐ **avantage**ᵐ	*management*	**gestion**ᶠ
birthrate	**taux**ᵐ **de natalité**	*maternity leave*	**congé maternité**ᵐ
branch office	**succursale**ᶠ	*member*	**membre**ᵐ
bubble	**bulle**ᶠ	*merchandise*	**marchandise**ᶠ
budget	**budget**ᵐ	*mismanagement*	**mauvaise gestion**ᶠ
challenge	**défi**ᵐ	*money exchange office*	**bureau**ᵐ **de change**
charity	**charité**ᶠ **bienfaisance**ᶠ	*mortgage*	**hypothèque**ᶠ
chart	**graphique**ᵐ **tableau**ᵐ	*over-the-counter*	**en vente libre**
committee	**comité**ᵐ	*phase*	**phase**ᶠ
commitment	**engagement**ᵐ	*pile*	**pile**ᶠ **tas**ᵐ
company	**entreprise**ᶠ	*priority*	**priorité**ᶠ
coin	**pièce**ᶠ **de monnaie**	*process*	**processus**ᵐ
consumer	**consommateur**ᵐ**/ consommatrice**ᶠ	*procrastination*	**procrastination**ᶠ
consumption	**consommation**ᶠ	*profits*	**bénéfices**ᵐ **profits**ᵐ
contract	**contrat**ᵐ	*progress*	**progrès**ᵐ
cost-of-living	**coût**ᵐ **de la vie**	*public holiday*	**jour férié**ᵐ
credit	**crédit**ᵐ	*quality*	**qualité**ᶠ
cubicle	**cabine**ᶠ **compartiment**ᵐ	*range*	**gamme**ᶠ
currency	**devise**ᶠ	*ratio*	**rapport**ᵐ **ratio**ᵐ
customer service	**service clientèle**ᵐ	*reminder*	**rappel**ᵐ
deadline	**date limite**ᶠ	*resignation*	**démission**ᶠ
dealership	**concessionnaire**ᵐ	*resource*	**ressource**ᶠ
debt	**dette**ᶠ	*retail (sales)*	**vente**ᶠ **au détail**
decline	**déclin**ᵐ **baisse**ᶠ **diminution**ᶠ	*reward*	**récompense**ᶠ
development	**développement**ᵐ	*rise*	**hausse**ᶠ **augmentation**ᶠ
digit	**chiffre**ᵐ	*scale*	**échelle**ᶠ
done deal	**affaire conclue**ᶠ **marché conclu**ᵐ	*scrap*	**ferraille**ᶠ

employment	**emploi**[m]	*skill*	**aptitude**[f] **compétence**[f]
entrepreneurship	**entrepreneuriat**[m]	*sponsor*	**sponsor**[m] **parrain**[m]
excess	**excès**[m]	*staff* *personnel*	**personnel**[m]
exchange rate	**taux**[m] **de change**	*stage* *step*	**stade**[m] **étape**[f]
executive	**exécutif**[m] **cadre**[m]	*statistics*	**statistiques**[f]
expenses	**dépenses**[f]	*street value*	**valeur marchande**[f]
expertise	**expertise**[f] **compétence**[f]	*stress*	**stress**[m]
exports	**exportations**[f]	*strike*	**grève**[f]
fair (exhibition)	**foire**[f] **salon**[m]	*success*	**succès**[m] **réussite**[f]
finances	**finances**[f]	*supplier*	**fournisseur**[m]
fixed schedule	**horaires fixes**[m]	*supplies*	**fournitures**[f]
flea market	**marché**[m] **aux puces**	*supply and demand*	**offre**[f] **et demande**[f]
fortune	**fortune**[f]	*surplus*	**excédent**[m]
franchise	**franchise**[f]	*talent*	**talent**[m]
fund	**fonds**[m]	*tax*	**impôt**[m] **taxe**[f]
Gross Domestic Product (GDP)	**Produit Intérieur Brut**[m] **(PIB)**	*trade*	**commerce**[m]
growth	**croissance**[f]	*unemployment*	**chômage**[m]
guarantee	**garantie**[f]	*unemployment benefits*	**allocations**[f] **de chômage**
headquarters	**siège**[m] **quartier général**[m]	*unfinished business*	**travail inachevé**[m]
hierarchy	**hiérarchie**[f]	*wealth*	**richesse**[f]
high season	**haute saison**[f]	*wholesale*	**vente**[f] **en gros**
human development	**développement humain**[m]	*windmill*	**moulin**[m] **à vent**
imports	**importations**[f]	*workday*	**journée**[f] **de travail**
income *revenue*	**revenu**[m]	*workshop*	**atelier**[m]

5. FAMILY II

We continue to add more to our vocabulary related to the family.

ancestor	**ancêtre**[m]	*orphan*	**orphelin(e)**
brother-in-law	**beau-frère**[m]	*parents*	**parents**[m]
clan	**clan**[m]	*single*	**célibataire**[m,f]
cousins	**cousins**[m]	*sister-in-law*	**belle-sœur**[f]
divorce	**divorce**[m]	*spouse* *partner*	**conjoint(e)**
divorced	**divorcé(e)**	*tribe*	**tribu**[f]
engagement	**engagement**[m]	*trouble* *hardship*	**difficulté**[f]
father-in-law	**beau-père**[m]	*twins*	**jumeaux**[m] **jumelles**[f]
grandparents	**grands-parents**[m]	*visitor*	**visiteur**[m]/**visiteuse**[f]
link (tie or bond)	**lien**[m]	*vow (marriage)*	**vœu**[m]
marital status	**état civil**[m] **état matrimonial**[m]	*wedding*	**mariage**[m]
marriage	**mariage**[m]	*widow*	**veuve**[f]
married	**marié(e)**	*widower*	**veuf**[m]
mother-in-law	**belle-mère**[f]	*will* *testament*	**testament**[m]

6. PEOPLE III

We add more vocabulary related to people that we encounter in our daily life.

acrobat	**acrobate**[m,f]	*homeless people*	**sans-abri**[m]
alien	**alien**[m] **extraterrestre**[m]	*interpreter*	**interprète**[m,f]
altercation	**altercation**[f]	*janitor*	**concierge**[m,f]
aristocrat	**aristocrate**[m,f]	*knight*	**chevalier**[m]
astronaut	**astronaute**[m,f]	*laborer*	**ouvrier**[m]/**ouvrière**[f]
baker	**boulanger**[m] /**boulangère**[f]	*manager*	**directeur**[m]/**directrice**[f] **manager**[m]
beggar	**mendiant(e)**	*mechanic*	**mécanicien(ne)**
blacksmith	**forgeron**[m]	*messenger*	**messager**[m]/ **messagère**[f]
bully	**brute**[f]	*miner*	**mineur**[m]
captain	**capitaine**[m]	*news anchor*	**présentateur**[m]/ **présentatrice**[f]
chemist	**chimiste**[m,f]	*nurse*	**infirmier**[m]/**infirmière**[f]

clown	**clown**[m]	*painter*	**peintre**[m]
crew (plane)	**équipage**[m]	*peasant*	**paysan(ne)**
dwarf	**nain(e)**	*peer*	**pair**[m]
farmer	**agriculteur**[m]**/-trice**[f] **fermier**[m]**/fermière**[f]	*physiotherapist*	**physiothérapeute**[m,f]
feature characteristic	**caractéristique**[f]	*pirate*	**pirate**[m]
feature trait	**trait**[m]	*plumber*	**plombier**[m]**/plombièr**[f]
firefighter	**pompier**[m]	*postman*	**facteur**[m]**/factrice**[f]
flight attendant	**steward**[m]**/ hôtesse**[f] **de l'air**	*prisoner*	**prisonnier**[m]**/ prisonnière**[f]
freelancer	**pigiste**[m,f]	*scholar*	**savant**[m] **érudit(e)**
gesture	**geste**[m]	*servant*	**serviteur**[m]
greeting	**salutation**[f]	*shepherd*	**berger**[m]**/bergère**[f]
guard	**garde**[m]	*slave*	**esclave**[m]
hairdresser	**coiffeur**[m]**/coiffeuse**[f]	*tailor*	**tailleur**[m]
hero	**héros**[m]**/héroïne**[f]	*witch*	**sorcière**[f]

7. WAR

War, or "**la guerre**," is another important topic in any language. Some related vocabulary is presented in the table below:

agreement	**accord**[m] **entente**[f]	*marshal*	**maréchal**[m]
ally	**allié**[m]	*military*	**armée**[f]
ambush	**embuscade**[f]	*morale*	**moral**[m]
armor	**armure**[f]	*mourning (grief)*	**deuil**[m]
army	**armée**[f]	*needs*	**besoins**[m]
atomic bomb	**bombe atomique**[f]	*order (command)*	**ordre**[m]
attack	**attaque**[f]	*pact*	**pacte**[m]
balance equilibrium	**équilibre**[m]	*panic*	**panique**[f]
barrier	**barrière**[f]	*parade*	**parade**[f]
battle	**bataille**[f]	*peace*	**paix**[f]
blast or gust (air)	**souffle**[m]	*poison*	**poison**[m]
bow (weapon)	**arc**[m]	*population*	**population**[f]
bullet	**balle**[f]	*poverty*	**pauvreté**[f]

burden	**fardeau**[m] **charge**[f]	*prison*	**prison**[f]
burial	**enterrement**[m]	*relief*	**secours**[m] **soulagement**[m]
cemetery	**cimetière**[m]	*result* *outcome*	**résultat**[m]
chaos *mess*	**chaos**[m]	*revenge*	**vengeance**[f]
circumstances	**circonstances**[f]	*rocket*	**fusée**[f]
collapse	**effondrement**[m]	*ruins*	**ruines**[f]
conqueror	**conquérant(e)**	*sacrifice*	**sacrifice**[m]
conquest	**conquête**[f]	*sadness* *sorrow*	**tristesse**[f]
consequences	**conséquences**[f]	*shelter*	**abri**[m] **refuge**[m]
control	**contrôle**[m]	*shooting*	**tir**[m]
corpse	**cadavre**[m]	*shortage*	**pénurie**[f]
crying	**pleurs**[m]	*siege*	**siège**[m]
dagger	**dague**[f]	*spear*	**lance**[f]
damage	**dommage**[m] **dégât**[m]	*support*	**soutien**[m] **appui**[m]
depletion *(resources)*	**épuisement**[m]	*sword*	**épée**[f]
despair	**désespoir**[m]	*tank*	**tank**[m]
disaster	**désastre**[m] **catastrophe**[f]	*tomb* *grave*	**tombe**[f] **tombeau**[m]
effort	**effort**[m]	*theft*	**vol**[m]
enemy	**ennemi**[m]	*tragedy*	**tragédie**[f]
famine	**famine**[f]	*trap*	**piège**[m]
fatality	**fatalité**[f]	*treason*	**trahison**[f]
genocide	**génocide**[m]	*trigger*	**gâchette**[f]
gun	**pistolet**[m]	*triumph*	**triomphe**[m]
homeland	**patrie**[f]	*troop*	**troupe**[f]
hunger	**faim**[f]	*veteran*	**vétéran**[m]
infrastructure	**infrastructure**[f]	*victory*	**victoire**[f]
killing	**meurtre**[m] **assassinat**[m]	*volunteer*	**bénévole**[m,f] **volontaire**[m,f]
lack of	**manque**[m] **de**	*warrior*	**guerrier**[m]**/guerrière**[f]
loss	**perte**[f]	*weapon*	**arme**[f]
march	**marche**[f]	*zone*	**zone**[f]

8. MEDIA II

Here is more vocabulary related to media and entertainment:

art	**art**[m]	*mania*	**manie**[f]
band (music)	**groupe**[m]	*masterpiece*	**chef-d'œuvre**[m]
broadcast	**diffusion**[f]	*maze*	**labyrinthe**[m]
cards deck	**jeu**[m] **de cartes**	*media coverage*	**couverture médiatique**[f]
cartoon	**dessin animé**[m]	*New Year's Day*	**jour**[m] **de l'An**
celebrity	**célébrité**[f]	*New Year's Eve*	**réveillon**[m] **de Nouvel An Saint-Sylvestre**[f]
circus	**cirque**[m]	*noise*	**bruit**[m]
comment remark	**commentaire**[m]	*orchestra*	**orchestre**[m]
concert	**concert**[m]	*painting*	**peinture**[f]
criticism	**critique**[f]	*plot (movie)*	**intrigue**[f]
crossword	**mots croisés**[m]	*poem*	**poème**[m]
debate	**débat**[m]	*poster*	**affiche**[f] **poster**[m]
dice	**dé**[m]	*protagonist*	**protagoniste**[m,f]
drum	**tambour**[m]	*rehearsal*	**répétition**[f]
entertainment	**divertissement**[m]	*review (movie or book)*	**critique**[f]
exhibition	**exposition**[f]	*riddle*	**énigme**[f]
fairy	**fée**[f]	*scene (movie)*	**scène**[f]
fame	**renommée**[f] **notoriété**[f]	*script (movie)*	**scénario**[m] **script**[m]
fantasy	**fantaisie**[f]	*shock*	**choc**[m]
fireworks	**feux**[m] **d'artifice**	*spectacle show*	**spectacle**[m]
gazette	**gazette**[f]	*subtitle*	**sous-titre**[m]
headline	**titre**[m] **manchette**[f]	*symphony*	**symphonie**[f]
image	**image**[f]	*tattoo*	**tatouage**[m]
journalism	**journalisme**[m]	*trend*	**tendance**[f]
magic	**magie**[f]	*tune melody*	**mélodie**[f]

9. RELIGION II

We add more vocabulary related to *religion*.

believer	**croyant(e)**	*nun*	**nonne**[f] **religieuse**[f]
blessing	**bénédiction**[f]	*pilgrim*	**pèlerin**[m]
Christmas Eve	**réveillon**[m] **de Noël**	*pilgrimage*	**pèlerinage**[m]
curse	**malédiction**[f]	*priest*	**prêtre**[m] **curé**[m]
Easter	**Pâques**[f]	*rabbi*	**rabbin**[m]
Good Friday	**Vendredi saint**[m]	*ritual*	**rituel**[m]
mass	**messe**[f]	*Scripture*	**Écriture**[f]
monk	**moine**[m]	*sect*	**secte**[f]

10. Sports II

More vocabulary related to sports is in the table below:

ball boy	**ramasseur**[m] **de balles**	*parachute*	**parachute**[m]
bat (baseball)	**batte**[f]	*performance*	**performance**[f] **rendement**[m] **représentation**[f]
betting	**pari**[m]	*physiotherapy*	**physiothérapie**[f]
bullfight	**corrida**[f]	*post (soccer)*	**poteau**[m]
commentator	**commentateur**[m]/ **commentatrice**[f]	*practice*	**pratique**[f]
competition	**concurrence**[f] **compétition**[f]	*prize*	**prix**[m]
contest	**concours**[m]	*rivalry*	**rivalité**[f]
cycling	**cyclisme**[m]	*running track*	**piste**[f]
defender	**défenseur**[m]	*score*	**score**[m]
diving	**plongée**[f]	*skydiving*	**parachutisme**[m]
draw (random selection)	**tirage**[m] **au sort**	*sled* *sledge*	**traîneau**[m]
fencing	**escrime**[f]	*stretching*	**étirement**[m]
friendly match	**match amical**[m]	*throw-in (soccer)*	**touche**[f]
helmet	**casque**[m]	*tournament*	**tournoi**[m]
horse riding	**équitation**[f]	*trophy*	**trophée**[m]
midfielder (soccer)	**milieu**[m] **de terrain**	*whistle*	**sifflet**[m]
on the bench	**sur le banc**	*wrestling*	**lutte**[f]

The following is a list of references that we found useful in writing this book:

Sagar-Fenton, Beth & McNeill, Lizzy (2018). How many words do you need to speak a language? Retrieved from https://www.bbc.com/news/world-44569277

Nation, Paul & Waring, Robert (1997). Vocabulary Size, Text Coverage, and Word Lists, by Paul Nation and Robert Waring. Retrieved from https://www.lextutor.ca/research/nation_waring_97.html

Francis, W. N., Kucera, H., Kučera, H., & Mackie, A. W. (1982). Frequency analysis of English usage: Lexicon and grammar. Houghton Mifflin.

Nation, Paul. (2019). 4000 Essential English Words 1-6. Compass Publishing.

Foreign Service Institute (FSI) https://www.state.gov/foreign-language-training/

Anki Webpage https://apps.ankiweb.net/

Vermeer, Alex. (2017). Anki Essentials v1.1: The complete guide to remembering anything with Anki [Kindle edition].

Heminway, Annie. (2008). Complete French Grammar. McGraw Hill.

Petrunin, Mikhail. (2018). Comparative Grammar of Spanish, Portuguese, Italian, and French. McGraw Hill.

Lawless French website.
https://www.lawlessfrench.com/

ThoughtCo website.
https://www.thoughtco.com/

FluentU website.
https://www.fluentu.com/

APPENDIX

Appendix A. Coupon Code for Free Flashcards

The Anki flashcards that accompany this book are available for free until December 31, 2023. Once you download the cards and back them up with the Anki account you create, the cards do not expire.

To download the free flashcards that accompany this book:

1. Visit the ADROS VERSE EDUCATION website at: https://www.adrosverse.com/books-and-flashcards/
2. Add the product **"French: Level I - Basic"** Anki Flashcards to the *Shopping Cart.*
3. Go to the *Shopping Cart* and use the following Coupon Code:

> # AMZNAVEFRY3

4. Proceed to *Checkout* and place your order.
5. Download the flashcards in ".zip" format and extract the ".apkg" files.

Appendix B. Verb Tenses and Conjugation Charts

We provide two useful cheat sheets that give you an overall perspective of most moods and verb tenses in French.

The two sheets are available **in color** in pdf format on the resources page of our website at https://www.adrosverse.com/resources/

The first cheat sheet is the Verb Conjugation Chart, which is structured as a comprehensive reference for the reader.

The second sheet dives into the irregular verbs of each tense, where applicable.

We recommend that you keep these two sheets handy by printing them out or having them available separately on your desk or electronic device.

VERB CONJUGATION CHART

FUTURE ↑ PRESENT ↓ PAST

CONDITIONAL

CONDITIONAL PERFECT

J'aurais parlé (I would have spoken)

The regular past participle is formed from the infinitive stem. In case of "être" conjugation, the past participle must agree in gender and number with the subject.

		-er	-ir	-re
je	aurais/serais	-é	-i	-u
tu	aurais/serais	-é	-i	-u
il/elle/on	aurait/serait	-é	-i	-u
nous	aurions/serions	-é	-i	-u
vous	auriez/seriez	-é	-i	-u
ils/elles	auraient/seraient	-é	-i	-u

SIMPLE CONDITIONAL

Je parlerais (I would speak)

The infinitive is used as a stem. In case of "-re" verbs, the final "-e" is dropped. The same suffixes are used for the three verb groups:

	-er	-ir	-re
je	-ais	-ais	-ais
tu	-ais	-ais	-ais
il/elle/on	-ait	-ait	-ait
nous	-ions	-ions	-ions
vous	-iez	-iez	-iez
ils/elles	-aient	-aient	-aient

INDICATIVE

FUTURE PERFECT

J'aurai parlé (I will have spoken)

The regular past participle is formed from the infinitive stem. In case of "être" conjugation, the past participle must agree in gender and number with the subject.

		-er	-ir	-re
je	aurai/serai	-é	-i	-u
tu	auras/seras	-é	-i	-u
il/elle/on	aura/sera	-é	-i	-u
nous	aurons/serons	-é	-i	-u
vous	aurez/serez	-é	-i	-u
ils/elles	auront/seront	-é	-i	-u

SIMPLE FUTURE

Je parlerai (I will speak)

The infinitive is used as a stem. In case of "-re" verbs, the final "-e" is dropped. The same suffixes are used for the three verb groups:

	-er	-ir	-re
je	-ai	-ai	-ai
tu	-as	-as	-as
il/elle/on	-a	-a	-a
nous	-ons	-ons	-ons
vous	-ez	-ez	-ez
ils/elles	-ont	-ont	-ont

SUBJUNCTIVE

PRESENT

que je parle (that I speak)

The stem is formed from the "ils/elles" form, by removing the final "-ent." For the "nous" & "vous" conjugations, the stem is formed from "nous" form by removing the final "-ons." The same suffixes are used for the three verb groups:

	-er	-ir	-re
je	-e	-e	-e
tu	-es	-es	-es
il/elle/on	-e	-e	-e
nous	-ions	-ions	-ions
vous	-iez	-iez	-iez
ils/elles	-ent	-ent	-ent

Je parle (I speak)

The stem is formed from the infinitive, by removing the final "-er," "-ir," or "-re." Regular verbs take the following suffixes:

	-er	-ir	-re
je	-e	-is	-s
tu	-es	-is	-s
il/elle/on	-e	-it	-
nous	-ons	-issons	-ons
vous	-ez	-issez	-ez
ils/elles	-ent	-issent	-ent

COMPOUND PAST

que j'aie parlé (that I spoke/ have spoken)

The regular past participle is formed from the infinitive stem. In case of "être" conjugation, the past participle must agree in gender and number with the subject.

		-er	-ir	-re
je	aie/sois	-é	-i	-u
tu	aies/sois	-é	-i	-u
il/elle/on	ait/soit	-é	-i	-u
nous	ayons/soyons	-é	-i	-u
vous	ayez/soyez	-é	-i	-u
ils/elles	aient/soient	-é	-i	-u

J'ai parlé (I spoke/ have spoken)

The regular past participle is formed from the infinitive stem. In case of "être" conjugation, the past participle must agree in gender and number with the subject.

		-er	-ir	-re
je	ai/suis	-é	-i	-u
tu	as/es	-é	-i	-u
il/elle/on	a/est	-é	-i	-u
nous	avons/sommes	-é	-i	-u
vous	avez/êtes	-é	-i	-u
ils/elles	ont/sont	-é	-i	-u

PROGRESSIVE TENSES

The French language does not have a present or past continuous tense equivalent to that in English, e.g., *"I am/was speaking."* It is common to use the simple present tense in French to talk about actions that are happening right now, e.g., "**Je parle**" *(I am talking)*.

To emphasize the continuous state of an action, one could use the expression "**être en train de**" *(to be in the process of)*, e.g., "**Je suis en train de parler**" *(I am speaking)*.

The Imperfect Subjunctive & the Pluperfect Subjunctive tense are mostly a literary tenses, and rarely used in daily spoken language.

SIMPLE PAST

Je parlai (I spoke)

The stem is formed from the infinitive, by removing the final "-er," "-ir," or "-re." Regular verbs take the following suffixes:

	-er	-ir	-re
je	-ai	-is	-is
tu	-as	-is	-is
il/elle/on	-a	-it	-it
nous	-âmes	-îmes	-îmes
vous	-âtes	-îtes	-îtes
ils/elles	-èrent	-irent	-irent

IMPERFECT

Je parlais (I spoke)

The stem is formed from the "nous" form, by removing the final "-ons." The same suffixes are used for the three verb groups:

	-er	-ir	-re
je	-ais	-ais	-ais
tu	-ais	-ais	-ais
il/elle/on	-ait	-ait	-ait
nous	-ions	-ions	-ions
vous	-iez	-iez	-iez
ils/elles	-aient	-aient	-aient

PLUPERFECT

J'avait parlé (I had spoken)

The regular past participle is formed from the infinitive stem. In case of "être" conjugation, the past participle must agree in gender and number with the subject.

		-er	-ir	-re
je	avais/étais	-é	-i	-u
tu	avais/étais	-é	-i	-u
il/elle/on	avait/était	-é	-i	-u
nous	avions/étions	-é	-i	-u
vous	aviez/étiez	-é	-i	-u
ils/elles	avaient/étaient	-é	-i	-u

IRREGULAR VERBS

PRESENT INDICATIVE TENSE

******-er Verbs******

1. Only one completely irregular "-er" verb
aller: vais, vas, va, allons, allez, vont

2. Minor spelling changes in some conjugation forms:
"-cer" verbs: e.g., "commencer" (nous commençons)
"-ger" verbs: e.g., "manger" (nous mangeons)
"-yer" verbs: e.g., "envoyer" (j'/il envoie, tu envoies, ils envoient)
"-eler" verbs: e.g., "appeler" (j'/il appelle, tu appelles, ils appellent)
"e" + consonant + "-er": e.g., "lever" (je/il lève, tu lèves, ils lèvent)

******-ir Verbs******

1. "-tir," "-mir," & "-vir" Verbs
dormir: dors, dors, dort, dormons, dormez, dorment
other examples: partir, servir

2. "-vrir," "-frir," & "-llir" Verbs
ouvrir: ouvre, ouvres, ouvre, ouvrons, ouvrez, ouvrent
other examples: ofrir, cueillir, couvrir, souffrir, découvrir, accueillir

3. "venir," "tenir," & their derivatives
venir: viens, viens, vient, venons, venez, viennent
other examples: tenir, devenir, obtenir, advenir, revenir, conevenir,
provenir, prévenir, survenir, intervenir, détenir, retenir, abstenir,
contenir, soutenir, maintenir, appartenir, entretenir

4. Irregular verbs ending in "-oir"
Verbs ending in "-oir" do not follow a single conjugation pattern
avoir: ai, as, a, avons, avez, ont
savoir: sais, sais, sait, savons, savez, savent
devoir: dois, dois, doit, devons, devez, doivent
pouvoir: peux, peux, peut, pouvons, pouvez, peuvent
vouloir: veux, veux, veut, voulons, voulez, veulent
voir: vois, vois, voit, voyons, voyez, voient
asseoir: assieds, assieds, assied, asseyons, asseyez, asseyent
décevoir: deçois, deçois, deçoit, deçevons, deçevez, deçoivent
recevoir: reçois, reçois, reçoit, recevons, recevez, reçoivent
falloir: il faut, pleuvoir: il pleut, valoir: il vaut

5. Other irregular "-ir" verbs
A few verbs are completely irregular and do not follow any pattern:
acquérir: acquiers, acquiers, acquiert, acquérons, acquérez, acquièrent
bouillir: bous, bous, bout, bouillons, bouillez, bouillent
courir: cours, cours, court, courons, courez, courent
parcourir: parcours, parcours, parcourt, parcourons, parcourez, parcourent
secourir: secours, secours, secourt, secourons, secourez, secourent
mourir: meurs, meurs, meurt, mourons, mourez, meurent

******-re Verbs******

1. "prendre" & its derivations
prendre: prends, prends, prend, prenons, prenez, prennent
other examples: enreprendre, surprendre, reprendre, méprendre

2. "mettre," "-battre," & their derivations
mettre: mets, mets, met, mettons, mettez, mettent
battre: bats, bats, bat, battons, battez, battent
other examples: promettre, débattre, admettre, commettre, abattre,
combattre, trasmettre, soumettre, permettre, compromettre

3. "rompre" & its derivations
rompre: romps, romps, rompt, rompons, rompez, rompent
other examples: corrompre, interrompre

4. "-aindre," "-eindre," & "-oindre"
peindre: peins, peins, peint, peignons, peignez, peignent
other examples: craindre, joindre, adjoindre, astreindre, atteindre,
ceindre, contraindre, dépeindre, disjoindre, empreindre, éteindre,
feindre, geindre, plaindre, rejoindre, restreindre, teindre

5. "-uire," "-dire," "-fire," & "-lire"
cuire: cuis, cuis, cuit, cuisons, cuisez, cuisent
lire: lis, lis, lit, lisons, lisez, lisent
other examples: dire, confire, conduire, constuire, contredire,
déduire, détruire, élire, induire, instruire, interdire, induire,
introduire, luire, médire, nuire, prédire, produire, reconduire,
reconstuire, réduire, séduire, suffire, traduire
One exception is the second-person plural of the verb "dire" (and its
derivatives), which is conjugated as "vous dites."

6. "-crire" verbs
écrire: écris, écris, écrit, ecrivons, écrivez, écrivent
other examples: inscrire, prescrire, proscrire, récrire, transcrire

7. "-aître" verbs (except "naître")
connaître: connais, connais, connaît, connaissons, connaissez, connaissent
other examples: apparaître, paraître, comparaître, disparaître,
méconnaître, reconnaître, reapparaître, transparaître

8. Other completely irregular "-re" verbs
clore, conclure, coudre, croire, dissoudre, distraire, exclure, inclure,
moudre, plaire, résoudre, rire, sourire, suivre, vivre

PRESENT SUBJUNCTIVE TENSE

1. The verbs "être" & "avoir" are completely irregular:
être: sois, sois, soit, soyons, soyez, soient
avoir: aie, aies, ait, ayons, ayez, aient

2. The following verbs have irregular stems but regular endings:
aller (aill-/all-): aille, ailles, aille, allions, alliez, aillent
faire (fass-): fasse, fasses, fasse, fassions, fassiez, fassent
pouvoir (puiss-): puisse, puisses, puisse, puissions, puissiez, puissent
savoir (sach-): sache, saches, sache, sachions, sachiez, sachent
valoir (vaill-/val-): vaille, vailles, vaille, valions, vailiez, vaillent
vouloir (veuill-/voul-): veuille, veuilles, veuille, voulions, vouliez, veuillent

3. The verb "falloir"
The verb "falloir" is impersonal and has only a third-person singular
form, which is irregular, i.e., "il faille" *(it is necessary)*.

SIMPLE FUTURE TENSE

The following verbs have irregular stem:
aller (ir-), avoir (aur-), courir (courr-), devenir (deviendr-), devoir
(devr-), envoyer (enverr-), être (ser-), faire (fer-), falloir (faudr-),
mourir (mourr-), pleuvoir (pleuvr-), recevoir (recevr-), savoir (saur-),
tenir (tiendr-), valoir (vaudr-), venir (viendr-), voir (verr-), vouloir
(voudr-)
Some verbs that undergo minor spelling changes, for example:
employer (emploier-), essuyer (essuier-), nettoyer (nettoier-), acheter
(achèter-), appeler (appeller-), jeter (jetter-)

SIMPLE CONDITIONAL TENSE

Same irregular verbs as in the future indicative tense.

IMPERFECT INDICATIVE TENSE

Only one irregular verb:
être: étais, étais, était, étions, étiez, étaient
Some verbs undergo minor spelling changes similar to
those in other tenses to maintain the proper pronunciation.

IMPERATIVE

1. Singular Informal (i.e., "tu" form)
être (sois), avoir (aie), savoir (sache), vouloir (veuille)

2. Plural and Singular Formal (i.e., "vous" form)
être (soyez), avoir (ayez), savoir (sachez), vouloir (veuillez)

3. Commands using "nous" form
être (soyon), avoir (ayon), savoir (sachon)

PAST PARTICIPLE

acquérir (acquis), apprendre (appris), avoir (eu), boire (bu),
comprendre (compris), conduire (conduit), craindre (craint), devoir (dû),
dire (dit), écrire (écrit), être (été), faire (fait), falloir (fallu), lire (lu),
mettre (mis), mourir (mort), naître (né), offrir (offert), ouvrir (ouvert),
peindre (peint), plaire (plu), pleuvoir (plu), pouvoir (pu), prendre (pris),
recevoir (reçu), rire (ri), savoir (su), suivre (suivi), vivre (veçu), voir (vu),
vouloir (volu)

SIMPLE PAST

avoir, être, boire, conduire, connaître, courir, couvrir, craindre, croire,
devoir, écrire, éteindre, faire, falloir, introduire, lire, mettre, mourir, naître,
obtenir, offrir, peindre, plaire, pleuvoir, pouvoir, prendre, recevoir, rire,
savoir, tenir, valoir, venir, vivre, vouloir

Appendix C. Acronyms and Abbreviations

Acronyms, initialisms, and abbreviations are common in French. Here, we summarize some basic rules and list some common examples.

Acronyms and Initialisms

Acronyms and initialisms are both utilized to shorten a phrase by using the first letter of each word. The difference between an acronym and an initialism is that the former is pronounced as one word, e.g., "NASA" and "LASER," whereas the latter is pronounced as separate letters, e.g., "ATM" and "UN."

In most cases, we follow the same rules to form acronyms and initialisms in French. For example:

United Nations	UN	Organisation des Nations Unies	ONU
International Monetary Fund	IMF	Fonds Monétaire International	FMI
World Health Organization	WHO	Organisation Mondiale de la Santé	OMS
Non-Governmental Organization	NGO	Organisation Non Gouvernementale	ONG
Value Added Tax	VAT	Taxe sur la Valeur Ajoutée	TVA

Abbreviations

An abbreviation is a shortened version of a word or phrase. It uses the initial part of a word or a combination of the initial and final parts and is often characterized by a period at the end.

Examples of such abbreviations are titles and professions, such as:

M.	monsieur	*Mr.*
Mme.	madame	*Mrs./Ms.*
Mlle.	mademoiselle	*Miss.*
Dr.	docteur	*Dr.*
Prof.	professeur	*Prof.*
Ing.	ingénieur(e)	*Eng.*

The months of the year are abbreviated as follows:

January	janv.	*July*	juil.
February	févr.	*August*	août
March	mars	*September*	sept.
April	avr.	*October*	oct.
May	mai	*November*	nov.
June	juin	*December*	déc.

Notice that the months of "**mars**" *(Mars)*, "**mai**" *(May)*, "**juin**" *(June)*, and "**août**" *(August)* are not abbreviated.

The days of the week are often abbreviated as follows:

Mon.	*Tue.*	*Wed.*	*Thur.*	*Fri.*	*Sat.*	*Sun.*
lundi	mardi	mercredi	jeudi	vendredi	samedi	dimanche
lun.	mar.	mer.	jeu.	ven.	sam.	dim.

The *Before Christ (BC)* era is referred to as "**avant Jésus-Christ**," and is abbreviated as "**av. J-C.**" The *Common Era (CE)* is often referred to as "**après Jésus-Christ**," and is abbreviated as "**ap. J-C.**"

The four cardinal directions are abbreviated as "**N**" for "**nord**" /noя/ *(north)*, "**S**" for "**sud**" /sμd/ *(south)*, "**E**" for "**est**" /est/ *(east)*, and "**O**" for "**ouest**" /west/ *(west)*. The four ordinal directions are abbreviated as "**NE**" for "**nord-est**" *(northeast)*, "**NO**" for "**nord-ouest**" *(northwest)*, "**SE**" for "**sud-est**" *(southeast)*, and "**SO**" for "**sud-ouest**" *(southwest)*.

In addition to the above, there are lots of abbreviated and shortened words that are often used in daily life in France, such as:

un/une coloc	un/une colocataire	*a roommate*
les actus	les actualités	*the news*
un appart	un appartement	*an apartment*
un ordi	un ordinateur	*computer*
le bac	le baccalauréat	*secondary education diploma*
la fac	la faculté	*university*
le foot	le football	*soccer (football)*

www.ingramcontent.com/pod-product-compliance
Lightning Source LLC
Chambersburg PA
CBHW080816170726
48000CB00021B/3131